Dear reader:

The AGO subscription series strives to provide spiritual guidance to people at all levels of faith, with the goal of helping them grow that faith. To that end, we choose very carefully the materials we make available to our customers. The selection process is often difficult, as there are many gifted authors and handlers of the Word. However, choosing to make the book you hold in your hands available to you was one of our easier selections.

Stephen Davey is especially adept at presenting scholarly biblical truths in bright and memorable ways. Through exhaustive research and careful organization, his messages flow clearly and logically to practical application. Along the way he illustrates God's truths with unforgettable colorations. When these messages are compiled into commentary form, as with this work, the logical flow is even more pronounced.

The Book of Job has always been particularly perplexing to me, for two reasons. First, for vast stretches through some of its chapters, the words spoken are not correct, but instead are the disparate voices representing wrong interpretations of the calamities afflicting Job. For me, the mental shift required in reading these passages has always been a challenge. Second, there are enormously deep theological truths to be gleaned from God's actions in Job's life, and some of these are easily misinterpreted or misunderstood.

Fortunately, Stephen Davey handles both the deep issues presented in Job and its unusual narrative style with care and precision. He illuminates Job's passages and ties them to broader truths with a virtuoso's mastery. What results is an easily readable but profoundly helpful book that I am hopeful will draw you closer to the One who laid the foundation of the earth.

Sincerely,

Chris Brady

Stephen Davey

Wisdom Commentary Series

Job

CHARITY HOUSE
PUBLISHERS

Wisdom Commentary Series: Job

Author: Stephen Davey
Editor: Lalanne Barber
Cover Design and Body Layout: Grace Gourley
Photo of Stephen: Sam Gray Portraits, Raleigh, NC (samgrayportraits.com)
ISBN 978 0 9851679 8 1

Published by Charity House Publishers

Charity House Publishers, Inc.
2201 Candun Street
Suite 103
Apex, NC 27523-6412
USA
www.wisdomonline.org

To my father

~Keith Davey~

who maintains tenacious optimism in the face of every trial,
faithfully declaring of his Redeemer—
to Whom he has given the right to both give and take away—
"Blessed be the name of the Lord."

CONTENTS

(Continued on next page)

CONTENTS

(Continued)

There was a man in the land of Uz whose name was Job; and that man was blameless, upright, fearing God and turning away from evil. [2]Seven sons and three daughters were born to him. [3]His possessions also were 7,000 sheep, 3,000 camels, 500 yoke of oxen, 500 female donkeys, and very many servants; and that man was the greatest of all the men of the east. [4]His sons used to go and hold a feast in the house of each one on his day, and they would send and invite their three sisters to eat and drink with them. [5]When the days of feasting had completed their cycle, Job would send and consecrate them, rising up early in the morning and offering burnt offerings according to the number of them all; for Job said, "Perhaps my sons have sinned and cursed God in their hearts." Thus Job did continually.

–Job 1:1–5

CHAPTER ONE

THE WISE MAN OF UZ

Job 1:1–5

It only took 39 seconds. In less than one minute, messengers tripped over themselves to deliver the news that Job had lost nearly everything. From that moment on, his name would become synonomous with suffering. The question still remains, "Why do God's children suffer?" Frankly, it's a question that begs some defining. Is a *trial* something large and life-threatening or can it represent smaller, everyday stuff, as well?

Like one author of a devotional for teenagers who entitled his booklet *If God Loves Me, Why Can't I Get My Locker Open?* Maybe it wasn't a locker that was stuck but a car door. Maybe you wondered why your washing machine broke down just before company arrived or why your alarm didn't go off on the day of your job interview; the timing of such irritations qualified them, at least in your mind, as *trials*. Perhaps they are.

A seminary student with whom I attended school told me of a wedding he had performed. It was in a small country church during the dead of winter. He arrived and found that it was almost as cold inside the little sanctuary as it was outside. The janitor had arrived with only thirty minutes to spare. He went to the basement and turned on the furnace. The church had the type of heat vents that ran along the baseboards of the sanctuary, blowing warm, dry air. The problem was he forgot to regulate it until it was too late.

During the processional, the trumpet player fainted. A little later a bridesmaid fainted and then the bride, as well. She was revived with a cold cloth, brought to her feet, and promptly fainted again. She and the groom spent the rest of the ceremony at the kneeling bench with a cold cloth on the back of her neck.

Afterwards, she refused to go on the honeymoon because she could not *remember* getting married. She had absolutely no recollection of the event, insisting that they watch the video so she could hear herself saying the vows. Satisfied, the two sped off to their honeymoon destination.

As irritating as these kinds of circumstances are, there are more serious problems that we would definitely consider *suffering*.

Jerry Bridges, a longtime missionary with the Navigators, wrote a book entitled *Trusting God: Even When Life Hurts*. He prefaced the book with these words:

> When I was fourteen years old, my mother died suddenly, without warning. I was in the adjoining room and rushed in just in time to see her gasp her last breath. I was stunned and devastated. My older brother was away at school, and my dad was too stricken with grief to help me. Worst of all, I did not know how to turn to God in times of trouble. I was alone in my adversity.[1]

A few years ago, a young man at our church sensed God calling him into vocational ministry. He and his wife were enthusiastic and made plans to attend Bible college. After months of preparation, they enrolled in an out-of-state school. During his first semester, he developed a nasal infection that required surgery. The doctor botched the surgery and cut through a group of sensitive nerves. What began as simple outpatient surgery became a nightmare.

He was wracked with incredible pain in his face—his eyes, nose, teeth, mouth, and jaws all screamed for relief. He was told that surgery would not repair anything and that only time could heal him. After two years, his recovery was still incomplete. He dropped out of school and was unable to work. He and his wife lost what little they had in the way of savings and eventually moved back home. When he came to see me, he could only sit for a few minutes. A morphine pack rested on his hip, and he sucked on a lollipop laced with more drugs to help the pain in his teeth.

What do you say to someone like that? What hope can you give them? How do you answer someone who is asking, "Where in the world is God?"

Our world loves to ask this question. Every time a hurricane blows in or a tornado levels homes or a killer goes on a shooting spree or terrorists carry out their murderous plans, the world screams this question in our ears: "If God is a loving God, why would He allow this to happen?"

Some authors try to answer the problem of suffering by taking God off the hook. Their conclusion is that if bad things happen in the world and God is supposedly a good God, then either God is *not* good or there is *no* God.

Elie Wiesel, the 1986 Nobel Peace Prize winner, is one such author. His biographical work entitled *Night* has sold an estimated six million copies. In the book, Wiesel describes his suffering as a Jewish boy interned at Auschwitz during World War II. I was again reminded of the demonically inspired hatred that the Nazis had for the Jews; even more tragic was Elie's response to it. He wrote:

> In that concentration camp, as I stood below the limp body of a little Jewish boy who had just been hung by the neck, I was convinced that God was dead.[2]

Wiesel's solace was a retreat into practical atheism. His argument is simply this: If terrible things like this happen in the world, then there can be no God.

Harold Kushner attempted to answer the problem of evil in the world in his best-selling book *When Bad Things Happen to Good People*. He offers something that seems better than atheism . . . but not by much. His readers are left with despair, confusion, and doubt as were Weisel's readers. Kushner's thesis is that God exists and is, indeed, loving but not sovereign. In defense of this idea, he writes,

> God wants the righteous to live happy lives . . . but it is too difficult even for God to keep cruelty and chaos from claiming innocent victims.[3]

Kushner's answer was not atheism, but it was a version of God that is just as empty and hollow.

So what is the answer? I won't give you one just yet. In fact, I am convinced that we are too quick with answers . . . too quick to spill out happy verses or hand out spiritual pats on the backs of those who are suffering immensely. In effect, they leave the sanctuary just as cold and desperate as when they arrived.

So before giving any answers, let's first identify the important questions:

- Why do the righteous suffer?
- Where is God when tragedy strikes?
- If God is all-loving, how can He allow human suffering?
- Does God really care about us?
- Does God demand some kind of payment or sacrifice in return for His goodness?
- Where is God when life hurts?
- Why is God silent while we suffer?[4]

These are only a few of the important questions to be answered, but they're a good start. These and many more are asked frequently throughout the Book of Job, which is where we begin our study of God's sovereignty and Christian suffering.

THE BOOK OF JOB

A man was driving across Texas late one night and scanned radio stations for something to keep him awake. He came across the voice of a preacher whose sermon title from Job was "I Can't Eat by Day, I Can't Sleep by Night, and the Woman I Love Don't Treat Me Right." As simple and humorous as this sounds, it's not a bad summary of the opening scene in Job's life.[5]

This eighteenth book in our Bible is really just a very long poem that stretches from chapter three all the way to chapter forty-two. The first two chapters form the prologue and the last eleven verses of the final chapter are the epilogue. J. Sidlow Baxter, a faithful pastor in Great Britain during the last century, wrote that this inspired account was a dramatic poem framed in an epic story.[6]

There are many things about this book which make it unique from others. It is believed by many to be the *oldest* book in the world. Although the Book of Genesis appears first in the Bible, the Book of Job may have been written years earlier and was, perhaps, edited by Moses. Most conservative scholars believe Job lived during the days of Abraham, Isaac, and Jacob . . . or maybe even earlier. He must have lived some time before the Law of Moses because he offers sacrifices for himself and his family. Once the Law came into being, only the priesthood of Aaron's descendants could offer sacrifices.[7]

Not only is this book the oldest in the world, but it also contains the longest account in the Bible of God's speaking to man: four chapters. If this isn't enough to stir your curiosity, it also reveals the longest account in the Bible of Satan's speaking.[8]

Job also uses many Hebrew words not found anywhere else in the Bible. His story will also provide a rare inside look into heaven, describing a conversation between God and Satan in the presence of the angels around the throne of God. Every time I read it, it leaves me amazed.

Think about it—the book that is not only the oldest book in the Bible but perhaps the oldest in the world is a book that deals with the issue that everyone still wants to know about: *suffering*. If there is one place which can provide the answers to our age-old questions, it is surely this book.

GOD OBSERVES JOB'S INTEGRITY

> ***There was a man in the land of Uz whose name was Job; and that man was blameless, upright, fearing God and turning away from evil*** (Job 1:1).

As we read this opening phrase, we might wonder if the story of Job is true. When I see the land of Uz, I think of *The Wizard of Oz*. Unlike Oz, which was a make-believe world, Uz was a very real place. It appears first in *Genesis 10:23* as the name of Shem's grandson—the great-grandson of Noah. The land of Uz was more than likely named after Noah's great-grandson; it occupied the southern region around the Dead Sea, later known as Edom.

If there was ever any doubt among the Jewish people that Job existed, the prophet Ezekiel settled the matter when he referred to Daniel, Noah, and Job as equally godly, righteous men *(Ezekiel 14:14)*.[9]

As the Book of Job opens, God wants to clear any doubt that Job was a real person in an actual time, in an actual region, with an actual wife, children, and friends. More importantly, God wants us to know that Job was a righteous man in everything. And if there was ever anyone who had the right to call life unfair, it was Job.

If you were to paraphrase the first four verses of ***Job 1***, you would find six words that describe the main character.

Righteous

This word refers to one's integrity, but it does not imply perfection. This adjective/noun appears two more times in Job—once when God is praising Job before Satan in ***Job 2:3*** and a second time when Job's wife asks him, ***"Are you still holding on to your integrity?"*** (Job 2:9). The Hebrew word is also used in *Genesis 20:5* in connection with moral innocence and later in *Judges 9:16* where the word is related to someone telling the truth.[10]

Real

The Hebrew word *yashar* which means ***upright*** indicates ethical behavior. It is a word that refers to relationships.[11] In other words, Job was not one person on the Sabbath and another on the job site. He was unlike one well-known executive who said, "On the weekend, my priorities are God, family, and business, but when I arrive at the office on Monday morning, the order is reversed to business, family, and God."[12]

Yashar is also used by the prophet Isaiah to refer to a straight path; a level road. There was nothing crooked about Job. His handshake meant something. He was a man of his word and people knew it.

Reverent

Fearing God brings to mind someone bowing before an authority. In the Old Testament, the concept of fearing God meant to hold Him in high esteem; to take Him seriously; to honor who He is; to obey what He says; to be in awe of and have respect and reverence for Him. In other words, Job did not take God lightly.[13]

So often we treat God as if He were not really important. We treat His Word flippantly and barely heed His commands . . . until something happens; then we begin to suffer. When trouble comes and pain runs through our front door uninvited, then we want to reverence Him—then we dust off our Bibles and become reacquainted with our sovereign, gracious Lord.

This is the magnificent thing about Job. He is already acknowledging God *before* trouble comes. He has not taken God for granted. He does not need great trial to bring him to his knees. He does not need pain to focus his perspective on God's glory. Job was constantly living in a state of reverence.

Resistant

Job is described as ***turning away from evil***; he didn't follow the way of the world. According to the world's philosophy, when someone is wealthy and powerful they are allowed to experiment with sin. They deserve a little sin and can easily get away with it. Everyone says, "Well, he owns the company; this is her business; he's at the top of his game . . ." but not Job. The more he owned and the greater his increase, the more concerned he was about pleasing God.

Rich

> ***Seven sons and three daughters were born to him. His possessions also were 7,000 sheep, 3,000 camels, 500 yoke of oxen, 500 female donkeys, and very many servants; and that man was the greatest of all the men of the east*** (Job 1:2–3).

This was a rare combination. Here you have a man who was both wealthy and godly, accumulating treasure in heaven while possessing treasure on earth.[14]

It is possible for someone to have treasures in heaven and have none on earth. There are many who die poverty-stricken after living godly lives of faith and character. It is also possible to have treasures on earth and have none in heaven. Many live only for themselves, pursuing wealth and power as their god. But it is a very rare thing to find someone who inherits a rich afterlife while maintaining a rich earthly one. Job was that man.

Reformer

> ***His sons used to go and hold a feast in the house of each one on his day, and they would send and invite their three sisters to eat and drink with them. When the days of feasting had completed their cycle, Job would send and consecrate them, rising up early in the morning and offering burnt offerings according to the number of them all; for Job said,***

> ***"Perhaps my sons have sinned and cursed God in their hearts." Thus Job did continually*** (Job 1:4–5).

We could call Job a reconciler; a revivalist; a reformer. He cared deeply about the spiritual condition of his children. And mark this—they were grown and on their own, having their own homes and families.

The text says that they used to have a feast ***on his day***. Perhaps this is a reference to a birthday, which they celebrated wholeheartedly. Job was concerned that in the midst of all the feasting and partying, one or more of his children had sullied their minds. He was worried that one of them might have drunk too much or have said something dishonorable to God.

Therefore, just as in the days of the Patriarchs, Job sacrificed on his children's behalf. What an example and challenge to every father who reads this passage. Our generation has much to learn from the parental responsibility displayed by Job. We have handed our children to youth leaders, Christian schools, camp directors, Christian artists, pastors, Sunday school teachers, and AWANA workers with the attitude, "Here, you teach 'em and train 'em. You instill godly values in 'em. That's *your* job."

Job becomes an example of a shepherd who cares about his family. He doesn't thrust his God-given responsibility upon others; he loves his children and cares for them as any father should. There is no better way to define Job than to simply say this about him: he was a man true to his calling as a father.

GOD DOESN'T OFFER IMMUNITY TO JOB

At conversion, Christians are not inoculated against grief, and there is no guarantee of health, wealth, and happiness. Those who teach such nonsense will themselves experience their own chapter of suffering. But doesn't this seem a bit unfair? Shouldn't Christians be exempt from suffering?

Perhaps you are struggling with this question right now. You have wondered if the godly life is worth the effort, the discipline, the commitment to marriage, the resistance to sin, the attempt at integrity and honesty, the reverence toward God and the things of God, and the struggle to parent with godly purpose . . . when it is only rewarded with severe trials.

In Steven Lawson's comments on Job, he retells the tragic event that occurred during the 1991 US Open at Hazeltine National Golf Club in Minnesota.

> It was a beautiful summer day, but the gray cloud front rushed in and within minutes, turbulent skies blackened and swirling banks of electricity collected overhead. Lightning was spotted—a golfer's worst nightmare. Storm sirens blasted as a fierce thunderstorm blew in, threatening the safety of one of the largest single-day crowds in the history of professional golf. Forty thousand spectators scrambled for any makeshift covering—a refreshment stand; an umbrella; a tree . . . anything.
>
> To keep from being drenched, one group of spectators sought shelter under a thirty-foot willow tree near the seventh tee. Just then, at the height of the storm, a lightning bolt struck that tree. A dozen bodies toppled like bowling pins. Six men got up while six others remained dazed on the ground. One died, his hands still in his pockets.
>
> One of the survivors recalled, "Somebody said it would be just our luck if lightning hit this tree. We all laughed. Seconds later, we were hit."
>
> This is a nearly perfect analogy to the story of Job. The tallest tree sometimes draws the most fire. The taller you stand, the more likely you are to feel the strike of the enemy.[15]

"Have you considered My servant Job?" God will soon say to Satan a few verses later. As if to say, "He's the tallest tree around . . . there is no one quite like him."

But what will happen when the lightning of Satan's temper falls upon Job? He will shudder and shake and split apart; his leaves will be stripped from their branches and his trunk will sway violently in the wind, but his roots will remain anchored—deep . . . grounded in faith. When the storm has passed, new branches and buds will spring from those roots, stronger and more fruitful than the ones stripped away.

But let's not get ahead of ourselves. We would miss a great deal of the treasure in this story if we merely race to the ending. So watch with me as the clouds darken over the land of Uz, making ready to release a furious deluge on a single tree—one that supposedly cannot be torn down.

Now there was a day when the sons of God came to present themselves before the
LORD, and Satan also came among them. [7]*The LORD said to Satan, "From*
where do you come?" Then Satan answered the LORD and said, "From roam-
ing about on the earth and walking around on it." [8]*The LORD said to Satan,*
"Have you considered My servant Job? For there is no one like him on the earth,
a blameless and upright man, fearing God and turning away from evil." [9]*Then*
Satan answered the LORD, "Does Job fear God for nothing? [10]*Have You not*
made a hedge about him and his house and all that he has, on every side? You
have blessed the work of his hands, and his possessions have increased in the
land.[11]*But put forth Your hand now and touch all that he has; he will surely*
curse You to Your face." [12]*Then the LORD said to Satan, "Behold, all that he has*
is in your power, only do not put forth your hand on him." So Satan departed
from the presence of the LORD.

–Job 1:6–12

CHAPTER TWO

EXHIBIT A

Job 1:6–12

The evangelist of the late 1800s, D. L. Moody, founder of Moody Bible Institute, once remarked, "I believe in the existence of Satan for two reasons: first, the Bible says so and second, I've done business with him."[1]

The average Christian goes through life without giving any thought to the war he or she is in.

One author wrote, "Many people get up, dress, eat, drive their cars to work, make phone calls, send emails, tend their children, clean the kitchen, and go to bed without giving one single thought to the existence of an unseen world and the fact that humanity is the staging ground in the greatest battle that has ever taken place."[2]

We have a tremendous advantage in this war, however. The powers of hell are no match for the power of heaven. This is not a battle between two equally strong forces in which we are left to wonder which will win. *No*! The power of God is supreme over the enemy and the conflict has *already* been won, though the forces of hell have yet to concede defeat.

Until the day of God's final display of power when He, with one word, silences the enemy and banishes them all to eternal hell, we must continue to fight our daily skirmishes with the defeated general. His favorite target is the child of God. If he is able to so much as squelch the praise and thanksgiving of one believer, then he has won a small victory. He hates the idea of God's receiving worship and glory from you and me; thus he will stop at nothing until we are silenced.

Isaiah writes that it was God's throne Satan coveted and God's glory he wanted. It was the worship of humanity he lusted for, which eventually sealed his doom. One-third of the angels joined him in his mutiny, and they were cursed with him. Their only aim now is to attack the work of God, the ways of God, and the workmen of God.

Peter tells us that Satan *is seeking someone to devour* (1 Peter 5:8); this means he wants to discredit the believer. Watch out—you are in his sights. The way Satan attacks the glory of God is through disobedient, disloyal, ungrateful, wayward children of God who refuse to glorify Him. The devil will use trials, tragedies, and temptations to try to mute the believer's worship of God. Just because God's throne is out of his grasp doesn't mean that we are.

When you hear the name Charles Spurgeon, many automatically think of him as the incredible preacher who ministered in London during the 1800s. Few of us remember him as the incredible *sufferer*. He battled greatly with physical ailments nearly his entire life. He preached almost one hundred sermons on the book of Job during his ministry and, for him, it was no exercise in homiletics. His bouts with ill health, causing him to live daily with continual pain and the need for extended bed rest, began in his twenties about the same time he began to pastor his church in London.

Spurgeon's wife Susannah was also a sufferer and became a semi-invalid in her thirties. She was rarely able to attend church on Sunday mornings to hear her husband, though 10,000 others walked through the doors each week. Spurgeon said in one of his sermons:

> Satan hates to see happy Christians glorifying God. He is well aware that mournful Christians often dishonor the glory of God by mistrusting it, and he thinks if he can worry us until we no more believe in the constancy and goodness of the Lord, he shall have robbed God of His praise. God said, *"Whoso offereth praise glorifieth Me,"* and so Satan lays the axe at the root of our praise, that God may cease to be glorified.[3]

Is this true? Is Satan's grand scheme really to silence the Christian's praise and destroy the worship the believer gives to his sovereign Lord? Yes. In the story of Job, Satan pulls back the curtain of his own inner desire and reveals his ultimate motive: to cause believers to curse God. Let's watch as God takes the life of Job and offers it up as evidence that there is at least *someone* on earth who will worship God through intense suffering.

The curtain is up; the tree is center-stage, standing tall beneath gathering gray clouds. The drama is about to take a devastating turn.

AN APPOINTMENT WITH GOD

One author said that at the end of verse five, there must have been a pause. If this were a play, the curtains would close, the audience would be given a few moments to stand and stretch, and then sit back down. The stagehands would then change the scenery from earth to heaven.[4]

While Job sleeps comfortably in his bed, God devises a plan that will alter his life. Job dreams of blessing and honor and peace; God formulates a nightmare that will bring the opposite. Scene II is chaotic; it unfolds tragedy after tragedy and in no way resembles the calmness of Scene I, which is filled with blessings.

> ***Now there was a day when the sons of God came to present themselves before the LORD, and Satan also came among them*** (Job 1:6).

The expression ***sons of God*** refers to angels in the Book of Job. It is later used in chapter 38 in reference to the angelic hosts who witnessed God's creation of the universe and rejoiced upon seeing it. Satan was also there at the time of creation and watched God perform His awesome work. Now, after his fall, he is standing in the presence of God again to give an account, along with the other angels.

If you have been led to believe that Satan does not have access to God because God cannot be in the presence of sin, you have been misinformed. There is nowhere that God is not. He is omnipresent. Satan stood in the Lord's presence and accused Joshua in *Zechariah 3:1*, and *Revelation 12:10* tells us that Satan accuses believers before God day and night. In *Luke 22:31*, the Lord also told Peter that Satan had come and asked if he could *sift you* [Peter] *like wheat*, which again shows that Satan still has access to God.

In other words, here is what Satan has the power to do:

- accuse you before God;
- accuse God before you;

- tell God you are not worth keeping;
- tell you that God is not worth following;
- remind God of your sin;
- remind you of God's wrath toward sinners;
- whisper in God's ear that you are unfaithful to Him;
- whisper in your ear that God is not interested in you.

The name Satan in this verse has the Hebrew definite article *he* before it, which can be translated "the Satan." This is actually referring to his activity as the adversary, not merely his character. In the New Testament, the article is dropped and he is simply referred to as Satan. Thus we often forget that his chief objective is to accuse and prosecute.[5]

Satan is not make-believe. He is not a funny cartoon character in red pajamas with a pitchfork, beard, pointed tail, and horns. Satan was created as part of the cherubim class of angelic beings. When we think of cherubs, we most often think of fat little babies with pink cheeks and soft curls. However, the cherubim were actually the angels that stood closest to the throne of God. In fact, when the Ark of the Covenant was crafted, it was constructed with two sculpted cherubim on either side of the lid (the mercy seat), with their wings spread toward one another.

The cherubim guarded Eden with their flaming swords as Adam and Eve were cast out in *Genesis 3*, and they were also the ones who were carved into the design of Solomon's magnificent temple in *1 Kings 6*. Ezekiel describes some cherubim as having four wings and four faces which faced north, south, east, and west; able to fly in any direction without ever having to turn around. Their faces are a man, a lion, a bull, and an eagle.

Other passages tell us that cherubim, as well as other angels, are able to change their appearance. Perhaps the four faces indicated the cherubim's mastery over travel and physical transformation. Satan, who is called the anointed cherub in *Ezekiel 28*, is also *the ruler of this world* (John 12:31); *the prince of the power of the air* (Ephesians 2:2); *the god of this world* (2 Corinthians 4:4)—*world* is translated from *aion*, which means "self-centered philosophy or system of thinking"; *Beelzebub the prince of devils* (Matthew 12:24 KJV)—which means "lord of the flies"; *Lucifer* (Isaiah 14:12 KJV)—which refers to his incredible beauty and to the aura of light that surrounds him; *the accuser of our brethren* (Revelation 12:10); *the enemy* (Matthew 13:39); *a murderer . . . the father of lies*

(John 8:44). This is the graphic description of the enemy who stood before God and the heavenly hosts to accuse Job.

> ***The LORD said to Satan, "From where do you come?" Then Satan answered the LORD and said, "From roaming about on the earth and walking around on it"*** (Job 1:7).

Satan did not somehow slip off God's radar—God knew *exactly* where he had been. It is similar to God's asking Adam in the Garden of Eden, *"Where are you?"* He already knew the answer. God knew where Adam was, but offered an opportunity for self-disclosure. In the same way, God knew exactly what Satan had been up to. He had been lurking behind the door of Job's house, watching closely for hidden malice.

In fact, the words ***roaming about*** and ***walking around*** refer to searching for something. Satan has been doing his homework; he has been carefully scrutinizing the ways of Job. So what does God do? He peers into Satan's heart and pulls out his hidden desire by asking a rhetorical question:

> ***"Have you considered My servant Job? For there is no one like him on the earth; a blameless and upright man, fearing God and turning away from evil"*** (Job 1:8).

This is a loaded question. It is as if God is saying, "Have you been watching Job's life carefully? Surely his life has caught your attention! He's quite a man, isn't he?" Try to imagine the implication of God's words to Satan. While Job slept, the adversary had been prowling around his estate, riffling through his files, checking his Internet locations, and reviewing his business contracts, searching tirelessly for the weak spot in Job's life. He found none.

Spurgeon wrote:

> As the worker in metals knows that one metal is to be worked at such a heat, and another at different temperature; as those who have to deal with chemicals know that at a certain heat one fluid will boil, while another reaches the boiling point much earlier, so Satan knows exactly the temperature at which to work us to his purpose. As the [hunter] has a gun for wild fowl, and another gun for deer and game, so has Satan a different temptation for various orders of men. The enemy, like a skilled fisherman, watches his fish, adapts his

> bait to his prey, and knows in what seasons and times the fish are most likely to bite.[6]

The problem for Satan was simply this: Job would not take the bait.

AN ACCUSATION AGAINST GOD

> ***Then Satan answered the LORD, "Does Job fear God for nothing? Have You not made a hedge about him and his house and all that he has, on every side? You have blessed the work of his hands, and his possessions have increased in the land"*** (Job 1:9–10).

Satan now moves from defense to offense in his conversation with God, as he makes an accusation about Job. In other words, Satan says: "Sure he's Your servant. Why wouldn't he be, with all the toys and trinkets you shower on him! That's why he loves You; that's *why* he worships You."

What if Satan and God had been talking about you? What if Satan had said something like: *The only reason he goes to church is because You gave him that pay raise* or *his favorite team won last night.*

Does that describe your loyalty to God? What happens to your spirit in the hospital . . . your prayer life in the emergency room . . . your walk with God in bankruptcy court . . . your faith beside an open grave . . . your attitude standing in the unemployment line? What happens when God doesn't pay up? This is the question that Job will wrestle with for almost 38 chapters.

If there were one man on earth who did not deserve the accusation, that man would be Job. He has walked with God for many years. As one author wrote,

> Job is called the servant of God. Satan could not care less. "Let him know what it is like to suffer the death of a child; let him go through the loss of all those possessions. Let all that hit him full force and then You will see what Job is made of."[7]

Satan is not only accusing Job in this passage, but he is also accusing God. Warren Wiersbe wrote these perceptive words:

> Satan's accusation was really an attack on God: "The only reason Job fears You is because You pay him to do it. You two have made a contract—You protect him and prosper him as long as he obeys You and worships You. You are not a God *worthy* of worship! You have to *pay* people to honor You."[8]

Don't ever forget that when you refuse to praise God in the midst of suffering, you not only fulfill Satan's accusation against you but also his accusation against your Savior. Every day you have the chance to prove to the devil that the Lord is worthy of your worship simply because of who He is.

God doesn't have to offer us possessions, promotions, or a good portfolio to be worthy of our praise; He has given us His person, which is worthy of all our adoration.

> ***"But put forth Your hand now and touch all that he has; he will surely curse You to Your face." Then the LORD said to Satan, "Behold, all that he has is in your power, only do not put forth your hand on him." So Satan departed from the presence of the LORD*** (Job 1:11–12).

Is God risking His own glory based on the response that Job will give? Is His glory really at stake? Hardly. Contrary to the popular writings of today, God risks nothing, needs to learn nothing, and is reckless in nothing. He is not some cosmic poker player betting all His winnings on Job's response; He has all the cards in His hand already and decides for Himself which ones He will play.

Satan, on the other hand, is not omniscient. He cannot know the future with perfect clarity as God does, and he has no clue what Job will do. God, however, knows everything from before time began and knows exactly how Job will respond. Satan is nothing more than a puppet in God's omniscient hands and God will use him to fulfill His own purposes. To this day, Satan hates to be reminded of his defeat by a mere man.[9]

Thus far, we have learned this of our enemy Satan:

1. He is loose on the earth but accountable to God.
2. He is brilliant and shrewd but not omniscient like God.
3. He is unable to touch the saint without the permission of God.
4. His influence and destructive power is limited by the will of God.
5. His ultimate defeat is found in the believer's praise of God.

There is less to fear than we thought.

Now on the day when his sons and his daughters were eating and drinking wine
in their oldest brother's house, 14 a messenger came to Job and said, "The oxen
were plowing and the donkeys feeding beside them, 15 and the Sabeans attacked
and took them. They also slew the servants with the edge of the sword, and I alone
have escaped to tell you." 16 While he was still speaking, another also came and
said, "The fire of God fell from heaven and burned up the sheep and the servants
and consumed them, and I alone have escaped to tell you." 17 While he was still
speaking, another also came and said, "The Chaldeans formed three bands and
made a raid on the camels and took them and slew the servants with the edge
of the sword, and I alone have escaped to tell you." 18 While he was still speak-
ing, another also came and said, "Your sons and your daughters were eating and
drinking wine in their oldest brother's house, 19 and behold, a great wind came
from across the wilderness and struck the four corners of the house, and it fell on
the young people and they died, and I alone have escaped to tell you."

20 Then Job arose and tore his robe and shaved his head, and he fell to the ground
and worshiped. 21 He said,
"Naked I came from my mother's womb,
And naked I shall return there.
The LORD gave and the LORD has taken away.
Blessed be the name of the LORD."

22 Through all this Job did not sin nor did he blame God.

–Job 1:13–22

CHAPTER THREE

NO SILVER LINING IN SIGHT

Job 1:13–22

On November 1, 1755, an earthquake rocked Lisbon, Portugal. Many of you will remember the tsunami at Christmas 2004, which swept away coastal villages from Southeast Asia to India and Thailand, and the March 2011 earthquake in Japan. These disasters might have been worse than the Lisbon earthquake in loss of life and possessions, but none was so widely discussed or had such profound ramifications. It is considered the most far-reaching and well-known natural disaster in modern history.

Ironically, it hit on All Saints Day, when churches were crowded with worshipers. After the first tremors, many people fled to nearby church buildings and cathedrals, hoping to be spared. Eyewitnesses watched in terror, and when the second shock wave began, priests and parishioners alike began to scream, calling out to God for mercy. When the earth stopped shaking, almost every church in Lisbon had been reduced to rubble, crushing the thousands inside.

Fires broke out across the city, followed by a tsunami which tore ships from their moorings and drowned hundreds of people. The death toll was in the tens of thousands—both the religious and the rebellious, the educated and the illiterate, the wealthy and the poor were killed. The earthquake proved to be no respecter of persons; seventy-five percent of Lisbon had been utterly wiped out.

Opinions were voiced throughout Europe as to why the disaster had occurred. Some believed the earthquake to be judgment from God, while others believed it was a sign of God's mercy—since Lisbon deserved much worse. Some claimed that God was trying to communicate to humanity that there is a world beyond this one . . . a world that could give meaning to the unpredictable and haphazard life on earth. Sermons on the earthquake were preached for years afterward, and historians have even claimed that the Revolution in France, as well as the Wesleyan revivals in England, was a result of the catastrophe in Portugal.[1]

Natural disasters and other types of suffering are often the most difficult tests of faith for a believer. A sobering truth for believers will echo loud and clear throughout Job's story; his faith will not separate him from suffering—it will *instigate* it.[2]

It is no wonder that preachers of the "prosperity gospel" ignore the Book of Job: the message is undeniable—Christians will suffer. They may preach and promise that if you mind your spiritual manners, give God everything you can, have unfailing faith and, of course, send them some money, God will hang a Do Not Disturb sign on the front door of your life. They must have overlooked the question that God asks Satan in the first part of chapter one: ***"Have you considered My servant Job?"*** They must have overlooked the Book of Job entirely, for it was God who allowed the suffering and God who initiated it in the life of His *faithful* servant.

Even the most optimistic Christian among us will say, "Job does go through an enormous cloud of suffering, but have you seen the silver lining? In the last chapter of the book, he gets everything back and more!"

That's easy for us to say!

Bill Walton, the sports announcer and former NBA basketball star once said, "I learned a long time ago that minor surgery is when they do the operation on someone else."[3]

Let me encourage you not to mentally skip to the end of the book. Even though you already know Job's children will die and he will have more children later, keep in mind that he will never get his first ten children back. Job will experience great suffering, with no silver lining in sight. There is no quick answer from God, no insight or reason from on high, and the clouds hover above the tree of his life for quite some time.

THE DEVASTATING MESSAGE

> ***Now on the day when his sons and his daughters were eating and drinking wine in their oldest brother's house, a messenger came to Job and said, "The oxen were plowing and the donkeys feeding beside them, and the Sabeans attacked and took them. They also slew the servants with the edge of the sword, and I alone have escaped to tell you"*** (Job 1:13–15).

Bandits from the kingdom of Sheba in southern Arabia (whose queen will one day visit Solomon) have come to pilfer Job's livestock, eliminating all traces of evidence.[4]

> ***While he was still speaking, another also came and said, "The fire of God fell from heaven and burned up the sheep and the servants and consumed them, and I alone have escaped to tell you"*** (Job 1:16).

Perhaps this was a lightning storm that swept into the region and continued to strike the ground. It must have been enormous, given the fact that Job owned 7,000 sheep. Notice how the messenger credits God for the fire that fell ***from heaven***. This message must have troubled Job greatly. The first tragedy came at the hand of bandits; the second came, evidently, from the hand of God.

> ***While he was still speaking, another also came and said, "The Chaldeans formed three bands and made a raid on the camels and took them and slew the servants with the edge of the sword, and I alone have escaped to tell you"*** (Job 1:17).

This is the third message which provided devastating loss for Job. He must be reeling under the staggering loss of his business, his fortune, and his work force. He considers for a moment the graves of his servants that must now be dug on his land, and the women and children who will be left widowed and orphaned. One author wrote, "Perhaps Job thought to himself, *At least I've got my kids.*"[5]

> ***While he was still speaking, another also came and said, "Your sons and your daughters were eating and drinking wine in their oldest brother's house, and behold, a great***

> ***wind came from across the wilderness and struck the four corners of the house, and it fell on the young people and they died, and I alone have escaped to tell you"*** (Job 1:18–19).

"It came so unexpectedly," the messenger panted, "the sound was deafening . . . there was nowhere to run or hide . . . it seemed as if the home of your oldest son where all your children had gathered was its target . . . the house exploded—and all your children were . . . killed."[6]

It is as if all the forces of heaven and earth conspired against Job and his family. His life will *never* be the same.

By the way, no voice speaks from heaven; no answers arrive from an angelic messenger saying, "Take heart, Job—Satan is testing your faith in God; and God already knows you will pass the test." The heavens are absolutely silent.

On the back cover of one of my commentaries on Job, there is a classic painting of this scene. Four messengers are standing around the doorway of Job's house. Three are there with the wind whipping about their robes and a fourth is pointing into the distance where trees are bent by a fierce wind. Job is prostrate on the ground; his sandals have fallen off; his arms and hands are covering his head in anguish.[7]

There is no such thing as a silver lining to this immense dark cloud.

THE DEFINING MOMENT

At this very moment, there is an invisible scene taking place that Job is unaware of. Satan and his minions are craning their necks to watch. They are hovering over this man of God to hear the first whisper of a curse toward God—to hear a word of blasphemy from Job . . . just one. Their ears are itching in anticipation of the bitter invectives that might escape his mouth—blasphemies that would prove God a liar and unworthy of praise.

> ***Then Job arose and tore his robe and shaved his head, and he fell to the ground and worshiped*** (Job 1:20).

By the way, we are not told the amount of time that passed between verses 19 and 20. It could have been a matter of moments or many hours. If it were minutes, I'm sure they felt like hours to the man who had just lost everything. But his response is remarkable. Five verbs appear in quick succession to indicate that the only cursing heard that day was from the mouth of Satan who had failed yet again.

Job prostrated himself and began to ***worship*** God, as the Hebrew language indicates. The amazing thing about this scene is not so much that Job suffered but that he didn't deserve it. Furthermore, while Satan is behind the peril, God is allowing it—all the while offering no explanation to Job.

Isn't this the biggest struggle we have with suffering ourselves? It's not usually about the degree of pain we have to endure but the fact that it seems unfair. We want a reason for why it's happening. We feel that we deserve answers but are given none. Can we really follow Job's example and worship God even in the midst of suffering? The answer is not only yes, but *absolutely*. We are to constantly worship God for His character because it is the one thing that never changes. He is to be praised at all times for He is always good and just, even when our circumstances tell us otherwise.

Job's response of worship should not be the exception; it should be the rule.

THE DEVIL'S MISFORTUNE

> ***He said, "Naked I came from my mother's womb, and naked I shall return there. The LORD gave and the LORD has taken away. Blessed be the name of the LORD"*** (Job 1:21).

Satan couldn't have seen this response coming in a million years. His best attempts at provoking Job to rebuke God made Job realize all the more his complete sufficiency in God. It does not get any clearer or more graphic than this. We were born with nothing in our hands, and we will die in the same manner.

Tragedies in life have a way of separating the meaningless from the significant, the desires from the necessities. In the wake of a massive hurricane, one author wrote:

> No one lamented a lost plasma TV or a submerged SUV. No one ran through the streets yelling, "My cordless drill is missing." If they mourned, it was for people lost. If they rejoiced, it was for people found. . . . Raging hurricanes have a way of prying our fingers off things that really don't matter.[8]

If that is not convicting enough, consider this:

> According to the Self Storage Association, the country now possesses about 1.9 billion square feet of personal storage space outside of the home. All this space is contained in nearly 40,000 facilities owned and operated by more than 2,000

> entrepreneurs, including a handful of publicly traded giants like Public Storage, Storage USA, and Shurgard.
>
> According to a recent survey, one homeowner out of every eleven also owns a self-storage space. This represents an increase of 75 percent since 1995. Most operators of self-storage facilities report 90 percent occupancy but, amazingly, as the amount of storage space required by homeowners has grown, so has the average size of the American house. The National Association of Homebuilders reports that the average American house grew from 1,600 square feet in 1973 to 2,400 square feet by 2004, and the number is increasing.
>
> So—houses got bigger, average family sizes got smaller, and yet we need two billion square feet of extra space to store our stuff?[9]

Job's comment is a startling reminder to all humanity: naked we entered life, and naked we will exit. With deep faith in the character of God, Job acknowledged the right of God over everything—his possessions, his health, his kids, his businesses, his employees, and his future.

As Job lies prostrate in the dust, he cries out these words, "The Lord gave me all I have and He has taken it all back." This may be easy to say—many of us may have said it. But I wonder how many of us have followed up that statement with this one: "And who does He think He is? It's not fair. Doesn't He know that I am a righteous person?"

Job, however, followed that statement saying, ***"Blessed be the name of the LORD."***

It is interesting that three times in his response, Job will use the name *Yahweh*—the personal name of God.[10] The thing that matters most to Job in the hour of his greatest sorrow is his relationship to his personal sovereign King. God is under no obligation to tell Job all that He has in store for him, and Job realizes that.

When there are no answers on earth; when it all seems so unfair; when life delivers one cruel message after another; when clouds are dark with no silver lining—*that* is when we worship God with childlike faith. That is when we learn to truly worship Him on the basis of who He is, rather than how we expect Him to act.

It is no wonder that the chapter ends with these powerful words:

> ***Through all this Job did not sin nor did he blame God*** (Job 1:22).

Why are we given this closing phrase? Because blaming God would have been the natural thing to do. Most people would have said, "Where were You, God? You could have stopped this from happening." Job refused to cast blame on God and as a result, Satan lost again. It may have been a devastating day for Job, but it was even more disastrous for the devil. Things aren't going so well for him at the moment.

In 1932, A.M. Overton was a pastor in Mississippi with a wife, three small children, and a fourth on the way. At the time of delivery, there were complications and his wife and baby died. During the funeral service, the officiating preacher noticed the bereaved young pastor writing something on a piece of paper. After the service, the minister asked him about it and was handed a poem entitled "He Maketh No Mistake." Overton's testimony was like Job's: no blame toward God. The poem's words became a song; the lyrics are powerful, reminding the storm-ridden Christian of his silver lining:

My Father's way may twist and turn,
My heart may throb and ache,
But in my soul I'm glad to know,
He makes no mistakes.

My cherished plans may go astray,
My hopes may fade away,
But still I'll trust my Lord to lead,
For He doth know the way.

Though the night be dark and it may seem,
That day will never break,
I'll pin my faith, my all in Him,
He makes no mistake.

There's so much now I cannot see,
My eyesight's far too dim,
But come what may, I'll simply trust,
And leave it all to Him.

For by and by the mist will lift,
And plain it all He'll make,
Through all the way, though dark to me,
He made not one mistake.[11]

Now on the day when his sons and his daughters were eating and drinking wine in their oldest brother's house, 14 a messenger came to Job and said, "The oxen were plowing and the donkeys feeding beside them, 15 and the Sabeans attacked and took them. They also slew the servants with the edge of the sword, and I alone have escaped to tell you." 16 While he was still speaking, another also came and said, "The fire of God fell from heaven and burned up the sheep and the servants and consumed them, and I alone have escaped to tell you." 17 While he was still speaking, another also came and said, "The Chaldeans formed three bands and made a raid on the camels and took them and slew the servants with the edge of the sword, and I alone have escaped to tell you." 18 While he was still speaking, another also came and said, "Your sons and your daughters were eating and drinking wine in their oldest brother's house, 19 and behold, a great wind came from across the wilderness and struck the four corners of the house, and it fell on the young people and they died, and I alone have escaped to tell you."

20 Then Job arose and tore his robe and shaved his head, and he fell to the ground and worshiped. 21 He said,
"Naked I came from my mother's womb,
And naked I shall return there.
The LORD gave and the LORD has taken away.
Blessed be the name of the LORD."

22 Through all this Job did not sin nor did he blame God.

–Job 1:13–22

CHAPTER FOUR

ACTS OF GOD

Job 1:13–22

WHAT'S NATURAL ABOUT DISASTERS?

The date was February 15, 1947. The sound was deafening. Although no one would hear it, ultimately it echoed around the world. None of the passengers in the DC-4 ever knew what happened . . . they died instantly. The Avianca Airlines flight bound for Quito, Ecuador, crashed clumsily into a 14,000-foot mountain peak near Bogotá . . . then dropped, a flaming mass of metal, into a ravine far below. One of the passengers was Glenn Chambers. He planned to begin a ministry with "The Voice of the Andes," but his lifelong dream suddenly ended. For his loved ones, his dream became their nightmare.

Before leaving the Miami airport earlier that day, Chambers had hurriedly dashed off a note on a piece of paper he found on the floor of the terminal. It was a scrap that had once been an advertisement; on one side was his note—on the other side was a single word typed across the face of that scrap of paper: "*WHY*?"

Between the mailing and the delivery of that note, Glenn died in that plane crash. When the letter arrived, there, staring up at his mother, was that haunting word—that lamenting question: "Why?"[1]

Perhaps the two most often asked questions of life are: "Why did this happen?" and "Where was God when it did?" Or perhaps it could be asked in this way: "Why did God let this happen in the first place?"

Had we been neighbors of Job and his wife, we would have been asking these same questions. In fact, most of the rest of the Book of Job is nothing less than an attempt by Job and his friends to answer these questions. If we didn't know the rest of the story, we would be asking the same things today.

In the first chapter of Job, we read in vivid detail how, in just one afternoon, Job's dreams turned into nightmares.

The first messenger came to tell Job that the ***Sabeans*** took his oxen and donkeys and killed his farm hands ***(Job 1:14–15)***.

The second messenger interrupted the first with the news that ***fire*** had fallen from heaven and consumed Job's 7,000 sheep and killed all his herdsmen ***(Job 1:16)***.

A third messenger broke into the group, bringing word that the ***Chaldeans*** raided Job's import/export business, stole all his camels, and killed all but one of his employees ***(Job 1:17)***.

The fourth and final messenger delivered the most horrifying news of all: a ***whirlwind*** struck Job's oldest son's house and all ten of his children are now dead. There was only one survivor: this messenger who stood, gasping for breath, wiping tears from his eyes ***(Job 1:18–19)***.

39 SECONDS

I reread these verses and timed myself, reading only the messages that were delivered one after another. The text clearly indicates that these messengers arrived virtually at the same time and interrupted each other with each new message. It took me only thirty-nine seconds . . . thirty-nine seconds for Job to have his heart crushed and his world crashed.

It takes a lifetime to build some things, so why can so much of life collapse in a matter of seconds?

The trouble Job will have for many months will not have anything to do with the Sabeans and the Chaldeans—they were thieves and brutal warriors. Job's trouble stems from the other two events: the whirlwind that seemed to target the house of his oldest son and the fire that fell from heaven.

Insurance agents and mortgage companies would call these events "acts of God." Were they? And is that enough of an answer?

- Is God involved in tragedies?
- Is God really interested in what happens on the planet He created?
- Is God powerful enough to control nature?
- Should natural disasters be called "acts of God"?

Haven't millions inside and outside the Church wondered at times if God is indifferent . . . calloused . . . uncaring?

Does God care? Does He watch the news?

Commenting on a recent natural disaster, one newscaster spoke for many skeptics when he said, "If this world is the product of intelligent design, then the Designer has some explaining to do."[2]

This kind of bold statement might make us cringe; however, isn't it interesting that those who do not believe in God immediately assume the existence of God as they rail against Him for allowing such disasters to occur.

RELIGIOUS ANSWERS TO ACTS OF GOD

The Eastern world has an answer that doesn't involve a personal, active God. They would say that anyone so affected is simply living out the Law of Karma. Hinduism's Law of Karma states that all the actions of life today are the result of the actions of a previous life. Blindness, poverty, hunger, and the behavior of others toward us are all the outworking of punishment for evil deeds in a previous existence. To attempt to alleviate pain and misery would be to *interfere* with justice.

This is one of the primary reasons that countries gripped by Hinduism do little for the unfortunate among them. Poverty and disease are rampant. Why not?—it's the individual's fault. This is a tidy, simple explanation for suffering.[3]

No matter what we believe, we normally attempt to *explain* natural disasters and suffering in general.

In recent years, many Muslims believed that Allah had struck Southeast Asia with a tsunami at Christmastime because the season is so filled with immorality and alcohol.

Hurricane Katrina of 2005 was the third strongest hurricane to reach landfall in American history. Nearly 2,000 people died in the storm. It has become the costliest natural disaster in United States history, at more than 81 billion dollars.

Erwin Lutzer reported in his book *Where Was God?* that after the hurricane, some Muslims said that Allah was heaping vengeance on the United States for the war in Iraq.

Christians piled on and said that the hurricane was judgment on New Orleans for Mardi Gras and the open acceptance of homosexual parades.

A Christian reporter in Israel said that the United States suffered a hurricane because it agreed with the Israeli policy that forced Jewish settlers out of the Gaza strip.

One Christian leader in America said that the Israeli Prime Minister suffered a stroke as a result of God's judgment against him for having divided God's land and given the Gaza Strip away.[4]

Frankly, this theology is horribly untrue; as if God couldn't stop the Middle east from being divided, but He could at least send the former Prime Minister a stroke to get even?!

When tragedy strikes, we have the natural tendency to interpret it in light of what we believe God is trying to say. And at times, we are terrible spokesmen for God.

What would *we* say about these *acts of God*?

What about the cruelty of man to mankind? Where was God on 9/11? When the bombs went off in Madrid and downtown London?

Was God any less involved in these than in the Asian tsunami which took the lives of 275,000 people? Was He missing from His post? Was He unconcerned when a massive earthquake and ensuing tsunami hit Japan killing tens of thousands of people and with economic losses costing more than 300 billion? Was He unable to head off the typhoon that flattened the landscape and flooded entire cities in the Phillipines that same year?

John Piper and Justin Taylor, in *Suffering and the Sovereignty of God*, posed similar questions about random acts of cruelty. They referred to the summer of 2005 when Dennis Rader was finally captured. He was called the BTK killer—Rader's acronym for "bind, torture, and kill." Piper posed the question, "Why does God allow such things to happen? While we begged God to make them stop, why didn't He?"[5]

Open any newspaper and read of drunken drivers crossing medians and killing entire families. Many of us know people who have experienced the pain of direct or indirect involvement with someone who has been mistreated, abused, raped, robbed, or murdered.

What do we say to them? What *would* we say to Job?

REACTIONS TO ACTS OF GOD

People react to tragedy in unique ways—many of which are *not* how we should respond.

Trivial

A person shrugs off the issue and says, "It really doesn't concern most people. God wants us to be happy, and I guess the devil gets in the way sometimes . . . you just gotta learn to deal with stuff."

Hypocritical

Those who use this approach are usually not even aware of their error. These are believers who are quick to defend, "God had nothing at all to do with that hurricane—it was just the forces of nature at work. God is in control, but He lets nature take its course."

The reason I call this hypocritical is because most of these Christians will pray for rain when needed for the crops and pray for sunshine on their wedding day. They will thank God for the nice weather, automatically acknowledging that God has *something* to do with it.

After a recent earthquake in California, a group of pastors met for a prayer breakfast. As they discussed impassable expressways and ruined buildings, they agreed that for all practical purposes, God had nothing to do with the disaster. When one of the ministers closed the meeting in prayer, he actually thanked God for the timing of the earthquake that came at five o'clock in the morning when there were fewer cars on the expressways and the sidewalks of cities and towns were empty. When he finished the prayer, his colleagues chimed in with a hearty, "Amen."[6]

How do you thank God for the timing of an earthquake if He is only an interested observer?

Knee-Jerk

When a prominent Christian was asked by a reporter why God wasn't around during certain disasters, he responded by saying, "Well, we've been telling God to get out of our classrooms, our schools, and our politics for some time . . . now that He's gone, you got your wish; and now you can't blame Him."

This sounds like a decent answer at first, but it leaves troubling questions lingering about the character of God. Is God pouting, since He has been blacklisted in our schools and public spaces? Has He taken His toys and gone home, since prayer is no longer allowed and political agendas ignore Him?

If this were true and God were just fed up with the planet, what does that say about His sovereign control and His omnipotent timing over the events of this world? What does it mean as it relates to this age of grace and the longsuffering of God?

In an attempt to get God off the hook by telling people that He left us just like we wanted all along, God becomes dependent on our actions, moods, legislations, and policies.

Shallow

This approach attempts to ignore the deeper questions about the nature and character of God and focuses, instead, on easier problems. The Church is struggling because of a lack of theological depth—perhaps a willful refusal to deal with the harsher realities of God's sovereignty.

John Piper commented further:

> The Church has not been spending its energy to go deep with the unfathomable God of the Bible. Against the overwhelming weight and seriousness of the Bible, much of the Church is choosing, at this very moment, to become lighter and more shallow and entertainment-oriented, and therefore has become irrelevant [while at the same time claiming to be so successful in being relevant. The truth is] the popular God of fun-church is simply too small and too sociable to hold a hurricane in His hand."[7]

Unwilling

When we don't care enough to try to give an answer, we find it hard to condense a solution into some short-and-sweet answer.

PRINCIPLES ON ACTS OF GOD

Consider these principles as you weigh your answer and acknowledge the sovereignty of God in the midst of natural disasters.

Suffering Is More Widespread than We Realize

News reports take us to cities and villages where people have died from mudslides, floods, and tornadoes. It may seem that we are surrounded by natural disasters and our news media take us from one crisis to another.

Asking why people die when natural disasters occur is similar to asking why people die . . . period.

Whether we know it or not, 6,000 people on this planet die every hour—most as a result of some sort of suffering. In the time it takes you to finish reading this sentence, 700 people will die—many of them from disease, crime, accidents, suicide, starvation, and natural disasters.

Actually, *more* children in the world under the age of five will die of starvation every day than the total number of children and adults who died when a major hurricane slammed into the Gulf Coast. The only reason natural disasters attract our attention is because they dramatically intensify the daily occurrence of death and destruction.[8]

There happens to be much suffering and death on earth, and it is more widespread than we can ever comprehend.

Today's World Isn't the World God Created

The Apostle Paul wrote to the Romans,

> *For I consider that the sufferings of this present time are not worthy to be compared with the glory that is to be revealed to us. For the anxious longing of the creation waits eagerly for the revealing of the sons of God. . . . For we know that the whole creation groans and suffers the pains of childbirth together until now. . . . even we ourselves groan within ourselves, waiting eagerly for our adoption as sons, the redemption of our body. . . . But if we hope for what we do not see, with perseverance we wait eagerly for it* (Romans 8:18–19, 22–23, 25).

In this paragraph, Paul makes a direct connection between the fall of man in sin and the curse of creation.

The world God originally created and the one that now erupts with earthquakes, mudslides, and floods is a different world system. It is out of joint. The created order is now waiting for God to make it right again.

One author wrote that nature is cursed because man is cursed; natural evil and brutality (which exist in the animal and physical world) is a reflection of moral evil, in that both are savage, ruthless, and damaging. Nature is a mirror in which we see ourselves.[9]

This could easily lead us to despair; the kind of despair evident in the words of Voltaire, the French skeptic, who wrote, "We are insects living for a few seconds on atoms of mud and cannot understand the designs of an infinite Creator."

He is correct . . . in part. Without the revealed Word of God, we would have no answer to pain and suffering at all. William James would be right when he said that we all are like dogs left in a library—seeing the print but unable to read the words.[10]

Mankind and nature are fallen, but neither has fallen out of the sovereign hand or plan and purpose of God. God has not walked away from the day-to-day control of His creation. While He certainly established physical laws by which He governs the forces of nature, those laws continuously operate according to His sovereign will.

Job will later hear this truth loud and clear:

> ***"He unleashes His lightning beneath the whole heaven and sends it to the ends of the earth. . . . He says to the snow, 'Fall on the earth,' and to the rain shower, 'Be a mighty downpour.' . . . The breath of God produces ice, and the broad waters become frozen. He loads the clouds with moisture; He scatters His lightning through them. At His direction they swirl around over the face of the whole earth to do whatever He commands them. Whether for correction, or for His world, or for lovingkindness, He causes it to happen"*** (Job 37:3, 6, 10–13 NIV; NASB).

One believing meteorologist has determined that there are over 1,400 references to weather terminology in the Bible. Many of them attribute the weather to the direct control and purpose of God.

> *He covers the sky with clouds; He supplies the earth with rain and makes grass grow on the hills. . . . He spreads the snow like wool and scatters the frost like ashes. He hurls down His hail like pebbles. Who can withstand His icy blast? He sends His word and melts them; He stirs up His breezes and the waters flow* (Psalm 147:8, 16–18 NIV).

The prophet Amos includes God's own testimony:

> *"I also withheld rain from you when the harvest was still three months away. I sent rain on one town, but withheld it from another. One field had rain; another had none and dried up"* (Amos 4:7 NIV).

All expressions of nature, all occurrences of weather—whether a devastating tornado or a gentle rain on a spring day—are acts of God. God controls all the forces of nature, both destructive and productive on a continuous, moment-by-moment basis—which means the believer is never the victim of the powers of nature or fate or chance.[11]

The *indirect* cause of our death or suffering might be nature or violence, but the *direct* cause behind it all is the plan and purpose of God.

Jesus Christ, in His Sermon on the Mount, said,

> *"He* [your Father in heaven] *causes His sun to rise on the evil and the good, and sends rain on the righteous and the unrighteous"* (Matthew 5:45*b*).

One theologian wrote, "Nothing—absolutely nothing—no evil thing or evil person or natural painful event falls outside God's ordaining will. Nothing arises, exists, or endures independently of God's will. So when even the worst of evils befall us, they do not ultimately come from anywhere other than God's hand."[12]

We sing the truth of this doctrine of God's sovereign control over nature and the affairs of mankind when we raise our voices with Isaac Watts' great hymn, "I Sing the Mighty Power of God."

There's not a plant or flow'r below
But makes Thy glories known;
And clouds arise and tempests blow
By order from Thy throne;
While all that borrows life from Thee
Is ever in Thy care,
And ev'rywhere that man can be,
Thou, God, art present there.[13]

The Character and Work of God on Earth Is Different from What We Imagined

If the Bible's description of God reveals that He is absolutely sovereign, then He is ultimately responsible.

When we watch someone sifting through the rubble of their home, which of the following responses would give them the most comfort?

- "Well, I don't know where God was when this tragedy struck."
- "I'm sure God didn't want this to happen."
- "This was allowed by God and one day He will will make His purposes clear."

Nahum introduces us to a mysterious God:

> [He is in] *the whirlwind and the storm* . . . (Nahum 1:3*b* NIV).

David writes of our God, who gives an account to no one:

> *But our God is in the heavens; He does whatever He pleases* (Psalm 115:3).

Isaiah's record agrees,

> *Surely, as I have planned, so it will be, and as I have purposed, so it will stand* (Isaiah 14:24 NIV).

God says an even more shocking thing when He declares:

> *"I form the light and create darkness, I bring prosperity and create disaster; I, the LORD, do all these things"* (Isaiah 45:7 NIV).

The Church today is trying desperately to let God off the hook while God is taking full responsibility.

This is God's universe. That was *His* storm; *His* lightning; *His* flood; *His* sunshine; *His* winter blast . . .

Would you rather believe that God is *not* in control of natural disasters? Tell that to Noah. Or Jonah. Or Pharaoah.

David wrote, *The heavens declare the glory of God* (Psalm 19:1*a* NIV).

Paul paraphrased that God's creation and the works of nature reveal His attributes of power and strength *(Romans 1:20).*

The Church needs to be reintroduced to an uncomfortable God—to a God, as David wrote, who is altogether unlike us *(Psalm 50:21).*

We need to embrace the God described by Solomon who considers it His *glory to conceal a matter* (Proverbs 25:2*a*).

This is the God of which we read, *Truly, You are a God who hides Himself* (Isaiah 45:15*a*). *The secret things belong to the Lord our God* (Deuteronomy 29:29*a*).

This is the God whose word to us might more often be simply: *"Be still, and know that I am God"* (Psalm 46:10*a* KJV).

C. S. Lewis said that God actually speaks loudest to us when we suffer. Have you noticed that?

Lewis wrote, "God whispers to us in our pleasures, speaks in our conscience, but shouts in our pain; it is His megaphone to rouse a deaf world."[14]

PURPOSES OF ACTS OF GOD

Why wouldn't God keep everything sunshine and roses? What does the record of Job's life thus far—and the perspective of Scripture as God has revealed Himself—tell us of His purposes for His creation's suffering under these *acts of God*?

To Remind Us What Is Truly Valuable

Augustine once wrote, "God would give us something, but does not because our hands are full."

When we are stripped of everything and our hands are emptied, we discover the most important things all over again.

I found it interesting that after a major hurricane swept through her state, Louisiana governor Kathleen Blanco called for a statewide day of prayer, saying, "We need to turn to God for strength, hope, and comfort."[15]

Had she said a few days before the hurricane that the state of Louisiana needed to turn to God in prayer for *anything*, she would have been mocked by the press and her colleagues and probably would have lost her credibility as a leader—and, perhaps, her job.

Acts of God remind us what truly matters matters in life.

To Release Our Claim on Expectations in Life

The things we thought we had a right to own or accomplish simply vanish. Bankruptcy, sickness, an accident all remind us that our expectation must be in Him and Him alone.

To Give Realistic Perspective on the Brevity of Life

Read the latest newspaper edition and consider: *we* could have been the victim of that calamity. It could have been any of *us* on the six o'clock news.

When things are going well, we are under the delusion that a comfortable life—or life itself—is a sure thing. Then our chest squeezes in pain and the next thing we know, we are hooked up to a dozen wires and the doctors are saying, "We got you here just in time."

The truth is whether we are aware of it or not, this could be our last day on earth.

To Warn Us about Eternal Judgment for All Life

Lutzer writes that ***Job 37:6, 10–13*** tell us, "Nature reflects God's gracious attributes, but also His attributes of wrath and justice."[16]

Accidents that take the lives of others are a reminder of a coming judgment from which there is no escape.

In *Luke 13*, the Lord was preaching just after a tower had fallen that had resulted in the death of eighteen people. Jesus used the incident as an illustration in His sermon that everyone was going to die. He said to them, in effect, "Are you ready for the judgment—have you repented of your sin?"

The suffering of people around the globe is intended to illustrate that fallen mankind will one day either be released from suffering in glory or condemned to suffer forever. The unexpected loss of life reminds us that we all have an appointment with God.

David Miller wrote, "Natural disasters provide people with conclusive evidence that life on earth is brief and uncertain."[17]

To Invite Us to Walk with God through Life

God does not promise the absence of storms, but He does promise His presence *in* the storms.

Don't be like that proverbial man who decided to get even. He'd been bitten by a dog and was informed by his physician that he was now infected with rabies. Upon hearing the diagnosis, the patient immediately pulled out a pad and pen and began to write feverishly. Thinking the man was making out his Last Will and Testament, the doctor said, "Listen, this doesn't mean you're going to die. There's a cure for rabies."

"I know that," said the man, "I'm making a list of people I'm gonna bite."[18]

As Warren Wiersbe encouaged us when facing trials, "Don't grow bitter; grow better."

The truth is, suffering is the megaphone through which God is inviting, "Walk with Me."

To Encourage Us That, for Believers, Suffering Will Be Replaced with Everlasting Joy

The Apostle Paul assures us that this present suffering cannot be compared to the glory that will be revealed to us *(Romans 8:18).*

When the *R.M.S. Titanic* went down, 1,517 people went to a watery grave. Among the dead were: 130 in First Class; 166 in Second Class; 536 in Third Class (Steerage); 685 crew members.

The immediate causes were human error, an iceberg, insufficient lifeboats, and frigid waters . . . but the ultimate cause was God, who had determined that their days on earth were completed.

After the news of the *Titanic* tragedy reached the countries of the passengers, the challenge was how to inform the relatives whether their loved ones were among the living or the dead. At the office of the White Star Line in Liverpool, England, a huge board was set up. At the top of one side a cardboard sign read KNOWN TO BE SAVED and on the other end was a sign with the words KNOWN TO BE LOST. Hundreds of people gathered to watch intently for updates. When a messenger brought new information, those waiting held their breath, wondering on which side of the board he would write and what name would be added to the growing list.

Although *Titanic*'s passengers had purchased tickets for First, Second, or Third Class arrangements and lodging, there were only two categories after the ship went down: the SAVED and the LOST.

At the end of human history when all of humanity is forever divided—there will be only two categories that will matter: those who were known to be saved and those who were known to be lost.[19]

For the saved, suffering will begin to make sense. For the lost, suffering will have just begun.

Make sure you are ready for the acts of God on earth *and* for the final act of God's judgment when you stand before Him on that day.

For those who believe, who are ushered into the heavenly city resting on a newly created earth, all suffering will make sense—in fact, it will probably no longer matter . . . for sorrow will be replaced with everlasting joy.

Again there was a day when the sons of God came to present themselves before the
LORD, and Satan also came among them to present himself before the LORD.
2 The LORD said to Satan, "Where have you come from?" Then Satan answered
the LORD and said, "From roaming about on the earth and walking around on
it." 3 The LORD said to Satan, "Have you considered My servant Job? For there is
no one like him on the earth, a blameless and upright man fearing God and turn-
ing away from evil. And he still holds fast his integrity, although you incited Me
against him to ruin him without cause." 4 Satan answered the LORD and said,
"Skin for skin! Yes, all that a man has he will give for his life. 5 However, put forth
Your hand now, and touch his bone and his flesh; he will curse You to Your face."
6 So the LORD said to Satan, "Behold, he is in your power, only spare his life."

7 Then Satan went out from the presence of the LORD and smote Job with sore
boils from the sole of his foot to the crown of his head. 8 And he took a potsherd to
scrape himself while he was sitting among the ashes.

9 Then his wife said to him, "Do you still hold fast your integrity? Curse God and
die!" 10 But he said to her, "You speak as one of the foolish women speaks. Shall
we indeed accept good from God and not accept adversity?" In all this Job did
not sin with his lips.

–Job 2:1–10

CHAPTER FIVE

A MONUMENT OF PRAISE IN THE VALLEY OF DESPAIR

Job 2:1–10

The citizens and farmers of Enterprise, Alabama, had a serous problem. Their entire economy rested on successfully growing cotton, but in the 1890s, small beetles migrating from Mexico had begun eating their way across the cotton fields of the South. They arrived in Alabama in 1910 and ravished all the cotton fields. The bug's official name is Anthonomus grandis, but we know him as the Boll Weevil. Because of the plague of weevils, the farmers faced certain bankruptcy and their economy was all but lost.

One farmer was a visionary, however, and saw the disaster as an opportunity. Rather than pack his bags and surrender to the cotton-eating pest, he listened to George Washington Carver, an agricultural scientist at the Tuskegee Institute, who told him to diversify his crops by planting peanuts, sweet potatoes, and soy beans. By following Carver's advice, Enterprise—in contrast to the rest of the state—rebounded economically by 1917 with the largest peanut harvest in the nation.

Mr. Fleming, a local businessman, came up with the idea of building a monument to the Boll Weevil, effectively thanking it for making them so prosperous. This monument stands more than thirty feet tall and, at the top, is a woman who resembles the Statue of Liberty. She was crafted in Italy and shipped to Alabama dressed in a flowing gown. With her arms raised, she holds in her hands a platter, on top of which is a large sculpture of the most famous beetle in the world. The monument was dedicated to the boll weevil on December 11, 1919, and has been standing for a hundred years.[1]

Imagine—people erected a monument to an agricultural pest. Did they forget about its desecration of their cotton fields? Did they forget about the bankruptcy it caused them? No! They saw the enormously positive effects that it had instigated on their town *after* the crisis was over.

There is a beautiful feature to the story of Job which is lost in the story of Enterprise, Alabama. Job will erect a monument of worship to God in spite of the fact that he is bankrupt, with no hope of a new crop or a glorious income. He raises a monument of praise *during* the trial, not afterwards.

FROM RICHES TO RAGS

Job was the wealthiest of men and the most prosperous of farmers, but unknown to him, a pest was moving into his territory. It wasn't a beetle, it was Beelzebub—the Lord of the Flies—and he brought with him pestilence like no man had yet seen or endured. In a matter of thirty-nine seconds, Job receives news that he is bankrupt, having lost his possessions, his livestock, and his children, and he experiences predictable, deep sorrow over his losses.

He's not the only one suffering loss. Satan, who was convinced that Job would respond to his crushing losses by *cursing* God, watched in agony as Job fell on his face and *worshiped* God instead. It is not certain who suffered more that day—Job or Satan.

Frankly, Job's response is almost unbelievable. In fact, if it were not recorded in the Bible, I would not believe it. How does someone pass this crisis of suffering and remain surrendered to the hand of God? Listen to the words of one author as he tells another story similar to Job's:

> It was late afternoon when the boat's engine sputtered, stalled, and refused to restart. Gallons of water surged into the craft as it pitched on six-foot swells. The five Jaeger men had done all they knew how to do, but it wasn't enough. An exciting family fishing trip was now becoming a thing of horror. They were going under. George Jaeger, his three sons, and his elderly father tightened the

> buckles on their life jackets, tied themselves together with a rope, and slipped silently into the dark and boiling Atlantic.
>
> George glanced at his watch as the boat sank out of sight—it was 6:30 p.m. One of his sons swallowed too much salt water, gagged, and then choked to death. Their helpless father heard his sons, one by one, and then his own dad, choke on the water, succumb to the waves, and drown.
>
> George never stopped swimming—in fact, he swam for eight hours, until he finally staggered onto the shore, still pulling the rope that bound him to the bodies of his sons and his father.
>
> Later, George told reporters, "My youngest boy, Clifford, was the first to go. I had always taught our children that death meant you would go to be with Jesus Christ. Before Cliff died, I heard him say, 'I can't go on fighting . . . I want to be with Jesus.' "[2]

Even in the midst of such agonizing losses, this man's crisis became a monument of faith, raised to his faithful God.

When invited to eat lunch with a pastor friend and his son, he told me some of the details of his wife's death, which had taken place only a few weeks before. It had been sudden and unexpected. Through tear-filled eyes, both he and his son spoke only of the faithfulness of Christ. These men joined the tribe of Job, having fashioned their crisis into a monument of praise to God.

Now if we take a step or two away from suffering, we would all agree that it is a skillful teacher. From painful circumstances we learn so many lessons about humility, eternal hope, enduring strength, where our true love lies, and God's truest, richest blessings.[3]

There is no doubt that God uses suffering to correct our thinking and conform our character. David wrote this principle on at least there occasions:

> *Before I was afflicted I went astray, but now I keep Your word* (Psalm 119:67).
>
> *It is good for me that I was afflicted, that I may learn Your statutes* (Psalm 119:71).
>
> *I know, O Lord, that Your judgments are righteous, and that in faithfulness You have afflicted me* (Psalm 119:75).

Paul also wrote,

> *And not only this, but we also exult in our tribulations, knowing that tribulation brings about perseverance; and perseverance, proven character; and proven character, hope* (Romans 5:3–4).

Christianity gave us *peace* with God, but it did not endow us with *patience.* That, Paul says, is created in the crucible of life and fashioned after the lightning strikes.

A REBUKE AND A REMATCH

> ***Again there was a day when the sons of God came to present themselves before the LORD, and Satan also came among them to present himself before the LORD. The LORD said to Satan, "Where have you come from?" Then Satan answered the LORD and said, "From roaming about on the earth and walking around on it." The LORD said to Satan, "Have you considered My servant Job?"*** (Job 2:1–3*a*).

God asks Satan another rhetorical question just as He did in the first chapter; He knows that Satan has placed all his destructive energy on Job and no one else. God asked him if he had considered his servant Job:

> ***"For there is no one like him on the earth, a blameless and upright man fearing God and turning away from evil. And he still holds fast his integrity, although you incited Me against him to ruin him without cause"*** (Job 2:3*b*).

In the Hebrew text, the *waw consecutive* does not mean "although you incited Me," but could be better rendered "and yet you incite Me against him without cause."[4]

In other words, the Lord is announcing that no matter what He allows Satan to do to Job, God is still in control.

Satan is still in denial. He can't believe Job has refused to curse God, so he raises the stakes even higher.

> ***"Skin for skin! Yes, all that a man has he will give for his life"*** (Job 2:4).

This phrase ***skin for skin*** is nothing more than a cruel, unfounded criticism of Job. Satan implies that Job is more than willing to sacrifice the skin of his children and his cattle and his employees, as long as he keeps his own skin intact. Satan, in effect, says, "Every man has a price . . . and I think I know what Job's is!"[5]

Satan offers:

> ***"However, put forth Your hand now, and touch his bone and his flesh; he will curse You to Your face"*** (Job 2:5).

Since one's bones were considered the seat of illness in ancient days, Satan has in mind a disease that will threaten Job's life.[6] Satan believed that Job would do anything to keep his *own* health. Most people will. Threaten to take a person's life and they will do most anything to live another day.

This is evidenced in no greater fashion than when Queen Elizabeth I said on her deathbed in 1603: "All my possessions for a moment of time."[7]

So Satan once again challenges God, unwilling to concede defeat. "Bring Job to the point of death and he will trade away his precious faith," Satan hissed. God replies to the challenge:

> ***So the LORD said to Satan, "Behold, he is in your power, only spare his life"*** (Job 2:6).

RAGE AND REVENGE

The horror of Scene II begins to unfold as Satan unleashes his fury.

> ***Then Satan went out from the presence of the LORD and smote Job with sore boils from the sole of his foot to the crown of his head*** (Job 2:7).

We have no idea how much time elapsed between the funerals of Job's ten children and the first sight of angry red bumps on his back, but we have every reason to believe that Satan would not have waited very long. He loves to strike the believer who is already suffering; Satan knows nothing of mercy or compassion.

His first punch: skin ulcers, which began to pop out all over Job's body—not an inch was spared. This meant that Job could not stand without pain or sit down—or even lie down—without aggravating the boils that covered his body. The Hebrew words translated ***sore boils*** are the same words used for one of the ten plagues in Egypt.

And this was only the beginning—the first of many such punches. Satan hoped he would bring about Job's downfall by a barrage of crushing blows:

- ulcerous sores ***(Job 2:7)***;
- persistent itching ***(Job 2:8)***;
- inability to eat ***(Job 3:24)***;
- sense of fear and dread ***(Job 3:25)***;
- insomnia ***(Job 7:4)***;
- worms ***(Job 7:5)***;
- hardened skin oozing pus ***(Job 7:5)***;
- difficulty breathing ***(Job 9:18)***;
- dark circles around his eyes (Job 16:16);
- loss of weight ***(Job 19:20; Job 33:21)***;
- constant pain ***(Job 30:17)***.

It is no wonder that when Job's friends came to visit, they didn't even recognize him. Satan had hooked the screws of suffering into Job's flesh, hoping to hear some syllable of blasphemy. It has yet to come.

> ***And he took a potsherd to scrape himself while he was sitting among the ashes*** (Job 2:8).

Keep in mind that Job wasn't at home lying in his own comfortable bed, being waited on by private medical staff. Hardly. He was where all the lepers would be found—quarantined at the town dump.[8] Towns in the Middle East had a landfill—a city dump outside the gates—where garbage and sewage were deposited. Periodically, the rotting garbage would be burned as a way of sanitation.[9]

To be sitting among the ashes was to be sitting near garbage and the dung heap. This was the place where beggars foraged for food . . . where dogs fought over scraps.

This was the city's sewer disposal site, and here sits Job in the ashes of a recent fire.[10]

Job's face, hands, feet, and every other visible part of his body seen through his torn clothing are oozing with open sores. His eyes are swollen from crying, shadowed by dark circles which made him look demented. His clothes are caked with filth and blood, and the bones in his shoulder blades poke through his dirty cloak. His breath comes in short, strained gasps, and his face is gaunt from the lack of food. Here in this ash heap sits the ***greatest of all the men of the east***, scraping his itching flesh with a broken piece of pottery, hoping for a few moments of relief.

And don't forget—Job's heart is still grieving over ten fresh graves and the loss of everything he owned. He recalls every child, every memory and how it once was when those precious ones were still with him. Surely Job will curse God now . . . surely he will cry out from the ashes, "God, You are no longer my God."

Much to the dismay of Satan, he does not.

But wait . . . an unhappy visitor has come to speak with Job, and Satan's hopes are lifted; this could be it . . .

> ***Then his wife said to him, "Do you still hold fast your integrity? Curse God and die!" But he said to her, "You speak as one of the foolish women speaks. Shall we indeed accept good from God and not accept adversity?" In all this Job did not sin with his lips*** (Job 2:9–10).

Are my eyes deceiving me?! Look at the wisdom and insight in Job's reply: ***"Shall we indeed accept good from God and not accept adversity?"*** From the first messenger's report, Job knew that his adversity was brought by none other than God Himself. Even still, Job praised Him unwaveringly.

There in the ash heap, he raises a monument of praise to God; through the ash and acrid fumes rose a fragrant aroma to the nostrils of the Almighty.

When Moses turned down God's calling for him to rescue the Israelites from Egypt, saying: "I am not good at speaking," God responded with a truth that Job evidently believed:

> *The LORD said to him, "Who has made man's mouth? Or who makes him mute or deaf, or seeing or blind? Is it not I, the LORD?"* (Exodus 4:11).

This is something we must grasp, as well. The immediate cause of our next trial may be a disease or disability or deformity or blindness or any number of things—but behind both sunshine and shadow is the sovereign plan of God. The disciples learned this lesson one day when they walked past a blind man and asked the Lord:

> "[W]*ho sinned, this man or his parents, that he should be born blind?" Jesus answered, "It was neither that this man sinned, nor his parents; but it was so that the works of God might be displayed in him"* (John 9:3).

The man was born blind so that God might be glorified in the restoration of his sight. Wait a minute . . . do you mean to say that God caused a child to be born blind? Yes. God knit him together in the womb, just as He did you and me and chose to leave him sightless.

All Jerusalem knew this man had been born blind. The religious leaders knew it and perhaps thousands of others who walked outside the temple knew this beggar by name. Month after month, year after year, he cried, "Alms for the blind; alms for the blind," making a living off the pity of people who assumed he had sinned to some great degree and was being punished by God because of it.

Jesus shocked their world when He opposed that view wholeheartedly. He told them that the sickness was ordained to bring glory to God, and the greater the number of people who knew the man, the greater the number of people who witnessed God's power when Jesus healed him.

In this way, the blind man becomes a picture of the suffering saint and a testimony of something that will one day happen to everyone who believes. For on the day of our glorification, all diseases and all suffering and all affliction will be set aside forever and our new and glorified bodies will be eternal testaments to the greatness and glory of God.

A RENEWAL IN THE RUINS

Are You Willing to Wait?

Job's initial praise demands personal introspection: are you willing not only to be patient but also to prepare for fresh challenges to your faith? Are you willing to prepare for those moments when the word *again* is written in your own life—when you are down for the count and still getting pounded by fresh trials? Are you willing to wait on God for direction . . . for a solution . . . for a divine rescue? Are you willing to wait and not grow bitter and ungrateful while God seems silent . . . distant . . . absent?

Are You Willing to Worship?

Worship is a word we use in our triumphs, but its greatest application is discovered in the midst of trials. Are you willing to roll up the sleeves of your faith and praise God when life doesn't make sense? Are you willing to trust Him during prolonged sickness, believing that He is in charge? At the graveside of your loved one, is He still in control? When a close relationship ends despite your attempts to salvage it, He is in command?

Maybe you don't understand the trial and you can't even quite explain it; maybe you feel you don't deserve it and you certainly didn't expect it—but the truth remains—you cannot escape it.

Will you lift your voice and praise Him in the midst of it? Will you erect a monument to the God who is behind the trial even while you are still suffering the bitter taste of salty tears? This, my friend, is worship in its purest form.

One author put it into the words of a prayer:

> O, God, I trust You. I don't know why I'm going through this. If there's something I can learn, wonderful. If there's something someone else can learn, great. Just get me through it . . . hold me close . . . deepen me . . . change me.[11]

This is what it means to turn your crisis into a testimony of praise—to raise a monument of praise in the valley of despair.

One of the men on our church elder team handed me this bit of prose written by Lehman Strauss, a converted Jewish man who went on to become a rather well-known Bible teacher and scholar:

> God does whatever He wants to do, whenever He wants to do it, for whatever purpose He chooses; He involves whomever He will, and whatever He does is right!

Peter said the same thing centuries earlier:

> *After you have suffered for a little while, the God of all grace, who called you to His eternal glory in Christ, will Himself perfect, confirm, strengthen, and establish you. To Him be dominion forever and ever. Amen* (1 Peter 5:10–11).

This is another way of saying, "Because of our sovereign Lord and the future of His glory and our own glorification, I will raise a monument of praise in the valley of despair—here and now!"

Then his wife said to him, "Do you still hold fast your integrity? Curse God and die!" [10] But he said to her, "You speak as one of the foolish women speaks. Shall we indeed accept good from God and not accept adversity?" In all this Job did not sin with his lips.

–Job 2:9–10

CHAPTER SIX

MRS. JOB: LESSONS IN SECONDHAND SUFFERING

Job 2:9–10

SECONDHAND SUFFERING

More than likely, you've been exposed to something very dangerous and you probably knew it.

As many as one million young people are affected with a variety of physical ailments because of it—including respiratory tract infections, asthma, and middle ear infections; some children have experienced permanent hearing loss because of it.

In adults, exposure to it is responsible for cancer and heart disease—in fact, there are 50,000 deaths attributed to it every year!

What makes it especially troubling is that the victims never did *anything* to bring this about; they just happened to be exposed to it.

If you haven't guessed by now, this culprit is *secondhand smoke.*

In the 1980s, Philip Morris conducted research that proved secondhand smoke was highly toxic—and kept their findings secret for twenty years.

By 2005, research had confirmed that secondhand smoke is responsible for 200,000 annual cases of respiratory tract infections in those two years old and under. Secondhand smoke causes 15,000 hospitalizations every year; it is the reason for one-half million asthma attacks and 1.6 million visits to a doctor *every* year.[1]

One Surgeon General even made an alarming statement that there is *no such thing* as a risk-free level of exposure.

Imagine someone having to suffer from any of these ailments or life-threatening diseases without ever having smoked a cigarette or a cigar or a pipe . . . not even once. But they lived with, commuted to work with, or ate lunch with people who did.

Medical studies have now proven that even the briefest exposure to secondhand smoke makes blood platelets become stickier, the lining of blood vessels is damaged, and coronary flow is decreased.[2]

Our culture has become concerned enough to pass a ledger book of laws to eliminate secondhand smoke from our lives.

It's troubling, though, that we can become so deeply concerned about the effects of secondhand smoke, yet make little effort to deal with something far more devastating, destructive, and life-altering—something far more life-threatening, dangerous, and debilitating than secondhand smoke: *secondhand suffering.*

Millions of people are affected by it every year. It is the cause of physical difficulties beyond number and fills bed after bed in hospitals. The calendars of doctors, counselors, and psychologists are full of appointments with tens of millions of inflicted people.

No laws have ever been passed to get rid of it. It wouldn't matter anyway—you can't eradicate it . . . no medicine can fully wipe out its effects.

Allow me to define secondhand suffering: *the adverse physical, emotional, and spiritual effects experienced by people who are involved with or regularly exposed to those who are suffering.*

THE PRIMARY SUFFERER

In ***Job 2:2***, we find Job on the ash heap. After the second wave of attacks by Satan, Job has suffered through the agony of grief. His children are dead, his businesses are bankrupt, and his health is gone.

Job is living a nightmare.

Evidently, he's moved out of his house, in so much agony that he really doesn't want to be around anyone.

Added to this was the fact that his reputation had been lost—the man people thought had lived for God had apparently been living a secret sinful life; now God was judging him severely.

There sits this once-great man, hunched over . . . perhaps rocking back and forth in despair as he weeps . . . oblivious to the dogs and the beggars. His heart is still grieving over his children.

Surely Job will validate the hopes of Satan and curse his God who obviously abandoned him. Surely he will raise his voice and blaspheme Jehovah.

But then a visitor arrives—his wife.

The person who gets lost in the usual retelling of Job's biography is the only other family member alive. She has already endured much but will experience still more as she not only agonizes over the sudden deaths of her children, but the ongoing suffering of her husband.

If Job is the epitome of suffering, she then becomes the poster child of *secondhand suffering.* Either form can be deadly to your faith. We will refer to this secondhand sufferer simply as Mrs. Job.

THE SECONDARY SUFFERER

At their wedding some forty years earlier, she and her husband could not have imagined this future tsunami of suffering. Everything had begun so smoothly; they had become well-respected, wealthy, busy, healthy grandparents enjoying their latter years in dignity and comfort.

Rabbinical tradition believes that Mrs. Job was Dinah, the daughter of Jacob. While there is biblical evidence that Job lived during the days of the Patriarchs (those men who, before the establishment of the priesthood, personally made ritual sacrifices on behalf of thier families), we can't say for certain that Mrs. Job was one of Jacob's daughters.

Another Jewish tradition states that one of Dinah's daughters, born to Job and Dinah after God restored Job's health, moved to Egypt and became the wife of Joseph after he was elevated to Prime Minister.

What we *do* know about Mrs. Job is that she appears briefly at the town dump where Job is living . . . perhaps in his desire to protect her from anything contagious.

When she arrives, she asks him, ***"Do you still hold fast your integrity?*** [Then she says,] ***Curse God and die!"*** (Job 2:9).

One translator renders it, "Renounce God, and die." Another puts it, "Bid farewell to God, and die." In other words, "Turn your back on God, abandon your testimony of faith, which is the only thing keeping you alive, and let God put you to death."[3]

The translation into modern parlance would be, "It's obvious that God has given up on you; why don't you give up on Him!"

Some might picture her as a conniving, serpentine woman. John Calvin believed she was spurred on by the devil to tempt her husband. Augustine believed she was the devil's accomplice, only allowed to live so Satan could induce her to tempt her husband to curse God.

After all my research and language study, I personally do *not* believe that she was trying to goad Job into sinning. I believe she was trying to *end* his suffering.

The Greek rendering of the Hebrew Scriptures (the Septuagint) was translated a few centuries before Christ. While the Septuagint is not inspired Old Testament scripture, it's interesting that the Apostle Paul, and even our Lord, quoted from it during their ministries.

In the Septuagint, Mrs. Job has a much longer speech which she delivers to Job, giving us potential insight into her motive for suggesting to her husband that he end his life by renouncing God—an act which she believes will cause God to move in judgment and take her husband's life.

It reads:

> *When a long time had passed,* [she asked] *"How long will you endure, saying, 'Behold, I will wait yet for a little time, looking for the hope of my salvation'? Behold, the memory of you has been blotted out from the earth,* [our] *sons and daughters, the travail and pain of my womb, who with toil I reared for nothing. And yet you yourself sit in the decay of worms, passing the nights under the open sky, while I am a wanderer . . . from place to place and from house to house, waiting until the sun goes down, so that I may rest from my toils and from the pains that now grip me."*

Later the text adds that she endured the humiliation of cutting off her hair and selling it to buy bread.[4]

What she's saying is, "All is lost . . . I can't bear to see you suffer any further . . . renounce God and let Him take your life—find release from your terrible misery."

While we can't defend what she recommends, we should try to understand it.

This once-wealthy woman has been reduced to begging for food. Her beautiful clothing has been sold, her jewelry has been pawned, and even her hair has been traded for bread.

Mr. and Mrs. Job, once respected and esteemed are now openly mocked. Their wealth is gone, their businesses have failed, their employees have been murdered, and their ten children have died in a freak accident.

A horrifically Perfect Storm had converged on husband and wife in a single day and changed them forever. No inner resource imaginable could be summoned to counteract the bitter poison they tasted as they helped each other up from wobbly knees. In a still-recent scene, both pairs of red-rimmed eyes willed the freshly dug graves to suddenly, somehow tremble and their ten resurrected children break through the tender, packed soil. *If only . . .*[5]

It's really too much for Mrs. Job to take. Her husband persists in his loyalty to a God who obviously has *not* been loyal to him.

Little wonder that her advice is to allow God to end his suffering . . . perhaps hers, too.

SUFFERING IS SERIOUS BUSINESS

There are four observations about anyone who endures secondhand suffering.

Secondhand Suffering Can Be As Painful As Firsthand Suffering

Though different, secondhand suffering can be equally as sharp and acute. The problem is that secondhand suffering is much more difficult to express. While someone suffering physical pain can say, "I'm hurting!" the one who watches the sufferer is unable to relieve the pain of their loved one—which is terribly distressing.

Secondhand pain is different . . . but just as deep.

Secondhand Sufferers Can Reach Points of Despair More Quickly than Those Who Are Suffering Firsthand

Mrs. Job is proof. She has already decided that life isn't worth living, and she is now advising Job to draw the same conclusion.

She's reached the point of despair. And why not? She's not only lost ten kids, but she's effectively lost her husband too.

Her husband once sat in the city gates as a respected leader of the people, one of the most renowned men of the Eastern region.

But now, their honor is gone . . . and as far as she is concerned, so is their hope.

In the Hebrew text, the verbs ***curse*** and ***die*** are imperatives. She is urgent in her counsel, no doubt delivered through tears and sobbing. I picture her having fallen to the ashes beside him as she weeps, "Job, just give in . . . give up!"

It's apparent here that secondhand suffering can be as toxic to your faith as it is to those directly affected by the trials of life.

Secondhand Sufferers Have Their Own Personal Sorrows to Endure and Lessons to Learn

A sign on the wall of a junior high classroom delivered this message, "Experience is the hardest teacher—it gives the test *first* and then the lesson."[6]

Have you ever felt like that? You're struggling to learn the lessons . . . but the testing never lets up.

For the secondhand sufferer, there are often *two* sets of tests, not just one. The first is how to biblically respond to someone you love who is suffering, and the second is learning what God wants to teach you personally as you suffer from the sidelines.

One woman in my church recently put her thoughts on paper as she witnessed her husband seeking a job—a process of ups and downs that lasted for more than two years. He had been laid off and the pressure was mounting . . . along with the bills. She wrote some interesting thoughts in a journal—one paragraph which began with the question, "Who will comfort *me*?" She added these words, "Both of us have been dramatically impacted by this layoff. Both of us have great needs. He has lost his job; I have lost my security. He thinks he has lost his identity because he lost employment; I think I've lost my identity because I feel like I'm losing him. He desperately wants a job and I desperately want him to have a job."[7]

This is the transparent vocabulary of a secondhand sufferer. This is the testimony of Mrs. Job.

She has relied on Job for everything: her economic existence, her social status, her moral standing in the community. But now, in a matter of moments, she, too, has lost everything. Her income is gone now that the cattle and servants have been destroyed. Her position as matriarch and wife of a prince has been lost as well.[8]

Keep in mind that none of this is her fault; she has been reduced to living off handouts, enduring the pity and stares of former friends who used to envy her good fortune. Worst of all, her husband sits at the town dump stripped of his honor, reputation, and dignity.

It's all gone.

Little wonder that she's concluded sudden death would be better than lingering pain. Isn't this cup too bitter to drink? Wouldn't God provide escape rather than demand endurance?

This is her Gethsemane.

Secondhand Sufferers May Reach Wrong Conclusions and Need Help Balancing a Biblical Perspective with Endurance

Secondhand sufferers may actually need the sufferer's help to grow during the crisis—even more than the sufferer needs the bystander to be strong.

Have you ever visited someone who was seriously ill or an invalid in the hospital or at home? You went to see them because you believed they needed encouragement. You were concerned about how they were going to get through the suffering—and they told you everything they had *gained* from having been in their circumstances. By the time you left their side, you were clearly aware that you didn't do them much good, but they had done you a world of good! This is exactly what takes place at the town dump.

LESSONS FOR THOSE AT LOSS

Mrs. Job has lost her biblical perspective and spiritual balance. She counsels Job to bury his testimony of faith, renounce God, and die.

As strange as it seems, Job the Sufferer becomes Job the Teacher. And if you're enduring suffering *firsthand*, draw several lessons from Job's response to his wife.

Suffering Is Never an Excuse to Lash Out at Others around You

Job's response began with the challenge,

> ***"You speak as one of the foolish women speaks"*** (Job 2:10*a*).

What seems at first to be harsh actually shows kind and gracious restraint. Notice that he does not call her a fool—or a foolish woman. He said to his wife, "You are speaking *as one of* the foolish women speaks."

In reality, Job is saying, "Sweetheart, I know you're not like one of *them* . . . even though you're talking like one of them; I know that's not really who *you* are."

The Hebrew word *nabbal* translated ***foolish*** is used in the Old Testament for someone who is impious and undiscerning. He's candidly telling her, "You are speaking words that are beneath you . . . you know God better than that . . . I know you're disillusioned . . . you have so much to grieve over . . . but this idea of cursing God is the talk of women who do not know God like you do."[9]

Job's response initially serves as a gracious reminder of what his wife already knew.

Suffering Is Often the Best Platform from Which Deep Truths Can Be Taught

Job continues to teach her:

> ***"Shall we indeed accept good from God and not accept adversity?"*** (Job 2:10*b*).

The Hebrew verb ***accept*** (qibbel) describes an active, positive participation in what God delivers . . . not just some sort of passive reception.[10]

In other words, the believer doesn't just throw up his hands and say, "Well, can you believe it? Look what's happened to me . . . and there's nothing I can do about it! I'll just grit my teeth and suffer through it."

No, this isn't what Job is suggesting. He's teaching his wife to have a spirit of acceptance as opposed to a spirit of bitterness.

Yes, Job will lose and then gain this perspective as time continues. He'll experience the cycle of grief and faith . . . he'll wish he'd never been born and he'll demand an audience with God.

But these comments to his wife are some of his finest moments . . . his most brilliant insights. And it seems to have served Mrs. Job well, for we never hear again of her demand that Job renounce his faith in God.

For now, however, she has signed off on God. Job is teaching her to receive and accept from God.

Another woman who suffered greatly in life wrote of the growth from her own desperate days of trial:

> Resignation and acceptance are two different things. Resignation is surrender to fate; acceptance is surrender to God. Resignation lies down in an empty universe. Acceptance rises up to meet the God who fills the universe; resignation says, "I can't" while acceptance says, "I can." Resignation says, "It's all over for me." Acceptance asks, "Now that I'm here, Lord, what's next?" Resignation says, "What a waste." Acceptance asks, "Lord, in what redemptive way can you use this mess?"

So wrote former missionary to the Auca Indians, Elizabeth Elliott.[11]

These deep truths aren't learned in the absence of pain and sorrow; they are learned in the *midst* of it.

Charles Spurgeon once preached on this text and said:

> O dear friend, when thy grief presses thee to the dust, worship there. If that spot has come to be thy Gethsemane, then present there thy strong crying and tears unto thy God. Remember David's words, "Ye people, pour out your hearts"—but do not stop there, finish the quotation—"Ye people, pour out your hearts *before Him*." Turn the vessel upside down; it is a good thing to empty it, for this grief may ferment into something more sour; turn the vessel upside down, and let every drop run out; let it run out before the Lord.[12]

Suffering Is the Proving Ground of Our Satisfaction with the Will of God

Job says, "Dear wife, are we going to receive good from God and not receive suffering and trial from God?"

Isn't it reassuring to know that *both* come through the open hand of God?

I am so encouraged that we have no record of a rebuttal from Mrs. Job—no heated words in response to his gentle lesson of God's right to give both joy and pain. It indicates to me that she agreed.

Perhaps she came under conviction . . . perhaps there was a revival in her own spirit there at the town dump, her tears spilling on the ashes where her broken husband sat.

ASSURANCE AT THE ASH HEAP

Imagine them huddled closely there; unable to rest her head on his shoulder for the pain it would cause him, she sits as close to him as she can . . . taking a turn for a few moments with that broken piece of pottery. Perhaps they spoke in quiet tones of a life that once was—and faith that must be.

They know *nothing* of the Divine contest. They hear no rustling movements of angels—both holy and evil—who swirl around them; they can't have imagined that God, whom they were tempted to believe had forgotten them, was intently watching them.

How could they have known that there in the middle of the ash heap, they were actually in the middle of the will of God.

The Apostle Peter wrote,

> *Those who suffer according to the will of God shall entrust their souls to a faithful Creator in doing what is right* (1 Peter 4:19).

Every Christian who endures adversity of any kind is suffering according to the will of God. God isn't absent; in fact, He's more aware than you can imagine.

And what does Peter say the sufferer should do? *Entrust your soul to your faithful Creator.*

What amazing advice! The word *entrust* is a banking term meaning *to deposit.* It's the idea of depositing treasure into trustworthy hands.

The FDIC insures a depositor's funds in the American banking system up to 250,000 dollars—I've never had an occasion to test their system. But your Creator has no limits on what *He* can insure. Whatever you deposit into His care is eternally safe.

God will never say to the sufferer, "You're putting more into my hands than I can guarantee to care for . . . sorry, that's over my limit."[13]

No, Peter says—and I paraphrase—"When you suffer . . . you can rest assured that every detail of your life is in the powerful hands of your Creator; your ash heap happens to be in the middle of the will of God."

Incidentally, that same Greek word *entrust* which Peter used was spoken several years earlier by the Lord Jesus as He hung on the cross. At one point He uttered the words,

> *"Father, into your hands I commit* [entrust, deposit] *my spirit"* (Luke 23:46).

Jesus spoke the same word that Peter used in his letter to encourage believers to entrust our suffering life into the care of our Creator, just as the Savior entrusted His Spirit into the hands of God the Father.

But it's more than that. For if at the hour of His greatest suffering Jesus could entrust His life to the will of the Father, then so can we.

When we do, we become a little more like our Savior as we come to truly know Him, not only in the power of His resurrection but in the *fellowship of His suffering.*

And in the meantime, we also become a little more like fellow sufferers Mr. and Mrs. Job.

[11]*Now when Job's three friends heard of all this adversity that had come upon*
him, they came each one from his own place, Eliphaz the Temanite, Bildad the
Shuhite and Zophar the Naamathite; and they made an appointment together to
come to sympathize with him and comfort him. [12]*When they lifted up their eyes*
at a distance and did not recognize him, they raised their voices and wept. And
each of them tore his robe and they threw dust over their heads toward the sky.
[13]*Then they sat down on the ground with him for seven days and seven nights*
with no one speaking a word to him, for they saw that his pain was very great.

–Job 2:11–13

CHAPTER SEVEN

THE MINISTRY OF PRESENCE

Job 2:11–13

Erma Bombeck was an American humorist and speaker who achieved great popularity for her newspaper column that described suburban home life from the mid-1960s until the late 1990s. Bombeck also published fifteen books, most of which became bestsellers.

She used her sense of realism and humor to encourage women, allowing them a vicarious opportunity to say what they thought. During that time period, most women weren't necessarily invited to speak their mind.

Although Erma was loyally and lovingly committed to her husband and children, her transparent honesty raised eyebrows. Two of her lectures have been recorded under the title *The Family That Plays Together Gets on Each Other's Nerves* (1977). That got a lot of attention! But it was her book *The Grass Is Always Greener over the Septic Tank* which made her a household name.

She spoke for millions of women when she sarcastically opined, "If a man watches three football games in a row, he should be declared legally dead." Women had finally found an advocate who dared to *say* what they were thinking.

Erma Bombeck died from complications from a kidney transplant in 1996, but several years before, she listed the following in a column entitled "If I Had to Live My Life Over":

- I would have cherished every minute of nine months of pregnancy instead of wishing it away . . . my only chance in life to assist God in a miracle.

- I would have invited friends over to dinner even if the carpet was stained and the sofa faded.
- I would have taken the time to listen to my grandfather ramble about his youth.
- I would have burnt the pink candle that was sculptured like a rose before it melted while being stored.
- I would have sat cross-legged on the lawn with my children and never worried about grass stains.
- I would have eaten less cottage cheese and more ice cream.
- I would never have said, "Later. Now, go get washed up for dinner" when my child kissed me impetuously.
- I would have said "I love you" . . . "I'm sorry" . . . "I'm listening" more.

I asked members of our church to send me their own personal lessons learned after their lives experienced that "39 seconds" of radical change—that period we have referred to as the length of time it took for Job to hear the messengers who came, one after another, telling him that he had lost everything and nearly everyone.

One woman's story included her husband being killed while a crime was being committed; another person struggled with the loss of his father who died suddenly.

One young man in our flock learned some profound lessons as a result of unexpected changes. He and his friend had been dropped off by a Super Cub plane in the wilderness of Alaska to hunt moose. They were experienced hunters and had carefully planned the expedition, including all the gear they would need for their hunt, as well as a satellite phone they had decided to rent at the last minute.

On the final day of the hunt, he spotted a bull moose and fired off one round. The moose didn't go down but, instead, charged toward him. He reloaded his gun and fired, and then felt intense pain. The gun had literally broken in half—one half had recoiled, severely lacerating his face and crushing one of his eyes.

After a rather amazing rescue by soldiers and an Army helicopter (thanks to that satellite telephone), he wrote out a list of questions while going through intensive recovery and still wondering about his impaired vision:

- What am I doing?
- Where am I going?
- What does God want me to do?
- What does God have in store for me?
- What should I do with God's blessings?
- What should I do with God's trials?
- Will I become resentful?

He concluded his thoughts by adding, "My only hope is the righteousness of Jesus Christ . . . I am of little strength . . . Lord, please help me."

How do you answer someone who asks such profound questions? How do you become part of God's solution in the life of someone immersed in sorrow . . . someone who has recently been diagnosed with a terminal illness and would love to have another shot at life?

I want to encourage you at the very outset of this chapter that everyone in the body of Christ qualifies to be an expert assistant to the suffering. You don't have to be brilliant, persuasive, articulate, or experienced. You can simply be involved in what we'll call The Ministry of Presence. Through the ministry of presence, you can have tremendous influence on those who are hurting . . . no ordination or certification necessary.

In fact, you don't have to *be* anything—except available. It's still true: the greatest ability is avail*ability*.

Observe what happens in the life of Job, a man shrouded in deep sorrow. These last few verses of ***Job 2*** show us exactly when—and how—those counselors of Job got it *right*:

> ***Now when Job's three friends heard of all this adversity that had come upon him, they came each one from his own place, Eliphaz the Temanite, Bildad the Shuhite and Zophar the Naamathite; and they made an appointment*** [a pact] ***together to come to sympathize with him and comfort him*** (Job 2:11).

They dropped everything, contacted one another and said, "Let's go to our friend in need and comfort him."

ELIPHAZ THE TEMANITE

Eliphaz is mentioned first, more than likely because he was the oldest. And deference in each of the cycles of speeches made by the three men (and later, by a fourth) seems to be given to Eliphaz, because he always speaks first.

He alludes to himself in ***Job 15*** as a grey-haired, aged man, much older than Job's own father. Job was probably around fifty years of age—with ten grown children—Eliphaz may have been anywhere from 75 to 80 years old.[1]

Add to that the fact that ***Job 2:15*** informs us that Eliphaz was a ***Temanite.*** Teman was famous for its wise men of the East and their profound sayings.

Jeremiah the prophet alluded to that when he wrote,

> *"Is there no longer any wisdom in Teman? Has good counsel been lost to the prudent? Has their wisdom decayed?"* (Jeremiah 49:7).

The wise men of Edom (Teman was the capital) are also referred to in *Obadiah 8.*

The name Eliphaz means "God is fine gold," and he would have been, more than likely, a powerful chieftain from this area of southern Arabia.[2] Wealthy enough to travel—revered and respected in his own right—he is one of Job's friends.

Of all the other men, Eliphaz will deliver not only the first but the longest speeches. God will later, in ***Job 42***, refer to him as the representative of the other counselors.[3]

So, picture in your mind a grey haired man—a man of wealth, dignity and experience—arriving at the scene of his friend's despair.

BILDAD THE SHUHITE

Bildad doesn't show up anywhere else in the Bible, although other documents speak of Suhu (the region named after Abraham's son Shuah), located on the Middle Euphrates River. It's likely that Bildad and Shuah knew one another and, if so, Bildad could have gleaned incredible life-lessons about the God of Abraham from Abraham's youngest son.

What we *do* know is that Bildad was a friend of Job. That alone speaks highly of him, serving as an excellent reference for his own character.

ZOPHAR THE NAAMATHITE

Zophar means "young bird," and he probably was the youngest in this trio of friends. He came from Naama, a region most likely named after the quintuple-great-granddaughter of Cain.

Many believe that Zophar's home was between modern day Beirut and Damascus.[4]

Keep in mind that Job lived during the days of the patriarchs. Many of these men were his contemporaries. It is likely that Job was known and respected by all who followed after the God of the patriarchs Abraham, Isaac, and Jacob.

These three friends heard the devastating news—which took some time to reach them—contacted one another (which took even more time to correspond back and forth), and agreed to come together to encourage Job.

One author said that if you have *one* friend who would drop everything and come running during your time of need, that would be wonderful—but to have *three* friends like that was truly amazing.[5]

Frankly, we have no idea how long it took them to locate Job. Perhaps they first went to his home and asked for him. It could have been one of the remaining servants of a now windswept and desolate estate who pointed the way to the city dump. Because of their shocked response, the implication here is that someone, indeed, needed to point Job out to them:

> ***When they lifted up their eyes at a distance and did not recognize him, they raised their voices and wept*** (Job 2:12*a*).

Maybe Job's wife led them to where he was sitting in the ashes at the town garbage heap. The text indicates that he was unrecognizable: "That man—the one sitting over there—that's Job."

"It can't be . . . that's impossible!"

The Hebrew text translated ***recognize*** (*hiphil perfect*) implies that it wasn't so much that these men doubted it was Job but, rather, that this man sitting on the ash heap did not look anything *like* Job. "How can this man be our friend, Job?"

"It's true." Their informant pointed from a distance, "That man with his cracked skin and open sores—the one scraping himself with broken pottery, moaning in unspeakable pain, suffering from fever and nausea, whose beard is now tangled and matted, eyes sunken and encircled with dark bands, clothing tattered and caked with blood and dirt—is, indeed, Job . . . your friend."

THREE FRIENDS—FIVE RESPONSES

1. They ***raised their voices and wept*** (Job 2:12*a*). The Hebrew text says that these men literally *wailed* in grief and shock.
2. Each ***tore his robe*** (Job 2:12*b*). Just as Job had done earlier to represent his broken heart, they also tore their robes in like manner (from the neck downward), representing the brokenness of their own hearts.
3. They ***threw dust over their heads toward the sky*** (Job 2:12*b*). This custom merely identified with Job in his great sorrow. Since he had been unable to bathe and had grown filthy, they would join him by soiling their own hair and clothing.
4. They ***sat down on the ground with him for seven days and seven nights*** (Job 2:13*a*). Seven days and nights was the customary period for mourning the dead.
    - The Men of Jabesh Gilead mourned the death of King Saul for *seven days (1 Samuel 31:13).*
    - Joseph mourned for his father Jacob for *seven days* after Jacob died in Egypt *(Genesis 50:10).* Job's friends are not merely mourning Job's condition, they are mourning the death of his children. And that's not all.
5. They were silent, ***with no one speaking a word to him, for they saw that his pain was very great*** (Job 2:13*b*). Even though the seven days of mourning for the loss of Job's family and servants eventually expire, out of great respect for their friend, they hold an impromptu memorial service of silence to commemorate further Job's intense suffering and pain.

HOW THE COUNSELORS GOT IT RIGHT

Identifying with His Sorrow

If Job's hair and clothing is dirty, then they'll get dirty. If Job is sitting on the ash heap at the town dump, then they'll sit out here with him. They will refuse to worry about all the stares and smirks from people who come to gawk.

Joining in His Grief

Earlier in ***Job 2:11***, we're told that these friends came to ***sympathize with him***. The Hebrew verb means much more than a quick hug.To ***sympathize*** or console means literally "to shake the head or to rock the body back and forth" as a sign of shared grief.[6]

You might do that today when you hear the news of someone's 39 seconds of unexpected suffering. All you can do is cover your mouth with your hand, shake your head, and rock back and forth in stunned silence and sorrow.

That's what they did with Job for seven days and seven nights. Job isn't crying alone here: there are four grown men, crying together at the city dump.

Another key word in ***Job 2:11*** is ***comfort***—an additional motive in their coming to visit Job. Someone who comforts is one who seeks to share the pain, as well as to lend a hand to physically and tangibly provide aid to the sufferer. Isaiah used the word to refer to a mother tending to the needs of her helpless child and thus comforting him *(Isaiah 66:13).*

This is the person who tenderly cares for the needs of the grieving—whether tending to physical wounds, cooking a meal, cleaning a house, caring for a child, cutting the grass, or paying the rent . . . these actions provide true comfort.

They also represent *true religion.* False religion *says* be warmed and filled but true religion, in the Biblical sense, puts on overalls, swings a hammer, washes dishes, writes a check, and cooks and delivers a meal.

True ***comfort*** in this text is seen in three friends sitting down at the dump, in the ashes, surrounded by rotting garbage, *with* Job.

Have you ever passed a town dump? Have you ever driven out to a landfill to drop off a truckload of trash? Try to take a breath. The smell of rotting garbage and the screeching of birds will make you want to drive away in less than seven minutes; I can't imagine staying there for seven days.

And you certainly wouldn't even consider eating a meal out there, much less curling up to sleep through the night.

They did . . . ***for seven days and seven nights***.

Showing Respect for His Grief

They are mourning *with* Job over the death of his children and servants. They are mourning the loss of financial assets, a home, businesses. They aren't just watching him weep. **[T]*hey raised their voices and wept*** (Job 2:12*a*).

Anyone who exercises the ministry of presence does that.

Have you ever noticed that no one is invited to a funeral; invitations are never mailed out.[7] Word spreads, and true friends just show up. And if they can't come, they send flowers, notes, or cards to communicate to the sufferer, *Listen, count me in; I want to show my respect and awareness of your grief . . . and I'm weeping with you.*

Allowing Job to Speak First

Don't miss this . . . underline it in your mind: they let Job speak *first.* Here's Warren Wiersbe's application to this passage in Job: "The best way to help people who are hurting is just show up; say little or nothing; don't try to explain everything because *explanations never heal broken hearts* [emphasis mine]."[8]

How quickly do we speak when in the presence of someone suffering . . . as if our words of wisdom will provide an explanation to take away their pain?

Ministers of Presence wait . . . watch . . . weep . . . and listen.

Earning the Right to Speak by Faithful Presence and Concern

Abraham Lincoln once admitted that he often regretted his speech, but he'd never regretted his silence.

And here's the good news: in order to exercise a ministry of presence, you don't have to have everything—or anything—figured out. Those grieving aren't looking for answers at that moment anyway.

You can be positively inspiring by your silence; truly ministering without one word . . . it's as if you're offering to them the gift of sacred silence.

Now before we leave this profound scene where three dignified, wealthy, revered men sit in the ashes with their weary, suffering friend, let's apply some practical lessons regarding the Ministry of Presence.

ENSURING AN EFFECTIVE MINISTRY OF PRESENCE

Reject the View that Quoting Scripture Will Eliminate Sorrow

This type of thinking pontificates, "You haven't represented truth if you haven't quoted Scripture."

While the Apostle Paul declares the sufficiency of Scripture to meet every need, the Book of Proverbs encourages the timely use of it.

Solomon recorded,

> *Like apples of gold in settings of silver is a word spoken in right circumstances* (Proverbs 25:11).
>
> *A man has joy in an apt answer, and how delightful is a timely word!* (Proverbs 15:23).

Don't walk into the presence of a sufferer and say, "Guess what I read this morning in my quiet time . . . man, this verse was perfect for you. Oh, by the way, I got you this coffee mug with a smiley face on one side and a cross on the other."

The Bible isn't a Band-Aid—don't go around sticking your favorite verse on those who are suffering, believing it will somehow eliminate their pain.

Scripture is not an aspirin: "Here, take two of these with a cup of tea in your new smiley face mug and call me in the morning to tell me how you're doing."

Physical injuries take time to heal . . . so do internal injuries of the heart. What the sufferer needs is the truth of Scripture demonstrated in and through your life as you minister to them with your presence, first and foremost.

Refrain from the Temptation to Say Something Profound

You might think you have to come up with that special nugget of truth in order to help—that you've got to be able to summarize the work of God in a sentence or two. The truth is suffering often exposes us to the *mystery* of God . . . not an explanation from God:

- *Oh, the depth of the riches both of the wisdom and knowledge of God! How unsearchable are His judgments and unfathomable His ways!* (Romans 11:33).
- *For "who has known the mind of the LORD that he will instruct Him?"* (1 Corinthians 2:16).
- *It is the glory of God to conceal a matter* (Proverbs 25:2*a*).

Here we are, running around trying to glorify God by *explaining* while He intends to be glorified by *concealing*. We've got to learn to say, "I have no idea what the Lord is doing, but I know He loves you. I want you to know I love you, too, and I'm here for you in every way possible."

Christians naturally have a hard time not coming up with answers—especially pastors. Imagine someone calling me, pouring out their story of suffering, and then asking me for an explanation. How good do you think it would go over if they hear me say, "Man, I haven't got a clue . . . I am completely stumped."

They'd probably start a petition to have me replaced.

By the time you get to the end of Job's story, he had demanded that God provide an explanation; instead, God will reveal His creation.

Job wanted a premise to *support* God's action; God will declared His power *behind* the action.

Refuse Any Expectation of Eliminating Grief with Your Insight or Wisdom

If you haven't learned it by now, learn it here in this scene. You don't eliminate sorrow—you share it. And shared sorrow has an amazing ability to lighten the load.

While you're at it, get rid of the idea that mature believers never grieve, or that deep Christians never break down and cry. If that were true, Jesus Christ was shallow; when He showed up at the tomb of Lazarus, He literally burst into tears *(John 11:35)*.[9]

Resist the Urge to Speak in Order to Express Love

When the Lord finally came to Lazarus's gravesite, He could have preached a sermon on His love for Lazarus. He could have made sure everyone knew how much He cared for His friend. But when He chose to weep instead of speak, the people said to each other, *"See how He loved him"* (John 11:36).

The Ministry of Presence is so powerful because you don't have to say anything. You just drop everything and drive two hours to be by the side of the sufferer.

In Chuck Swindoll's commentary on Job, he quoted from Joseph Bayly's book entitled *The Last Thing We Talk About*:

> Joe and his wife Mary Lou lost three of their children: one son following surgery when he was only 18 days old; their second son at age five from leukemia; their third son at age 18 after a sledding accident. Joe wrote, "I was sitting, torn by grief. Someone came and talked to me of God's dealings; of why it happened; of hope beyond the grave. He talked constantly, saying things I [already] knew were true. I was unmoved, except I wished he'd go away. He finally did. Another came and sat beside me for an hour and more—listened when I said something, answered briefly, prayed simply, and left. I was moved. I was comforted. I hated to see him go.[10]

That's the power of presence. You don't have to be brilliant, articulate, scholarly, seasoned, or winsome

You just show up. You just offer this amazing Ministry of Presence.

Afterward Job opened his mouth and cursed the day of his birth. [2]And Job said,
[3]"Let the day perish on which I was to be born, and the night which said, 'A
boy is conceived.' [4]May that day be darkness; let not God above care for it, nor
light shine on it. [5]Let darkness and black gloom claim it; let a cloud settle on it;
let the blackness of the day terrify it. [6]As for that night, let darkness seize it; let
it not rejoice among the days of the year; let it not come into the number of the
months. [7]Behold, let that night be barren; let no joyful shout enter it. [8]Let those
curse it who curse the day, who are prepared to rouse Leviathan. [9]Let the stars
of its twilight be darkened; let it wait for light but have none, and let it not see
the breaking dawn; [10]because it did not shut the opening of my mother's womb,
or hide trouble from my eyes. [11]Why did I not die at birth, come forth from the
womb and expire? [12]Why did the knees receive me, and why the breasts, that I
should suck? [13]For now I would have lain down and been quiet; I would have
slept then, I would have been at rest, [14]with kings and with counselors of the
earth, who rebuilt ruins for themselves; [15]or with princes who had gold, who were
filling their houses with silver. [16]Or like a miscarriage which is discarded, I would
not be, as infants that never saw light. [17]There the wicked cease from raging, and
there the weary are at rest. [18]The prisoners are at ease together; they do not hear
the voice of the taskmaster. [19]The small and the great are there, and the slave is
free from his master. [20]Why is light given to him who suffers, and life to the bitter
of soul, [21]who long for death, but there is none, and dig for it more than for hid-
den treasures, [22]who rejoice greatly, and exult when they find the grave? [23]Why is
light given to a man whose way is hidden, and whom God has hedged in? [24]For
my groaning comes at the sight of my food, and my cries pour out like water. [25]For
what I fear comes upon me, and what I dread befalls me. [26]I am not at ease, nor
am I quiet, and I am not at rest, but turmoil comes."

–Job 3:1–26

CHAPTER EIGHT

HITTING ROCK BOTTOM

Job 3:1–26

William Wilberforce, an English abolitionist, was a committed believer and a man of conviction. His uncle and aunt were saved under the ministry of George Whitefield and, in turn, had a great influence on William who eventually came to faith in Christ as a young man. He was later discipled and encouraged by John Newton, a pastor and the author of the hymn "Amazing Grace."

Wilberforce's embracing of the anti-slavery cause was the direct result of his Christian worldview. In 1807, he saw his bill passed by Parliament which would prohibit slave trading in the West Indies.

He did not stop with the passage of this bill. William spent another twenty-six years passionately defending the bill to abolish slavery entirely. That bill was finally passed in 1833, three days before he died.

While many will only see the heroic side of his efforts in the name of Christ, they will never know that he suffered greatly. Early in his life, doctors prescribed daily opium pills to help him cope with the incredible pain of his ulcerative colitis. The medicine in his day was considered a "pure drug," but the effects wore him down. He had colon distress, could not see without difficulty, lung problems, painful episodes with ulcers, and suffered from degenerative curvature of the spine.

One author wrote of William as a middle-aged man:

> One of his shoulders began to slope; and his head fell forward a little more each year until it rested on his chest unless lifted by conscious movement; he would have looked grotesque were it not for the charm of his face and the smile about his mouth. For twenty years, he wore a brace beneath his clothing that most people knew nothing about—a steel brace around his waist, cased in leather, which supported his back and arms.[1]

GOING, GOING, ALMOST GONE

Most of the time, we don't mind if our heroes suffer a bit; we're somewhat distressed to discover that they suffered greatly. And we are troubled most to discover that our heroes of the faith often struggled with despair and even depression.

When a great theologian in the nineteenth century lost two of his sons in the space of a month, he was brought to a moment he had never experienced before. He wrote,

> When Jimmy died, the grief was painfully sharp, but the acting of faith, the embracing of consolation, and all the cheering truths which ministered comfort to me were just as vivid. [*This is a great place to stop, is it not? This is what we like to hear: a great man of God hit rock bottom but came back up with smile.*] But when the stroke was repeated, and thereby doubled, I seem to be paralyzed and stunned. I know that my loss is doubled, and I know also that the same cheering truths apply to the second as to the first, but I remain numb, downcast . . . without hope and interest."[2]

This is *not* the way we are supposed to talk, is it?

We are somewhat uncomfortable with the transparency of Charles Spurgeon, the great preacher of the nineteenth century, who once wrote, "I am the subject of depression so fearful that I hope none of you ever get to such extremes of wretchedness as I go to."[3]

Steven Lawson writes in his commentary on Job, "Every person has a breaking point; even genuine believers have a point at which they can become severely discouraged and even depressed. Such despair can cause a person to want to give up on life."[4]

If you have ever experienced despair like this and wondered how you could be a Christian and feel that way; if you have ever been hurt so badly that you wished you could go on to heaven; if you have suffered so long with pain and are so tired that all you want to do is lie down and die; if you have ever looked for an escape hatch in life—some way out, an exit sign, relief—you may have more in common with the heroes of the faith than you ever dreamed.

We see this example in heroic King David, who wrote *Psalm 88*, beginning and ending with despair.

We also see this in John the Baptizer—the heroic prophet who stood against the world for the Gospel of the Lamb of God—who became totally despondent and disillusioned. There he sits in a prison cell, hours away from being beheaded by Herod for having condemned his immorality, wondering if all his efforts have been misguided. In fact, he wonders aloud if he had even been following the wrong Messiah. It seemed that Christ was not fulfilling the prophecies of the Old Testament after all—prisoners were not being freed; the yoke of bondage was not being lifted.

So John sends a delegation of his disciples to Christ. They ask this question on behalf of the imprisoned prophet,

> *"Are You the Expected One, or shall we look for someone else?"* (Matthew 11:3).

John had hit rock bottom. Now, even though he had baptized Jesus—he heard the Voice from heaven, watched the Spirit descend like a dove, listened to the Savior preach, and saw Him perform miracles that only God could do—John the Baptizer had reached his breaking point there in prison. He asked, "Lord, are You really the Messiah or should we pack our bags and look for someone else?"

This is not the way we expect heroes of the faith to talk.

Perhaps this is the reason ***Job 3*** makes us uncomfortable. Perhaps this is the reason most students only study ***Job 1–2*** and marvel at the man who said,

> ***"Blessed be the name of the LORD"*** (Job 1:21*b*).

> ***"Shall we indeed accept good from God and not accept adversity?"*** (Job 2:10*a*).

That's the way heroes speak in the face of incredible pain. And maybe that's why we would rather move past ***Job 3***, where he speaks from the bottom of the pit. Think about it—have you ever met anyone who has memorized any verse from ***Job 3***? Who wants to memorize the verse where Job says,

> ***"Let the day perish on which I was to be born . . ."*** (Job 3:3*a*).

How's that for a Happy Birthday card?

What about, ***"Why did I not die at birth?"*** (Job 3:11*a*).

Or the last verse,

> ***"I am not at ease, nor am I quiet, and I am not at rest, but turmoil comes"*** (Job 3:26).

Can't you see this framed and hanging in the church lobby: I AM NOT AT EASE, NOR AM I QUIET.

This might work in the nursery department; in fact, it might just be a terrific theme verse! However, this verse will never make it on as many tee shirts and coffee mugs as *Romans 8:28* or *Jeremiah 29:11*.

So let's just rush to the end of this book where Job is comforted by God and restored to health and given a new family. Why spend time dissecting the less-than-heroic words of Job?

Not so fast.

JOB CURSES THE DAY HE WAS BORN

By taking a quick scan of the first section of chapter three, we can see the repetition of the words ***let*** and ***may***. In Hebrew syntax, these words are known as *jussives*; that is, they are words that refer to "desire," as if they could issue commands. We could translate them *I wish*:

- I wish the day had never come on which I was born ***(v. 3)***;
- I wish the night had never been on which I was conceived ***(v. 3)***;
- I wish the day had been darkness when I was born ***(v. 4)***;
- I wish God had kept the light from ever dawning on that day ***(v. 4)***;
- I wish the blackness of night and gloom had blotted it out ***(v. 5)***;
- I wish to never celebrate my birthday again because I wish it had never happened ***(v. 6)***.

This continues on and on.

Why would Job ever say such things? Because he is depressed; he has hit rock bottom and wants his sorrowful life to end.[5]

No wonder Robert Alden wrote,

> The third chapter of Job must be one of the most depressing chapters in the Bible; few sermons are made from this chapter; few verses are claimed as promises and few are remembered for their warmth . . . it [may very well be] the lowest point in the Book.[6]

The truth is that Job has arrived at the point at which he cannot see any good reason or explanation for his trials; he does not have any idea what to do next; he does not see any end to his suffering; he assumes that God has abandoned him—and for no good reason—he can see no escape or exit door out of his suffering and pain.

In this first section of Job's lamentation, we also notice the repeated use of words for darkness:

- ***darkness (v. 4);***
- ***darkness and black gloom (v. 5)***;
- ***let darkness seize it (v. 6)***;
- ***let the stars of its twilight be darkened (v. 9)***.

I have read two stories recently of people who suffered greatly and found it interesting that they both wanted to be left alone in the dark.

Joni Eareckson Tada was paralyzed from the neck down and lay in a hospital bed that was flipped every three hours; she was strapped into the bed to keep from falling to the floor. She hung suspended, face down, looking directly at the tiles of her hospital room floor—three hours at a time. She finally demanded that everyone leave and the lights be turned off; she wanted to be left alone in the dark.

This is what we do when we hit rock bottom.

JOB WISHES HE HAD DIED AT BIRTH

The second section of Job's lament is no more hopeful than the first. Job, in effect, says, "Okay, since I can't turn back the clock and not be born, I wish I had at least been stillborn" ***(Job 3:11–12a)***. In other words, "Why couldn't I just have died and been spared all this misery?"

One of the dominant themes of this second stanza of Job's lament is his desire for rest. He is exhausted physically, emotionally, intellectually, and spiritually ***(Job 3:13)***. "I am tired. I just want rest from this trouble. I need relief from my sorrow. I need rescuing by someone . . . anyone."

JOB LONGS FOR DEATH TO COME *NOW*

The third section can be entitled "I Just Want to Die Now!"

> ***"Why is light given to him who suffers, and life to the bitter of soul, who long for death, but there is none, and dig for it more than for hidden treasures"*** (Job 3:20–21).

Job thinks a casket would be better than a treasure chest. ***Death*** is a treasure to Job. In his mind, it would be better than gold. By the way, this is not a cry of defiance against God—it is a cry of despair to God.[7]

Job is not doubting the existence of God; in fact, he refers several times to God and assumes He is the one who has surrounded him with all this suffering.

Job is not talking about ending his life; he wants *God* to take his life. There is a vast difference in these two desires. Both desires are for life to end, but one leaves it up to God and the other takes matters into our own hands.

Maybe you are reading this and thinking, *Wow, I thought I had it bad; I thought I was suffering and depressed—but not like Job. I'm better off than I thought!* Or this may be your situation: *I know exactly what Job is talking about; I think I know just how he feels. Heroes of the faith aren't supposed to talk like this so I've kept quiet, but Job has spoken for me.*

The truth is that if someone with Job's character and integrity and faith can hit bottom, so can we . . . and we probably have, at some point or another.

Is it any wonder that so many people through the ages have turned to the Book of Job when they themselves are crushed by suffering?

Joni Eareckson Tada wrote:

> As I lay immobilized in the hospital, my mind swirled with questions. When I learned that my paralysis was going to be permanent, I was desperate for answers. One of the first places I turned after my diving accident was to the Book of Job."[8]

SURFACING AFTER HITTING BOTTOM

Are there any solutions? Yes!

Ascribe to God Only Those Thoughts Clearly Supported by Scripture

We demolish arguments and every pretension that sets itself up against the knowledge of God, and we take captive every thought to make it obedient to Christ (2 Corinthians 10:5*a* NIV).

Take every thought into captivity—run every thought through the scanner—make sure the baggage is not carrying dangerous things into the mind. Your mind is where the battle is fought, so guard it well.

When C. S. Lewis was losing his wife to cancer, he wrote,

> I am not in danger of ceasing to believe in God. The real danger is to believe terrible things *about* God. The conclusion I dread is not, "So there's no God after all," but, "So this is what God is really like?"[9]

Refuse Counsel—Including Your Own— That Doubts the Sovereign Plan of God

This was the downfall of Eve, who believed that God was keeping from her what was best, and of the Israelites who were convinced that God was not worth following in the wilderness.

Suffering makes us forget the joys of the past and convinces us of the hopelessness of the future.[10]

Any feelings that drive you deeper into that pit—any counsel that raises doubts about your past, present, and future not being under the guidance of the Sovereign God of the universe—is false counsel and wayward emotion.

Cultivate a Deeper Love and Desire for Sacred Substance

It might be the assembly of believers whom you may be tempted to avoid when you hit rock bottom. Perhaps you will be tempted to neglect your reading the Scriptures . . . or refuse the friendship of another believer.

You open yourself to developing a habit for unhealthy things that only add to your misery.

Cultivate a deeper love and taste for sacred substance even before you hit rock bottom, so that when you are down, you will have ready resources at hand.

You Are Not the First Believer Who Desires to Suffer Alone

Take heart! You are not the only one to walk through such deep sorrow that you want the lights turned off, the door closed, and to be left alone.

One author made a great connection to Christ—who was portrayed for us in the Gospels as one *made like his brothers in every way* (Hebrews 2:17 NIV); of whom was written that He *began to be deeply distressed and troubled . . . overwhelmed with sorrow to the point of death* (Mark 14:33–34 NIV). As B. B. Warfield comments on this passage:

> In these moments our Lord [experienced] the ultimate depths of human anguish, and vindicated by the intensity of His mental sufferings the right to [be called] The Man of Sorrows.[11]

Give Your Energy to Bring Help and Hope to Others

Joni Eareckson Tada wrote:

> Trapped face down, staring at the floor hour after hour, my thoughts grew dark and hopeless. All I could think was, *God, I prayed for a closer walk with You; if this is Your idea of an answer to prayer, I am never going to trust You with another prayer again. I can't believe that I have to lie face down and do nothing but count the tiles on the floor of this torture rack. I hate my existence.* I asked the hospital staff to turn off the lights, shut the blinds, and close the door.

She writes that a friend came and listened to her rant and rave and cry. Then, she put a Bible on a little stool in front of her and turned to this verse:

> *In my distress I called upon the LORD, and cried to my God for help* (Psalm 18:6*a*).

Now, years later, Joni is determined to provide an estimated 18 million wheelchairs, along with the Gospel of Jesus Christ, to the disabled around the world.

Recently, she received an email from a woman named Beverly, who wrote:

> Dear Joni,
>
> I'm out of hope. But I am wondering if you might be able to help my husband Ron who was in an accident last year that left him a quadriplegic. He's a pastor, and he continued to [work] for a time, but now, he has resigned. He no longer wants to get out of bed. He doesn't talk. He doesn't want the lights on in his room and no TV. He doesn't want to live and he doesn't care about our family anymore. We all seem to be falling through the cracks. My husband feels useless and hopeless. We need help.

Joni gave this account of her reply:

> I responded by calling information and tracking down Ron and Beverly and gave them a call. Beverly answered and [after sharing and praying with her] I asked if I could talk to Ron. She knocked on his door and he let her tuck the phone under his ear. Although he would not respond, I talked a little bit of shop about quadriplegia.
>
> I wanted to move beyond these topics, however, and bridge the conversation to spiritual things. So I started to share favorite Scriptures that have sustained me through the toughest of times, like Romans 8:18: *For I consider that the sufferings of this present time are not worthy of being compared with the glory that is to be revealed to us.*
>
> Silence on the other end. I even sang to him. Nothing.
>
> Finally, I did the only thing I could think of that I had not already tried. I asked Ron if he had ever seen a movie called *The Shawshank Redemption.*
>
> "Why, yes, I have," he said.
>
> I couldn't believe it—Ron had responded.
>
> "Well, Ron, do you remember when Red found Andy's letter? Do you remember what it said?"
>
> "I think so…umm, 'Hope is a good thing . . . and no good thing ever dies.' "

> "Ron, there are ten thousand other quadriplegics like you and me across America . . . and all of them were lying in bed this morning wondering whether or not they should get busy living or get busy dying. Ron, I'm going to make a choice to get busy living. Do you want to join me today?"
>
> He said, "Yes, ma'am, yes, I do."
>
> The last Joni heard was that Ron and Beverly were active in sharing their testimony to everyone, preaching far and near.[12]

He had hit rock bottom but surfaced with hope. Ron had decided to get busy with living—and help others surface from their own episode when they hit the bottom, too.

Remember, Job thought he was forgotten. He had no idea that he was under the watchful gaze of God.

And he certainly had no idea that he would be remembered by millions of believers throughout the course of human history as an example of how to hit rock bottom and surface with hope . . . someone who would make the choice to get busy living.

Then Eliphaz the Temanite answered, 2"If one ventures a word with you, will
you become impatient? But who can refrain from speaking? 3Behold you have
admonished many, and you have strengthened weak hands. 4Your words have
helped the tottering to stand, and you have strengthened feeble knees. 5But now it
has come to you, and you are impatient; it touches you, and you are dismayed. 6Is
not your fear of God your confidence, and the integrity of your ways your hope?
7Remember now, who ever perished being innocent? Or where were the upright
destroyed? 8According to what I have seen, those who plow iniquity and those
who sow trouble harvest it. 9By the breath of God they perish, and by the blast
of His anger they come to an end. 10The roaring of the lion and the voice of the
fierce lion, and the teeth of the young lions are broken. 11The lion perishes for lack
of prey, and the whelps of the lioness are scattered. 12Now a word was brought to
me stealthily, and my ear received a whisper of it. 13Amid disquieting thoughts
from the visions of the night, when deep sleep falls on men, 14dread came upon
me, and trembling, and made all my bones shake. 15Then a spirit passed by my
face; the hair of my flesh bristled up. 16It stood still, but I could not discern its
appearance; a form was before my eyes; there was silence, then I heard a voice:
17'Can mankind be just before God? Can a man be pure before his Maker? 18He
puts no trust even in His servants; and against His angels He charges error.
19How much more those who dwell in houses of clay, whose foundation is in the
dust, who are crushed before the moth! 20Between morning and evening they are
broken in pieces; unobserved, they perish forever. 21Is not their tent-cord plucked
up within them? They die, yet without wisdom.'"

–Job 4

(Continued on next page)

(Continued)

“Call now, is there anyone who will answer you? And to which of the holy ones
will you turn? 2 For anger slays the foolish man, and jealousy kills the simple. 3 I
have seen the foolish taking root, and I cursed his abode immediately. 4 His sons
are far from safety, they are even oppressed in the gate, and there is no deliv-
erer. 5 His harvest the hungry devour and take it to a place of thorns, and the
schemer is eager for their wealth. 6 For affliction does not come from the dust, nor
does trouble sprout from the ground, 7 for man is born for trouble, as sparks fly
upward. 8 But as for me, I would seek God, and I would place my cause before
God; 9 who does great and unsearchable things, wonders without number. 10 He
gives rain on the earth and sends water on the fields, 11 so that He sets on high
those who are lowly, and those who mourn are lifted to safety. 12 He frustrates the
plotting of the shrewd, so that their hands cannot attain success. 13 He captures the
wise by their own shrewdness, and the advice of the cunning is quickly thwarted.
14 By day they meet with darkness, and grope at noon as in the night. 15 But He
saves from the sword of their mouth, and the poor from the hand of the mighty.
16 So the helpless has hope, and unrighteousness must shut its mouth. 17 Behold,
how happy is the man whom God reproves, so do not despise the discipline of the
Almighty. 18 For He inflicts pain, and gives relief; He wounds, and His hands also
heal. 19 From six troubles He will deliver you, even in seven evil will not touch
you. 20 In famine He will redeem you from death, and in war from the power of
the sword. 21 You will be hidden from the scourge of the tongue, and you will not
be afraid of violence when it comes. 22 You will laugh at violence and famine,
and you will not be afraid of wild beasts. 23 For you will be in league with the
stones of the field, and the beasts of the field will be at peace with you. 24 You
will know that your tent is secure, for you will visit your abode and fear no loss.
25 You will know also that your descendants will be many, and your offspring as
the grass of the earth. 26 You will come to the grave in full vigor, like the stacking
of grain in its season. 27 Behold this; we have investigated it, and so it is. Hear it,
and know for yourself.”

–Job 5

CHAPTER NINE

AVOIDING THE ERROR OF ELIPHAZ

Job 4–5

MISERY LOVES COMPANY

There is something wonderful about well-timed words. Solomon was right when he said,

> *Pleasant words are a honeycomb, sweet to the soul and healing to the bones* (Proverbs 16:24).

He also wrote:

> *Anxiety in a man's heart weighs it down, but a good word makes it glad* (Proverbs 12:25).

He adds: *How delightful is a timely word* (Proverbs 15:23).

Solomon also warned of the deadly power of words:

> *A soothing tongue is a tree of life, but perversion in it crushes the spirit* (Proverbs 15:4).

This sounds similar to James, in his New Testament epistle, where he compared the tongue to a forest fire:

> [The tongue] *sets on fire the course of our life and is set on fire by hell* (James 3:5–8).

Frankly, there isn't anything more destructive, defeating, discouraging, deflating, or depressing than ill-timed, unwise, uncaring, unfeeling, self-centered, self-promoting words.

And there isn't anything more refreshing than timely, encouraging, uplifting, instructive words.

On the ash heap outside his hometown, one of the greatest and godliest men of the East sits in pain. His name has already become a nickname for suffering.

For one week, his three esteemed friends who traveled from afar sit with him in silence.

Finally, after seven days of shared grief, Job speaks, pouring out his confusion, sorrow and grief. While he doesn't curse God, he definitely curses the day he was born. He asked,

> ***"Why did I not die at birth?*** (Job 3:11) ***. . . like a miscarriage which is discarded, I would not be"*** (Job 3:16).

Job effectively laments the fact that he was allowed to be born and then grow up to suffer the worst of anyone's fears:

> ***"For what I fear comes upon me, and what I dread befalls me"*** (Job 3:25).

This is explosive language; lamenting sorrow; depressed and despairing agony from a man who wished he'd never been born.

What follows Job's eruption of misery is the response from the oldest of his three friends: Eliphaz. His ill-timed and discouraging words are not what Job needed to hear.

PRETENDED CONCERN

> ***Then Eliphaz the Temanite answered, "If one ventures a word with you, will you become impatient?"*** (Job 4:1–2).

That's not putting your best foot (or word) forward. What Eliphaz begins with is a question that can be paraphrased, "Are you going to get mad at me if I say something you don't like?"

Job will reserve his anger for much later. He won't interrupt Eliphaz, even though the words are arrogant, uncaring, and unjust.

Eliphaz continues,

> ***"Behold, you have admonished many, and you have strengthened weak hands. Your words have helped the tottering to stand, and you have strengthened feeble knees"*** (Job 4:3–4).

In other words, "Job, you've done a wonderful job in the past helping people who are discouraged; you've admonished them to walk the right path; you've strengthened people who were defeated and filled with despair."

Nice recovery, Eliphaz!

And what you would *want* to read next is, *"And now Job, it's time for someone to come along and strengthen your hands—to put wind into your sails; to steady your frail body and strengthen your crushed heart."*

Job hungered to hear that. But alas, Eliphaz continues :

> ***"But now it has come to you, and you are impatient; it touches you and you are dismayed"*** (Job 4:5).

In other words, "Job, you can dish out advice, but you can't receive it; you can tell others what to do to get back up on their feet, but you won't do it yourself. And because of that, you, Job, are ***dismayed***—literally, in a panic."

What Eliphaz *should* be saying is something like, "Now it's my turn, Job, to encourage you!" But he doesn't. Why? Because he doesn't think Job needs *encouragement* . . . he's convinced that what Job really needs is *discipline.*

PERSONAL CONDEMNATION

Eliphaz continues,

> ***"Remember now, who ever perished being innocent? Or where were the upright destroyed? According to what I have seen, those who plow iniquity and those who sow trouble harvest it"*** (Job 4:7–8).

This is the classic response to human suffering—promoted by Christians and preached in churches: innocent Christians are never in a crisis and the godly never suffer.

In other words, "The good guys always win and the bad guys always lose."[1]

You could summarize everything Eliphaz will say to Job with these words: "Job, this is all *your* fault!"

Can you imagine? Even if it were true, the time to deliver that verdict is not when someone's covered with boils and mourning the loss of ten children.

Eliphaz wins a gold medal in tactless, heartless, unfeeling, uncaring, untimely counsel.

Later in ***Job 5:4***, Eliphaz even implies that Job's children died because of his own foolish sin, evidently covered up and hidden away.

What makes it even more devastating is that Job is likely to believe him. What parent hasn't suffered the loss of a child and wondered if they were unworthy parents? Maybe they didn't deserve that child . . . maybe it *was* their fault!

I've had parents weep in my arms, asking, "Did God take my son [or daughter] because of something I did?" That's a common response of a parent who would have gladly taken their child's place!

Instead of words of comfort, Eliphaz crushes Job's heart with words of condemnation. His basic premise (and that of his many descendants) is this: sin = suffering; suffering = judgment.

Job is suffering—*therefore* Job is sinning; since Job is sinning, his suffering has brought about judgment.

What Eliphaz failed to consider was that Job was not sinless—no one is—but Job *was* innocent.

Eliphaz has overlooked the fact that even though unrepentant sinners will *ultimately* be judged by God, they are not all *immediately* judged. Even pagans can live a long life of wickedness and ease. Unbelievers often die at an old age with plenty of money in the bank and plenty of children to sue each other over the inheritance.

That was Asaph's quandary when he wrote:

> *For I was envious of the arrogant as I saw the prosperity of the wicked. For there are no pains in their death and their body is fat. They are not in trouble as other men, nor are they plagued like mankind. Surely in vain I have kept my heart pure and*

> *washed my hands in innocence;. for I have been stricken all day long and chastened every morning* (Psalm 73:3–5, 13–14).

While sinners may not be judged immediately, they will be judged ultimately. Contrary to the advice of Eliphaz, the righteous may not prosper immediately, but they will prosper ultimately . . . finally!

PROUD CONDESCENSION

So what kind of evidence does Eliphaz, the original prosperity preacher, bring to the table to prove that sinners suffer and saints succeed?

I find it ironic that his first—and foundational—evidence is from a vision he'd experienced.

Eliphaz mystically pounces on Job:

> ***"Now a word was brought to me stealthily, and my ear received a whisper of it. Amid disquieting thoughts from the visions of the night . . . then a spirit passed by my face; the hair of my flesh bristled up. It stood still, but I could not discern its appearance; a form was before my eyes; there was silence, then I heard a voice: 'Can mankind be just before God? Can a man be pure before his maker?'"*** (Job 4:12–13, 15–17).

These are rhetorical questions and the answers are supposed to be obvious: Job can't possibly be blameless and honest in the eyes of God.

How do you argue with someone whose counsel begins with, "I had a vision from God and I know the truth about your life." Who can escape such inspired advice?

Frankly, Christians use this approach all the time. I can't tell you how many times over the years I have heard from people who have heard from *God*. You've probably bumped into your share of the same: televangelists, teachers, and preachers alike who spend more time telling you what God told *them* than what God already said in His Word.

When people declare that God told them something, there's really nothing *you* can tell them! Frankly, anytime a conversation begins with the sentence, "God has spoken to me," there is no room for discussion.[2]

And don't miss the painful fact (which makes it doubly hard for Job): this condescending counsel has kernels of truth inside all the rhetoric. It *is* true that:

- no man is justified before God ***(Job 4: 17)***;
- men and angels err ***(Job 4:18)***;
- we live in bodies made of dust ***(Job 4:19)***;
- life is short ***(Job 4:20–21)***.

The theological *observations* from Eliphaz are correct. But he's completely wrong in his personal *applications* to Job's condition. How do we know? Because of what *God* said.

Earlier in chapter one, God made it clear that Job was *not* being punished for unrighteousness; he was going to suffer because he *was* righteous!

Eliphaz, the condescending counselor, had it absolutely turned around. Job wasn't suffering because he was a sinner; he was suffering because he was a saint.

Still, Job's friend moves from pretended concern to personal condemnation to proud condescension and, now, he offers another twisted gem.

PERVERTED COUNSEL

Eliphaz is caught up in his own perverse diagnosis—his own preconceived opinion, buttressed by a personal vision which he'll expound on, ad nauseum, throughout chapter five. And in the meantime, he accomplishes the very thing Solomon warned us to avoid if we truly cared for others:

> *A soothing tongue is a tree of life, but perversion in it crushes the spirit* (Proverbs 15:4).

We could summarize the words of Eliphaz: "I understand God more than you do . . . and you have gotten on His wrong side."

He advises Job,

> ***"But as for me, I would seek God, and I would place my cause before God"*** (Job 5:8).

In other words, "If *I* were *you*, I'd confess my hidden sins before God, repent, and get back in His good and prosperous graces."

He promises Job:

- God will set on high those who are lowly ***(Job 5:11a)***.
- God will lift you up after you've mourned over your sin ***(Job 5:11b)***.
- God will turn the lights back on and remove your dark despair ***(Job 5:14)***.
- You'll get your hope back ***(Job 5:16)***.
- Then you can be happy again ***(Job 5:17)***.
- Even though God has disciplined you and inflicted pain on you, He will give you relief ***(Job 5:18)***.
- God has wounded you, but His hands will also heal you ***(Job 5:18)***.

Eliphaz, the messenger of God via visions and dreams, informs Job that if he admits and repents of his hidden sins, he'll be saved from seven things that God never allows to touch the righteous:

> ***"From six troubles He will deliver you, even seven evils will not touch you"*** (Job 5:19).

1. Famine ***(Job 5:20)***
2. Defeat in war ***(Job 5:20)***
3. Physical abuse or violence ***(Job 5:21)***
4. Harm from wild beasts ***(Job 5:22)***
5. Financial loss ***(Job 5:24)***
6. Barrenness ***(Job 5:25)***
7. An early death ***(Job 5:26)***

Eliphaz is guaranteeing, "Job, if you lay out your cause before God and walk with Him, you will have everything you've ever dreamed of and you will never need to fear anything! And what's more, ***you will come to the grave in full vigor*** (Job 5: 26). You're not even going to get sick before you die!"

Evidently *all* saints cross the finish line without disease or aching joints or weary limbs . . . in fact, godly Christians die in such good shape and forward mobility that when their body hits the ground, it leaves skid marks!

Who wouldn't want that?

"Listen Job," he adds, ***"we have investigated it, and so it is. Hear it, and know for yourself"*** (Job 5:27).

The bad news is simply that Eliphaz bases his advice on a wrong assumption: Job was not suffering because he lacked holy living—it was his holy living that caught Satan's attention.

Now, Eliphaz meant well, but the effects of his words will be, as we'll see in the next chapter, devastating. His words do not help his friend . . . they deepen the hurt.

How do we avoid the error of Eliphaz? For those who will offer counsel to others, what observations can we make to guide our own words?

Acknowledge the Sufferer's Pain before You Challenge Their Perspective

Someone who is suffering will need your ear and your heart before they can receive anything out of your mouth. And that goes for those who *are* facing difficult and painful lives because they have sinned against the Lord.

Even then, begin with statements such as these:

- I can't imagine how difficult it must be for you to be a single mother.
- It must be agonizing to be facing a 10-year sentence.
- I'm so sorry that you lost your family in the car accident when you were driving under the influence.
- I'm grieving with you that you lost your family over decisions you made that ended up hurting all of you.

Listen—even when it *is* their fault and their suffering *is* the result of sinful behavior, you will not be viewed by them as condoning their sin just becuase you sympathized with them over the consequences of their actions.

It's actually okay to say, "I'm really sorry you're going to jail." Acknowledge their pain before you challenge their perspective.

Don't Dissect Someone's Speech—Deal with Their Spirit

Job's counselor earns the nickname, Eliphaz the Exterminator![3] Eliphaz hears the despair of Job's grief and pain and then criticizes what he says, rather than dealing with Job's crushed spirit.

We need to listen to what is being *felt* and not just to what is being *said.*

A wise counselor and comforter must listen with his heart and respond to feelings as well as to words. You do not heal a broken heart with logic; you heal a broken heart with love.[4]

Base the Content of Your Counsel on Biblical Truth, Not Personal Experience

You can illustrate truth with personal experience whenever it's helpful, but the basis of lasting hope and genuine healing is not what *you've* experienced—it's what *God* has revealed. It is not what *you've* seen but what *God* said.

When someone tells you how much they're hurting and you respond by telling them what happened to you, you miss the mark as badly as Eliphaz.

Every time you hear the name Eliphaz, think of an elephant—because when he finished his diatribe, Job felt like he'd been stepped on by one.

People who are in pain don't necessarily mind hearing a sermon, but they appreciate some sympathy, as well. So, put a spoonful of sugar in your medicine.

As we've gone through this speech, perhaps you haven't identified with Eliphaz at all; maybe you feel like Job. You don't want to *give* counsel . . . you'd just love to *receive* some. As you've climbed into this passage with me, your thoughts have mirrored Job's; you find yourself sitting beside him and asking the same questions he does. If that's true, let me warn you with several cautions.

Well-Meaning People May Only Add to Your Pain

One book in my library calls these people well-intentioned dragons. Oh, yes, they intend well enough . . . they're just unable to walk in your sandals. They can't grasp the depth of your pain. In fact, they really don't want to hear about it! They've got God all figured out . . . and you, too.

If you bare your soul to people like this, they'll more than likely deliver a rebuke . . . and then a truckload of correction. Or worse, they'll ignore what you even said because they don't like dealing with difficult questions.

People with pat answers aren't equipped, or interested, to explore the deeper issues of life.

I read a testimonial of a woman who was diagnosed with cancer. When she shared the devastating news with her mother and complained that she didn't know what to do or think, her mom sat there for a few moments and then said, "What do you think we should cook for dinner?"

In other words, "I'm not capable of handling a saint who's suffering . . . so let's just wave our emotional and theological remote at this drama and change the subject as quickly as we change the channel." Her daughter was crushed—as if an elephant had just stepped on her heart.

The disregard and unkindness of Eliphaz will pin Job to the ground rather than lift him up on his feet.[5]

Well-meaning? Yes. In fact (get ready for this), Eliphaz is the most *compassionate* of the counselors who will address Job. If you can imagine, he will give Job the most sympathy of the three men who traveled great distances to help Job get his life back on track.

Which takes me back to my point: well-meaning people may only add to your pain.

Wrong Counsel Is More Readily Available than Wise Counsel

Since bad counsel didn't end with the days of Eliphaz, make sure you don't give equal weight to everyone's advice.[6]

Having trouble with your marriage? The guy in the next cubicle may be ready with advice, but he might be out to lunch. Don't tell him that . . . but don't listen to him, either.

The neighbor who lives across the street may be eager to give you her perspective and counsel, but she might be biased by her own experiences and failure.

I have had couples come to my office who had been advised to divorce; others, to remain unmarried and yet live together; still others who were told to clearly violate Scripture in a variety of ways.

One pastor said that faithful members of his church had been carrying a secret for years. They had struggled financially and faced bankruptcy and the loss of their home. Their former pastor had advised them to get a divorce and put all the assets in her name, thus avoiding the loss of their possessions. They agreed, got a divorce in Las Vegas, and continued living together, thus keeping their home from bankruptcy foreclosure in the process. For the next fifteen years they maintained an unmarried, yet intimate relationship . . . that is, until their grown children came out with it and challenged them to make things right. Fortunately, they repented, were remarried, and reconciled to their family.

The warning for us all is to choose our counselors carefully—whether they wear a collar, have a cross hanging on the wall, or host a television program on cable TV. Make sure you filter their advice through the Word of God, prayer, and common sense . . . which doesn't seem to be all that common any more.[7]

The Path of Pain Often Runs Parallel to the Mystery of God's Plan

Pain and the mystery of God are often traveling companions; the path of suffering often runs parallel to the mystery of God's will for our lives. Just remember: your path of pain is not a mystery to *God.* Job will say it: ***"He knows the way I take"*** (Job 23:10).

God knows which path you'll take, which way it twists and turns, how long it takes, and how deeply it will impact your life.

He also knows *why.*

A young theological student came one afternoon to receive counsel from the famous London pastor C. H. Spurgeon. Spurgeon was himself a sufferer with many pressures and physical ailments, primarily the painful suffering with gout. The student was struggling with his own setbacks and the inability to figure out what God was doing with his life. Spurgeon said to him, "Young man, allow me to give you this word of advice: you must expect to let God know some things which you will never understand."[8]

Sometimes the wisest thing to say is, "God knows . . . and *He* understands.

Eliphaz, you *don't* know . . . you elephantine spirit-crusher with your untimely words and unwise counsel—you *think* you know everything, but you don't know anything about the mystery of God in the life of Job.

But God knows! And in the end, that's all that matters.

Then Job answered, 2 "Oh that my grief were actually weighed and laid in the balances together with my calamity! 3 For then it would be heavier than the sand of the seas; therefore my words have been rash. 4 For the arrows of the Almighty are within me, their poison my spirit drinks; the terrors of God are arrayed against me. 5 Does the wild donkey bray over his grass, or does the ox low over his fodder? 6 Can something tasteless be eaten without salt, or is there any taste in the white of an egg? 7 My soul refuses to touch them; they are like loathsome food to me. 8 Oh that my request might come to pass, and that God would grant my longing! 9 Would that God were willing to crush me, that He would loose His hand and cut me off! 10 But it is still my consolation, and I rejoice in unsparing pain, that I have not denied the words of the Holy One. 11 What is my strength, that I should wait? And what is my end, that I should endure? 12 Is my strength the strength of stones, or is my flesh bronze? 13 Is it that my help is not within me, and that deliverance is driven from me? 14 For the despairing man there should be kindness from his friend; so that he does not forsake the fear of the Almighty. 15 My brothers have acted deceitfully like a wadi, like the torrents of wadis which vanish, 16 which are turbid because of ice and into which the snow melts. 17 When they become waterless, they are silent, when it is hot, they vanish from their place. 18 The paths of their course wind along, they go up into nothing and perish. 19 The caravans of Tema looked, the travelers of Sheba hoped for them. 20 They were disappointed for they had trusted, they came there and were confounded. 21 Indeed, you have now become such, you see a terror and are afraid. 22 Have I said, 'Give me something,' or, 'Offer a bribe for me from your wealth,' 23 or, 'Deliver me from the hand of the adversary,' or, 'Redeem me from the hand of the tyrants'? 24 Teach me, and I will be silent; and show me how I have erred. 25 How painful are honest words! But what does your argument prove? 26 Do you intend to reprove my words, when the words of one in despair belong to the wind? 27 You would even cast lots for the orphans and barter over your friend. 28 Now please look at me, and see if I lie to your face. 29 Desist now, let there be no injustice; even desist, my righteousness is yet in it. 30 Is there injustice on my tongue? Cannot my palate discern calamities?"

–Job 6

(Continued on next page)

(Continued)

"Is not man forced to labor on earth, and are not his days like the days of a
hired man? 2 As a slave who pants for the shade, and as a hired man who eagerly
waits for his wages, 3 so am I allotted months of vanity, and nights of trouble
are appointed me. 4 When I lie down I say, 'When shall I arise?' But the night
continues, and I am continually tossing until dawn. 5 My flesh is clothed with
worms and a crust of dirt, my skin hardens and runs. 6 My days are swifter than a
weaver's shuttle, and come to an end without hope. 7 Remember that my life is but
breath; my eye will not again see good. 8 The eye of him who sees me will behold
me no longer; your eyes will be on me, but I will not be. 9 When a cloud vanishes,
it is gone, so he who goes down to Sheol does not come up. 10 He will not return
again to his house, nor will his place know him anymore. 11 Therefore I will not
restrain my mouth; I will speak in the anguish of my spirit, I will complain in
the bitterness of my soul. 12 Am I the sea, or the sea monster, that You set a guard
over me? 13 If I say, 'My bed will comfort me, my couch will ease my complaint,'
14 then You frighten me with dreams and terrify me by visions; 15 so that my soul
would choose suffocation, death rather than my pains. 16 I waste away; I will not
live forever. Leave me alone, for my days are but a breath. 17 What is man that
You magnify him, and that You are concerned about him, 18 that You examine
him every morning and try him every moment? 19 Will You never turn Your gaze
away from me, nor let me alone until I swallow my spittle? 20 Have I sinned?
What have I done to You, O watcher of men? Why have You set me as Your target,
so that I am a burden to myself? 21 Why then do You not pardon my transgression
and take away my iniquity? For now I will lie down in the dust; and You will
seek me, but I will not be."

–Job 7

CHAPTER TEN

ESCAPING THE DUNGEON OF GIANT DESPAIR

Job 6–7

John Bunyan was a pastor who, because of his biblical convictions, refused to align himself with the Church of England in the 1600s. In 1678, while in prison for holding unauthorized services, he wrote a book entitled *The Pilgrim's Progress from This World to That Which Is to Come*—better known today as *The Pilgrim's Progress.*

One of the most powerful dramas of Christian faith ever written, this captivating allegory of man's religious journey in search of salvation follows a pilgrim as he travels an obstacle-filled road. Bunyan's book would become an enormously influential seventeenth-century classic, universally known for its insight, passion, and beauty of language.

Bunyan portrays the adventures of a young disciple named Christian, who left his home in the village named City of Destruction and traveled to the Celestial City—or heaven.

In one chapter, Christian and his traveling companion Hopeful are captured by Giant Despair and thrown into a dungeon cell inside Doubting Castle. In the morning, they are taken to the castle yard and shown the bones of other pilgrims who never escaped from Giant Despair.

Christian and Hopeful refuse the Giant's demands to recant and are returned to their cell after being severely beaten. As the pilgrims begin to sucumb to despair, Christian remembers a way to escape. He is able to unlock their cell door with a key he'd been given earlier and they escaped with their lives.

Christian and Hopeful escape Doubting Castle and Giant Despair—not by a show of force or innate determination but by a key given to Christian . . . a key called Promise.

By the time you reach this particular chapter in the Book of Job, you discover him imprisoned in Doubting Castle, under the control of Giant Despair. As Job speaks, he will ask questions . . . questions without answers. And Giant Despair will nearly do him in.

The heavy chains of despair are now wrapped tightly around Job's body and spirit; the iron bars of discouragement hem him in; his response to the counsel of his friends is nothing less than the lamenting of an imprisoned believer held captive in Doubting Castle.

JOB SPEAKS TO HIS FRIENDS

Job Apologizes for His Rash Communication

> ***Then Job answered, "Oh that my grief were actually weighed and laid in the balances together with my calamity! For then it would be heavier than the sand of the seas; therefore my words have been rash"*** (Job 6:1–3).

In spite of his agony, Job offers his friends an apology.

What incredible character this displays! We see it peeking through every now and then, even though Job is racked with pain and frustration.

To paraphrase Job, he responds, "Listen, men, I know I'm speaking reckless words, but understand that if you put my grief and calamity on the scales, it would outweigh the sands of the seas."

You know how heavy wet sand is; Job's spirit is even heavier.

This is a good reminder to us as we help people who are crushed in spirit; one author said, "Cut them a little slack." We are to give them a measure of grace. Remember, don't just deal with their speech, take into consideration their wounded spirit, which is revealed in their bitter words.

Job Admits to His Raw Condition

It is as if Job says, "There's nowhere left to hide."

> ***"For the arrows of the Almighty are within me, their poison my spirit drinks; the terrors of God are arrayed against me"*** (Job 6:4).

Job says, "If God is firing His arrows at me, where am I going to hide? He never misses. He has perfect aim and has found my spirit. Furthermore, His arrows are dipped with poison and I am now filled with bitterness."

Then he admits, "There's nothing left for me to enjoy."

> ***"Does the wild donkey bray over his grass, or does the ox low over his fodder? Can something tasteless be eaten without salt, or is there any taste in the white of an egg? My soul refuses to touch them; they are like loathsome food to me"*** (Job 6:5–7).

These wild animals do not complain when they are satisfied with food. However, "As for me," Job says "there's nothing in life I can enjoy—not even the simple pleasure of a boiled egg."

Job's final remark about his condition is, "There's no one left to help."

> ***"Oh that my request might come to pass, and that God would grant my longing! Would that God were willing to crush me, that He would loose His hand and cut me off! But it is still my consolation, and I rejoice in unsparing pain, that I have not denied the words of the Holy One"*** (Job 6:8–10).

How Satan must have hated to hear these words! He and his demons have been longing to hear Job blaspheme the character of God, yet Job will not do it.

I am periodically reading the sermons of Joseph Caryl, a Puritan pastor who preached through the Book of Job several centuries ago. He took more than twenty-three years to finish that sermon series!

On this text in Job, Caryl observed:

> "Although the spirit hath no weight at all; only flesh and material substances are weighty; but a wounded spirit is

> heavier than wounded flesh." Then, he made this interesting insight, "The spirit is strong enough to bear the burden of wounded flesh; but the flesh is not strong enough to bear the burden of a wounded spirit."[1]

This is the reason that when we are discouraged, we are also tired. Our flesh cannot support a weary, despairing soul. When we find rest for our souls, we will find strength for our flesh.

Job says, "This is more than I can take. I am not made of stone or brass. I am a human . . . a weak, frail, faltering human being."[2]

Job admits to his friends his condition: his emotions are raw. He cannot take much more of a beating from Giant Despair.

Job Appeals for Real Compassion

> ***"For the despairing man there should be kindness from his friend; so that he does not forsake the fear*** [reverence] ***of the Almighty"*** (Job 6:14).

What pity this *should* have stirred in the hearts of Job's friends.

Nothing stirs our hearts quite like the personal observation of someone suffering. Nothing moved me to empty my pockets more than the children in India who scrambled after our luggage and followed us everywhere we walked, begging for small coins.

In New Delhi, I was riding with my window down, approaching a curb at a busy intersection; a young woman was standing there with a baby in her arms. Her face was blotched with leprosy, her eyes revealing the hopelessness of her soul; she held her thin arm and bony fingers outstretched toward me. All these years later, I cannot forget that image.

Can you imagine Job? Covered in boils, racked with pain, bereft of his children, sitting on the ash heap at the town dump, appealing not for money ***(Job 6:22)*** or physical help or deliverance ***(Job 6:23)***—only for kindness.

Job's friends, however, are afraid ***(Job 6:21)***. They are afraid that if they associate too closely with Job, God will send the same judgment upon them. They refuse to give him sympathy because it might anger God.

Job says to these friends,

> ***"My brothers have acted deceitfully like a wadi"*** (Job 6:15).

A wadi is a desert stream bed that rushes with water during the rainy season, but dries up in the heat of the summer.

Caravans from Tema and travelers from Sheba (Job 6:19) were known to travel across the desert. They would often be desperate for water and would travel along a wadi in hopes of finding it. Sometimes the search was in vain and the travelers died of thirst.

Job says, "I'm following after you, hoping for refreshing water, but at the end of the day, you have nothing to offer me. You haven't even given me one little drop of compassion."

Job Says His Friends Haven't Offered Realistic Correction

> ***"Teach me, and I will be silent; and show me how I have erred"*** (Job 6:24).

The Hebrew word for ***erred*** refers to unintentional sins. Job never denies sinning—he just doesn't know where he sinned and refuses to repent so that God would now judge him.[3]

Job says to his friends, "Listen, I don't need accusation—I need illumination. Show me my fault; show me my sin, and I'll readily confess!"[4]

Of course, these friends don't do this because they can't. Instead, they offer trite advice and condescending counsel.

Do you feel weary when someone gives you advice but you know they don't care, and their words are trivial and insufficient?

Charlie Brown, that transparent cartoon character, provides a poignant illustration as he complains that his team always loses their baseball games: "We always lose; we are always defeated."

Lucy comes along and, in her know-it-all way, offers this counsel: "Remember, Charlie Brown, you learn more from your defeats than you do from your victories."

Charlie then replies, "Well, then, that would make me the smartest person in the whole world!"

True compassion opens the door to wise counsel, even when it is challenging and reproving. *Identifying* with the sufferer is the first part of giving *insight* to the sufferer.

One of our young people at church—a middle schooler—was diagnosed with Crohn's disease. One of the most encouraging things to this boy as he battled his disease was receiving an email from David Garrard, then quarterback for the Jacksonville Jaguars:

> Dear David,
>
> My name is David Garrard and I'm a professional football player. Three years ago I was diagnosed with Crohn's disease, just like you. I am here to tell you that I know first-hand the circumstances that you are going through. I will be praying for you and for a speedy recovery. Remember that God puts things in our lives to teach us to trust Him. Keep your eyes on Him and trust Him with all your heart. I know that some days can be worse than others . . . but keep your head up. Feel free to contact me anytime.
>
> Sincerely,
> David Garrard #9

What encouragement and wise counsel. David Garrard first identified with young David and then provided encouraging insight.

JOB SPEAKS TO GOD

Now Job turns from speaking to his friends and speaks to his God.

Job Mourns the Misery of His Suffering

"Listen, Lord, even a slave who works in the hot sun eventually gets a chance to rest in the shade, and a hired hand who works hard at least has his paycheck to look forward to, but I don't have any relief—there is no shade tree under which my sorrow can find rest" ***(Job 7:2–3*** paraphrase*)*.

We are informed that Job's physical condition is worsening.

> ***"My flesh is clothed with worms and a crust of dirt, my skin hardens and runs"*** (Job 7:5).

Literally, Job's skin is now oozing with pus. It is not just that it's not letting up—it's getting worse! The beatings of Giant Despair are only growing harder for him to endure.

Job Bemoans the Brevity of His Life

> ***"My days are swifter than a weaver's shuttle . . . Remember that my life is but breath . . . I waste away; I will not live forever. Leave me alone, for my days are but a breath"*** (Job 7:6–7, 16).

Job is saying, "Since my life is short anyway, why let me linger—why not end it, Lord? The grave would be better than my painful life."

> **"[M]*y soul would choose suffocation, death rather than my pains*"** (Job 7:15).

It is this verse that John Bunyan put into the mouth of Christian as he languished in the cell deep in the dungeon of Doubting Castle.

Christian says to his companion, "Shall we be ruled by this giant? . . . I know not whether it is best to live like this or to die . . . the grave is easier for me than this dungeon!"

At this place in the original manuscript of *The Pilgrim's Progress*, John Bunyan, himself languishing in a prison cell, pencils into the margin the reference ***Job 7:15***.

The natural cry of the believer under great suffering is, "How long, O Lord? If it is for the rest of my life, take me on to heaven."

Job Laments a Loss of Communion with God

> ***"Have I sinned? What have I done to You, O watcher of men? Why have You set me as Your target, so that I am a burden to myself? Why then do You not pardon my transgression and take away my iniquity? For now I will lie down in the dust; and You will seek me, but I will not be"*** (Job 7:20–21).

Perhaps the greatest injury to Job is not his misery in suffering or his brevity in life, but that which he admits in this third and last portion of his prayer.

Make no mistake—Job is bound, deep in the cavernous depths of Doubting Castle, his spirit ruled by Giant Despair. All we can do is observe him there . . . and learn.

We can learn from the writings of John Bunyan, as well, who found a way for Christian and Hopeful to escape Doubting Castle; it happens to be the same method of escape for us all.

Earlier in *The Pilgrim's Progress*, Christian had been given a small key and told that whenever he needed to open a door, he should use this gift. The special key had a name: Promise.

That night in their dungeon cell, Christian suddenly remembers he has the key in his pocket. He pulls it out and, indeed, he is able to unlock the cell door and the outer gate, as well. He and his companion escape Doubting Castle and Giant Despair, not by their own strength or determination, but by the key, representing the promises of God.

GOD SPEAKS TO US

Should you find yourself locked in a similar dungeon, remember the gifts of promise given to those who follow Christ. Use these keys to defeat Giant Despair.

When You Conclude God Isn't Present, He Is

"I will never leave you nor forsake you" (Hebrews 13:5*b* NKJV).

This is God's promise key; there is no loophole or fine print. God means it.

When You Feel Life Is Hopeless, It Isn't

"'For I know the plans that I have for you,' declares the LORD, 'plans for welfare and not for calamity, to give you a future and a hope'" (Jeremiah 29:11).

Corrie ten Boom was a young Dutch Christian who helped hide Jewish people from the Nazis during World War II. She survived the horror of her imprisonment in Ravensbrück concentration camp. She later said, "There is no pit so deep but that God is not deeper still."

No matter how deep your dungeon, God is deeper still.

When You Believe God Doesn't Care, He Does

[C]*asting all your anxiety on Him, because He cares for you* (1 Peter 5:7).

Cast your cares upon Him because He *continually* cares—the tense declares: He constantly, without ever stopping, cares and is concerned for you. This is the key. It is His gift to you.

When You Think You Know Better than God Does, You Don't

> *As for God, His way is blameless; the word of the LORD is tried; He is a shield to all who take refuge in Him* (Psalm 18:30).

God's Word has never missed the mark . . . His promises are backed by the experience of the ages. His promises have been tried, tested, and found true.

When You Believe God Hasn't Heard Your Cry, He Has

> *You who seek God, let your heart revive. For the LORD hears the needy and does not despise His who are prisoners* (Psalm 69:32*b*–33).

With God, even when nothing is happening, *something* is happening—even for those in wretched conditions.

When You Don't Feel Loved, You Are

> *For I am convinced that neither death, nor life, nor angels, nor principalities, nor things present, nor things to come, nor powers, nor height, nor depth, nor any other created thing, will be able to separate us from the love of God, which is in Christ Jesus our Lord* (Romans 8:38–39).

I challenge you to contemplate the connection you have in your suffering to others who have suffered—past and present:

- If you are struggling, read the biographies of Christians who have gone before you.
- When you feel your circumstances are beyond the love of Christ, read *Foxe's Book of Martyrs.*
- Experience the fellowship of Christ's sufferings, as He was humbled when He voluntarily came to this land of sorrow, taking the form of a servant and dying the death of a despised, unwanted, unloved criminal *(Philippians 2).*

See your connection to the body of Christ—His Church. We all share in the sufferings of believers around the world *(1 Peter 5)*, and we desperately need wisdom to handle our own temptation to despair *(James 1).*

You are *not* alone and you are deeply loved—whether you sense it, conclude it, feel it, or even believe it.

Ask Job.

We all appreciate the testimony of sufferer Fanny Crosby, the blind hymn writer whose hymns have brought strength and joy to many. But there is another blind hymn writer who was not so well known:

> When George Matheson was a teenager, he learned that his poor eyesight would deteriorate until he could no longer see. The diagnosis was discouraging but not defeating. He continued his studies at Glasgow University in his native Scotland.
>
> He graduated from college when he was nineteen, but when pressing on in his graduate studies, the prognosis became reality. In 1862, at the age of twenty, Matheson became totally blind.
>
> His sisters closed ranks with him, learning Greek and Hebrew so they could assist him in his studies. He persevered, even after his fiancée broke off their engagement, stating that she was unwilling to marry a blind man.
>
> The pain of that rejection never totally left him, and George never married. However, he did enter the ministry and served in the pastorate for thirty-one years.
>
> Queen Victoria often invited him to preach to the royal court. In fact, she paid to have his sermons on Job published.
>
> After his youngest sister married, leaving him entirely alone, George became overwhelmed with sorrow. Instead of languishing, however, he sat down and wrote the words to a poem that since has become a beloved hymn of the Church. Even more, the words of this poem reflect the keys of promise that kept George Matheson from self-pity and defeat.[5]

O Love that wilt not let me go,
I rest my weary soul in Thee;
I give Thee back the life I owe,
That in Thine ocean depths its flow
May richer, fuller be.

O Joy that seekest me through pain,
I cannot close my heart to Thee;
I trace the rainbow through the rain,
And feel the promise is not vain,
That morn shall tearless be.

O Cross that liftest up my head,
I dare not ask to fly from Thee;
I lay in dust life's glory dead,
And from the ground there blossoms red,
Life that shall endless be.[6]

This is the way we escape Doubting Castle . . . this is the way we flee Giant Despair.

*Then Bildad the Shuhite answered, 2 "How long will you say these things, and
the words of your mouth be a mighty wind? 3 Does God pervert justice? Or does
the Almighty pervert what is right? 4 If your sons sinned against Him, then He
delivered them into the power of their transgression. 5 If you would seek God and
implore the compassion of the Almighty, 6 if you are pure and upright, surely now
He would rouse Himself for you and restore your righteous estate. 7 Though your
beginning was insignificant, yet your end will increase greatly. 8 Please inquire of
past generations, and consider the things searched out by their fathers. 9 For we are
only of yesterday and know nothing, because our days on earth are as a shadow.
10 Will they not teach you and tell you, and bring forth words from their minds?
11 Can the papyrus grow up without a marsh? Can the rushes grow without water?
12 While it is still green and not cut down, yet it withers before any other plant.
13 So are the paths of all who forget God; and the hope of the godless will perish,
14 whose confidence is fragile, and whose trust a spider's web. 15 He trusts in his
house, but it does not stand; he holds fast to it, but it does not endure. 16 He thrives
before the sun, and his shoots spread out over his garden. 17 His roots wrap around
a rock pile, he grasps a house of stones. 18 If he is removed from his place, then it
will deny him, saying, 'I never saw you.' 19 Behold, this is the joy of His way; and
out of the dust others will spring. 20 Lo, God will not reject a man of integrity, nor
will He support the evildoers. 21 He will yet fill your mouth with laughter and
your lips with shouting. 22 Those who hate you will be clothed with shame, and
the tent of the wicked will be no longer."*

–Job 8

CHAPTER ELEVEN

CALLING THE KETTLE BLACK

Job 8

Has it ever occurred to you that when God wants to teach us how to be satisfied in sorrow, contented in chaos, and trusting in trials, He doesn't give us a theological treatise—He gives us a biography.

More than likely, the Lord has given you someone—a living biography of grace and truth—in your life who has demonstrated the perseverance of Job. That person (or persons) has marked you . . . inspired you . . . convicted you. When you think of suffering, your thoughts often turn to them and you're deeply encouraged by their testimony of trust.

The dignified, winsome leadership of Dr. Richard Seume was a weekly reminder to us young seminarians that God was awesome, and worshiping Him was a privilege.

It came as a surprise to learn that this gracious, positive leader was on dialysis several times a week due to kidney failure. I remember one afternoon watching him walk across the seminary parking lot toward the clinic where he would receive treatment. He was dressed, as always, in a suit, gracious dignity and quiet confidence emanating from his bearing. It was little wonder that he impacted thousands of students for God's glory.

In my last year of seminary, Dr. Seume's successor was appointed. Talk about positive—the new man made us all think we needed a shot of adrenalin and a big dose of laughter just to keep up. Bill Bryan has now served for decades as the chaplain at Dallas Seminary. I still remember his joy in leading the student body in singing, his trumpet stashed conveniently nearby.

No student left Bill Bryan's presence without a positive word and a big handshake. He told me personally of his childhood . . . scenes from his past that would not normally create the optimistic, joyful man he would become.

In Charles Swindoll's commentary on the Book of Job, I was reminded of one particular scene from Chaplain Bill's story:

> Bill's dad struggled with the dark emotional tunnel of depression. Back in those days, any kind of emotional or mental struggle was rarely brought out of the closet and there was very little treatment known for people who suffered in this way.
>
> Bill remembers going week after week to the Medical Arts building in Springfield, Missouri, where they would take the elevator to the sixth floor. He waited with his mother as his father went through counseling sessions. As a little boy he didn't understand what was happening. He just knew his dad was troubled and that his dad's [spirit] was bleak and barren.
>
> On one occasion, Bill recalls his father being escorted out of the doctor's office and asked to stay with little Bill (who was only four at the time) while his wife went into the private office of the physician. Since his father's depression was advancing, they were making plans to admit him to what was then called an "insane asylum." Every word of the consultation could be heard in the hallway. One of the doctors made the unfortunate comment that "this man will probably never get out."
>
> Bill said, "I remember as my mother walked out with several doctors in tow, my dad picked me up and held me close and said, "I love you, son." He then put me down on the floor, turned and ran the hallway, jumping through the six-story window as the glass shattered, and falling to his death."
>
> These were the last, lingering memories Bill had of his father. From that time on, Bill was primarily cared for by his grandparents and his aunt as his mother tried to recover from the tragedy.

> All of us who know this joyful servant of God would have never expected a man like Chaplain Bill Bryan to have emerged from such a sad, sorrowful beginning.[1]

I couldn't agree more. Frankly, the more I learn about Job's suffering and the more I study the unfortunate words of Job's counselors, the more amazed I am that Job didn't turn and run away. The fact that he *stayed* amazes me.

And all the while, God is silent . . . no reassuring answer from above.

No wonder James summarized this ancient man's testimony by writing *You have heard about the endurance of Job* (James 5:11*b*).

Job is in the examining room and one doctor after another makes his diagnosis. Dr. Eliphaz hints at Job's secret sin. He suggests that Job need only repent and admit his hidden rebellion against God, and all will be well.

The second doctor now pronounces his opinion. If you thought Eliphaz *the Elephant* was crushing, you will be stunned by Bildad *the Brutal.* That's the best way I can describe his treatment of Job.

LET ME TELL YOU WHO GOD IS!

> ***Then Bildad the Shuhite answered*** [Job]***, "How long will you say these things and the words of your mouth be a mighty wind?"*** (Job 8:1).

Moffat translates this "[you are using] wild and whirling words."[2]

As Job defends himself against the accusations of Eliphaz, Bildad becomes angry and self-righteous. He waits for Job to catch his breath before jumping in . . . and striking back.

At least Eliphaz began with some tact when he said, ***"If one ventures a word with you, will you become impatient?"*** (Job 4:2).

Not Bildad *the Bruiser.* He pounces immediately, asking two questions:

1. **"When are you going to stop running your mouth?"** With arrogance and unconcern for his patient, he effectively calls Job a windbag: "Job, you're filled with hot air!" Bildad is upset because Job didn't accept the diagnosis of Eliphaz. Job had responded by saying, effectively, "God doesn't appear to be fair . . ." Bildad concludes that Job's view of God needs to be corrected—perhaps that's his problem!

2. **"When are you going to stop distorting and twisting the character of God?"** This is a paraphrase of ***"Does God pervert justice? Or does the Almighty pervert what is right?"*** (Job 8:3). The Hebrew word translated ***pervert*** means *to distort or twist.* In other words, since God is *always* fair, you've obviously sinned!

The brutality of Bildad's counsel cuts even deeper: he accuses Job's children of sin.

> ***"If your sons sinned against Him, then He delivered them into the power of their transgression"*** (Job 8:4).

That is, "If Eliphaz is wrong and your children didn't die because *you* sinned, then it's rather obvious they died because *they* sinned."

Remember, this had been the great concern of Job. In the first chapter, he is seen sacrificing for the possible sins his children might have committed as they gathered to celebrate their birthdays at one another's homes:

> ***Job would send and consecrate them, rising up early in the morning, and offering burnt offerings*** [for the unintentional sins of his children] ***. . . Thus Job did continually*** (Job 1:5).

His greatest concern had been that his children walked in fellowship with God.

Bildad bruises Job's heart with the implication, "None of your sacrifices did any good, Job. You didn't satisfy God with your burnt offerings on their behalf and, apparently, they were such great sinners that they had to be killed by God's judgment after all."

Unbelievable. This is a knife driven directly into the heart of a grieving dad. This is equally the heartbreak of any godly parent: their children will walk away from God and then face severe consequences because of their sin. Certainly every committed, godly, praying parent is crushed by thoughts that perhaps what they did as parents wasn't good enough.

Honestly, it's amazing that Job doesn't get up and run directly off a cliff to silence his agony . . . and the voice of this accuser.

But wait—unfortunately, Bildad isn't finished yet.

Bildad's Counsel

- **Let me tell you who God is *(Job 8:1-7).***

He goes even further in his arrogance as he pretends to speak on behalf of God:

> ***"If you would seek God and implore the compassion of the Almighty; if you are pure and upright, surely now He would rouse Himself for you and restore your righteous estate"*** (Job 8:5–6).

Bildad counsels, "Trust me, Job, I know what God will do if you just follow my advice." He then offers, as proof of his knowledge of God, the traditions of the past.

- **Listen to what our forefathers believed *(Job 8:8–10).***

Bildad expounds:

> ***"Please inquire of past generations, and consider the things searched out by their fathers"*** (Job 8:8).
>
> ***"Will they not teach you and tell you, and bring forth words from their minds?"*** (Job 8:10).

He implies that the thoughts of the forefathers would all line up with his own personal opinion that the righteous do *not* suffer and God *only* punishes pagans.

Besides, he asserts: "We were only born yesterday and we don't know anything and life is too short to ever figure anything out anyway" ***(Job 8:9*** paraphrase*)*.

In a way, Bildad is right. We don't learn enough in life to fully prepare for life. For example, by the time we've discovered how to do a decent job of parenting, our children are grown and gone.

Thank God for grandchildren! Maybe that's why we can't wait to be grandparents—we finally have enough experience to make up for all our mistakes.

One anonymous pundit put it this way: *Experience is a comb after you've lost your hair.*

Stephen Pile has written a book entitled *The Book of Failures.* There is an interesting story from 1978 when the British Army had assumed the task of emergency firefighting. They were new at it, lacked experience, and it showed. On January 14, they were called out by an elderly lady in South London to rescue her cat. Arriving with impressive haste, they very cleverly and carefully rescued the cat and prepared to leave the scene. The lady was so grateful she invited the men in for tea. When driving away later with fond farewells and waving of arms, they ran over her cat and killed it.[3]

Someone wrote, "Experience is what it takes to recognize a mistake the second time you make it."

Another reminds us all, "The problem with learning by experience is that it charges so much for tuition."

Bildad scolds Job: "You *think* you know something about God and life and suffering and trouble? You don't know anything. You haven't lived long enough to gain the experience. So learn from what our fathers knew and our forefathers before them—terrible things in life are the result of sinning against God."

This is the wisdom of the ages: somebody at your address sinned!

And as if Job needs more evidence to buttress this ancient principle, Bildad plows ahead.

- **Look at what nature teaches *(Job 8:11-19)*.**

Here he assumes Job does, in fact, need more convincing. In this third section of his counsel, Bildad provides three illustrations from the natural world:

> ***"Can the papyrus grow up without a marsh? Can the rushes grow without water?"*** (Job 8:11).

Obviously, the answer is no. Without water, papyrus withers ***(Job 8:12)***. Job is likened to a stalk of ***papyrus***; for some time, he might have looked healthy, but when the water (God's favor) dried up, Job began withering, as well, proving that God and he were disconnected ***(Job 8:13)***.

Next, Bildad illustrates the frailty of Job's life with a spider's web: it looks magnificent, but it's so ***fragile*** that you'll fall over if you lean on it for support ***(Job 8:14)***.

Notice the gourd, Bildad continues,

> ***"He thrives before the sun, and his shoots spread out over his garden . . . If he is removed from his place, then it will deny him, saying, 'I never saw you'"*** (Job 8:16, 18).

The vine and its roots will totally rot away, leaving no evidence that it was ever in the garden.

"Three parables for you, Job; listen carefully to me," Professor Bildad *the Blunt*, intones:

1. You've run out of water and you're withering away.
2. You're leaning on a spider's web and you've collapsed.
3. You're a vine that God has uprooted and all the evidence that you even existed is rotting away.

How terribly encouraging . . . thank you, Bildad *the Belittler.*

One of the strangest war incidents I've ever read was the arrest, trial, and imprisonment of an American serviceman in World War II. He struck no blow for the enemy; he was not disloyal to his country; he was just a *discourager* at a very critical time in the battle. While the fate of his company hung in the balance, he would travel along the front lines and say disheartening words *[We're not going to make it . . . we're all going to be killed . . . this war is hopeless . . . we shouldn't be out here, etc.]* to the men on duty. The court marital judged it a crime to speak disheartening words at such critical times. He was sentenced to one year in military prison.[4]

Bildad should have been locked up!

At the most critical time in Job's life—in the heat of battle—Bildad comes along with discouraging, belittling words. He may have begun by accusing Job of being a windbag, but the fact of the matter was far different: Bildad was the one full of hot air, not Job.

Bildad was the pot calling the kettle black! He was blinded by the beam in his own eye as he spouted off about the speck in Job's.

But true to form, Bildad stumbles on . . .

- **Think of what lies ahead *(Job 8:20–22).***

  "God will not reject a man of integrity, nor will He support the evildoers" (Job 8:20).

Again, this is his basic equation (along with Eliphaz and the others): sin = suffering, and since Job is suffering, he's obviously in sin.

How do we know this assumption is true? Bildad harrumphs,

> ***"God will not reject a man of integrity."***

That's just the way it works! So confess, Job—and if you do, look what lies ahead:

> ***"He will yet fill your mouth with laughter and your lips with shouting"*** (Job 8:21).

"Trust me Job . . . confess your sin and you'll be laughing again in no time."

How arrogant . . . how tactless. Laughter is the farthest thing from Job's mind. Job doubts he will *ever* laugh again.

Bildad is like a doctor telling a man with acute appendicitis that he should try not to feel so much pain.[5]

For those who want to analyze Bildad's blunders, he made several:

- his arrogance led him to an unkind approach;
- his lack of pity caused a severe lack of perspective;
- his self-assured counsel eclipsed gracious correction.

LET ME TELL YOU HOW LIFE IS!

Like Eliphaz, much of what Bildad said contained parcels of truth; however, incomplete truths that sound so clever can quickly lead to error.

Life Is Too Short to Grow Wise!

Bildad proposed in ***Job 8:9***:

> Life is so short *(true)*, you don't have enough time to get wisdom on your own—especially at a young age *(false)*.

Solomon, another wise man from the East inspired by God's wisdom, counseled with these words,

> *My son, if you will receive my words and treasure my commandments within you . . . the LORD gives wisdom . . . wisdom will enter your heart* (Proverbs 2:1, 6, 10).

Wisdom speaks and says,

> *"By me kings* [older men] *reign . . . By me princes* [young men] *rule. I love those who love me; and those who diligently seek me will find me"* (Proverbs 8:15–17).

Paul could tell Timothy with confidence that he shouldn't be ashamed of his youthfulness but that he could, in fact, be an example to the believers in his speech, conduct, love, faith, and purity *(I Timothy 4:12)*. He could demonstrate wisdom—the application of truth to life.

You don't have to grow old to grow wise.

Only the Perfect Can Approach God!

Bildad challenges Job to get God's attention by becoming pure before He approaches Him ***(Job 8:6)***. He was saying, "You gotta get your act together before you can grow close to God." To someone who is desperately trying to figure out why God doesn't seem to be listening, this advice can be devastating.

This type of counsel led to the monastic order . . . asceticism . . . self-inflicting wounds . . . penance . . . purgatory . . . and a thousand other tragic and unbiblical errors.

False teaching like this belongs on the ash heap alongside Bildad. The truth is you do *not* pursue perfection in order to get God's attention.

Jesus Christ said:

> *"It is not those who are healthy who need a physician, but those who are sick"* (Matthew 9:12).

If you'd like an appointment with the Great Physician, the only thing you need to understand is that you're sick and needy. That's all!

Things Will Always Be the Way They Were!

Job is told by Bildad that the past always dictates the present; you're to learn your cues from past generations ***(Job 8:8)***. In modern parlance, if something was good enough for them way back when, it's good enough for us.

This is the same sound bite that discourages churches and defeats progress. This is the congregant or deacon whose typical response to innovation is, "We've never done it that way before." As if there were something sinful about trying something novel.

One author put it so well: God never intended the past to become a parking lot—it's a launching pad.

There's one final observation on the counsel from Bildad *the Bruiser*.

We Always Get What We Deserve!

"Surely God does not reject a blameless man or strengthen the hands of evildoers" (Job 8:20 NIV).

There is a half-truth expressed here in the principle of reaping what you sow. But according to Bildad, there are no exceptions to this rule. He hasn't yet learned what God had to say about the matter.

LET ME TELL YOU WHAT GOD SAID!

We thank God there are final and eternal exceptions to the rule. And *we* are the exception, by the grace of God.

We sowed sin and deserved hell. *But* we have been redeemed by Christ who was Himself an exception: receiving in His body the punishment for sins He never sowed, for iniquity He never committed. Yet *He Himself bore our sins in His body on the cross, so that we might die to sin and live unto righteousness* (1 Peter 2:24).

Jesus Christ got what He did *not* deserve so we could receive what we do not deserve: forgiveness and eternal life.

Bildad said, ***"God does not reject a blameless man."*** Oh, but He did! For Christ, the blameless Man, was forsaken by the Father.

And because Christ was forsaken, we can be forgiven.

A word to Bildad: grace has opened up an eternity of exceptions. And we will live forever in heaven because of it.

> A man in Dundee, Scotland, in the late 1800s was confined to bed for forty years, having broken his neck in a fall at age fifteen. But his spirit remained unbroken, and his cheer and courage so inspired people that he had a constant stream of guests.
>
> One day a visitor asked him, "Doesn't Satan ever tempt you to doubt God?"
>
> "Oh, yes," replied the man; "he does try to tempt me. I lie here, and see my old schoolmates driving along in their carriages and Satan whispers, 'If God is so good, why does He keep you here all these years? Why did he permit your neck to be broken?'"

> The guest asked, "What do you do when Satan whispers those things to you?"
>
> "Ah," replied the invalid, "I take him to Calvary and show him Christ and say, 'You see, He does, indeed, care for me.'"[6]

Bildad, you're wrong . . . *thank God*:

- We don't have to grow old to grow wise.
- We don't have to be perfect to approach God.
- Things will not always be the way they were.
- We don't always get what we deserve.

One day, we who believe by faith in Christ alone will receive eternally and entirely what we do *not* deserve!

Then Job answered, [2]"In truth I know that this is so; but how can a man be in
the right before God? [3]If one wished to dispute with Him, he could not answer
Him once in a thousand times."

–Job 9:1–3

[22]*"It is all one; therefore I say, 'He destroys the guiltless and the wicked.' [23]If the*
scourge kills suddenly, He mocks the despair of the innocent. [24]The earth is given
into the hand of the wicked; He covers the faces of its judges. If it is not He, then
who is it? [25]Now my days are swifter than a runner; they flee away, they see no
good. [26]They slip by like reed boats, like an eagle that swoops on its prey."

–Job 9:22–26

[32]*"For He is not a man as I am that I may answer Him, that we may go to court*
together. [33]There is no umpire between us, who may lay his hand upon us both.
[34]*Let Him remove His rod from me, and let not dread of Him terrify me."*

–Job 9:32–34

CHAPTER TWELVE

THE GOSPEL ACCORDING TO JOB

Job 9–10

It might strike you as unbelievable, but there are actually people in the world who want to take God to court. One news article from Athens, Greece, told the story of a Romanian prisoner who served time in jail while at the same time filing suit against God. State television picked up the story of the inmate named Pavel M. who was sentenced to serve twenty years in the west Romanian city of Timisoara. He apparently blamed God for the troubles in his life and demanded that God be held accountable for failing to keep His end of the bargain. According to Greek authorities, the plaintiff claimed that when he was baptized in childhood, he entered a contract with God. The contract—according to Pavel—had legal effects. God was obligated to protect him from the devil but had not followed through. The lawsuit was submitted, but the civil court responded, tongue in cheek, that it was unlikely the case would ever be heard since it was impossible to subpoena God.[1]

That reminded me of a legal organization that defends people against "size discrimination." Their mission is to provide legal protection for children and adults who face prejudice because they are overweight. This is well and good, but reading further into their mission statement, I found that they actually make a claim against God:

> The largest offender of size discrimination is God. He gives them heart disease and stroke, high blood pressure, diabetes, cancer . . . gout, and breathing problems . . . [We are] suing God . . . because God discriminates." Then this organizatino sarcastically asks, "Hey, God, do you think defibrillators and insulin are free!?" There follows a place to sign up to "join [our] class action suit against God for the burden he is placing on the health care system . . ."[2]

A secretary in Oakland, California, recently took God to court. A lightning bolt struck near her home, creating a fire and destroying four houses. The six-figure damage suit charges God with careless and negligent operation of the universe. The scathing indictment included the mismanagement of the weather. Her attorney said he would try to collect the money by attaching a claim to property that had been deeded to a church nearby. She said that the money should be rewarded to her if God failed to show up in court.[3]

If you want to know how Job is feeling at this point in the progression of his story, these people from Romania, Canada, and California answer the question: Job wants to take God to court.

Legal jargon begins to appear as Job vents his frustration at what he believes to be the injustice of God:

- ***dispute*** – to enter into litigation ***(Job 9:3)***;
- ***answer*** – to give testimony in court ***(Job 9:15)***;
- ***judge*** – an opponent at law ***(Job 9:15)***;
- ***set a time*** – subpoena to appear in court ***(Job 9:19)***.
- ***umpire*** – an arbitrator or judicial mediator ***(Job 9:33)***;
- ***reason*** – the argument of a legal case ***(Job 13:3)***;
- ***prepare*** – make ready his legal case ***(Job 13:18)***;
- ***contend*** – dispute in court ***(Job 13:19)***.

Basically, Job laments, "Even if I could get God to appear in court, what would I be able to say that would make Him listen?" ***(Job 9:14–16*** paraphrase***)***.

Job is frustrated with the fact that God will not show up in court and allow him an opportunity to state his case. He says:

- God is *invincible* ***(Job 9:10)***.

- God is *invisible* ***(Job 9:11)***.
- God is *unaccountable* ***(Job 9:12)***.
- God is *unanswerable* ***(Job 9:15a)***.

In other words, "I would not be able to state my case in court before this invincible, invisible, unaccountable God even if I could somehow get Him to show up."

Furthermore, Job has almost reached the conclusion that God is *unmerciful* in the way He treats the human race:

> ***"It is all one; therefore I say, 'He destroys the guiltless and the wicked.' If the scourge kills suddenly, He mocks the despair of the innocent. The earth is given into the hand of the wicked; He covers the faces of its judges. If it is not He, then who is it?"*** (Job 9:22–24).

Job's pain is being replaced with anger. Satan hasn't succeeded in provoking Job to blaspheme God, but he has succeeded in distorting Job's perception of God, making God Job's enemy.

People in deep pain often arrive at this same conclusion. They think, *God must not love me . . . He must not care about me . . . so He must be against me.*

Job has become convinced of three things:

1. God is all-knowing but refuses to share His insight ***(Job 10:1–7)***.
2. God created Job but no longer cares about him ***(Job 10:8–17)***.
3. God brought Job to life but offers no hope ***(Job 10:18–22)***.

In spite of Job's despair and anger, his words are filled with deep truths. Without even realizing it, he delivers the salient points of the Gospel in prophetic form.

For those of us who live with completed revelation, we can look at the anguish of Job, hear his demands for justice, and read in his complaint the future promises of the Gospel of Christ.

When Jesus Christ walked on the Emmaus Road with two disillusioned disciples, He worked His way through the Old Testament, beginning with Moses and the prophets, delivering the truth about Himself.

I am fairly certain that Job's own words would have formed a few texts for our Lord to expound upon. Job raises questions that find answers only in Christ. He makes statements that find fulfillment in Christ alone.

First, he presents the dilemma of the entire human race in his opening response to Bildad:

"But how can a man be in the right before God?" (Job 9:2*b*).

Some would say that Job is not referring to salvation but to vindication. It doesn't matter to me—for in either case, the question remains the same, "What would ever give a human being the right to be accepted by a holy, righteous God?"

This is the question of the ages; this is the most important question you will ever have to answer. What is it that you think gives you the right to enter the presence of God and be accepted forever?

The world today is telling us that anything you want to believe will get you to heaven. This is as foolish as going to the airport and saying, "I'd like a ticket to visit my cousins in Georgia—any plane will do as long as the pilot is sincere, I feel good when I get in my seat, and I sense deeply that this is the plane for me."

Are you kidding? We want an exact flight . . . an exact gate . . . an exact destination. We even want the time of departure and arrival. We do not need to meet the pilot or feel good about our seat.[4]

Why is it that when it comes to traveling from earth to eternity, any path will do—any gateway will suffice, as long as we feel good that this is the religion for us?

THE GOSPEL TELLS MANKIND HOW TO BE RIGHT WITH GOD

The Gospel does not apologize for its exclusive claim through Christ alone:

> *Jesus said to him, "I am the way, and the truth, and the life . . ."* (John 14:6).

The Gospel reveals,

> *Therefore there is now no condemnation for those who are in Christ Jesus* (Romans 8:1).

Peter preached,

> *"And there is salvation in no one else; for there is no other name under heaven that has been given among men by which we must be saved"* (Acts 4:12).

Paul wrote to the Galatian church,

> *Grace to you and peace from God our Father and the Lord Jesus Christ, who gave Himself for our sins so that He might rescue us* (Galatians 1:3–4*a*).

Jude put a great exclamation mark on his answer to this question, "How do I stand before God?" A question that haunts the human race and long ago troubled the heart of Job:

> *Now to Him who is able to keep you from stumbling, and to make you stand in the presence of His glory blameless with great joy, to the only God our Savior, through Jesus Christ our Lord, be glory, majesty, dominion, and authority, before all time and now and forever. Amen.* (Jude 1:24–25).

This is the Gospel, and this Gospel answers the question of Job. We are both justified and vindicated in the presence of God the Father by the advocacy and atonement of God the Son.

THE GOSPEL SILENCES MANKIND'S SELF-DEFENSE MECHANISMS

> ***"If one wished to dispute with Him, he could not answer Him once in a thousand times"*** (Job 9:3).

Again, Job delivers a gospel truth. The Gospel silences the sinner. At the moment of his conversion, he is utterly empty of self-help, self-defense, self-support, self-vindication, self-promotion, and self-justification.

The whole of unbelieving humanity will one day be silenced as it stands accountable before God *(Romans 3:19)*. The very thing the world resists—the very thing the world hates to consider—will one day take place.

All the world will become, before God, *accountable*.

Paul is saying that all the world will be brought to trial before God and is, even now, guilty before God.

Notice in this future scene that Paul doesn't say everyone will have their chance to articulate a defense, but rather that *every mouth* [will] *be closed.*

"Even if we exhaust our legal options" [and land in prison], one author commented, "we can still write letters, we can even write a book . . . we can argue . . . we can refuse to be silenced!"[5] But this is not the case in the courtroom scene that Paul is describing. He is referring to the coming judgment of all who are without Jesus Christ when they stand before God at the Great White Throne Judgment *(Revelation 20:11-15).*

Before this great white throne, described by John in *Revelation 20*, there will be no defense; no series of alibis; no plea bargaining; no prayer for judgment—just silence!

This is not a trial by peers; this is a trial by Providence. There are no extenuating circumstances for sin; God was an eyewitness to everything ever thought, said, or done.

The Gospel warns that the host of unbelievers will stand before Him in silence. It will be too late to pray. Paul writes that mankind without Christ is without an advocate; without a defender—condemned to everlasting torment without any hope of parole.

Job says, "Suppose mankind could get an audience with God, we would have no answer or excuse. Even if we had a thousand chances to speak, we would come up short."

THE GOSPEL WARNS MANKIND OF THE BREVITY OF LIFE

> ***"Now my days are swifter than a runner; they flee away, they see no good. They slip by like reed boats, like an eagle that swoops on its prey"*** (Job 9:25–26).

Job had watched boats made of papyrus and light bark skim across the water. These were the speed***boats*** of the ancient world.

He had watched an ***eagle swoop on its prey***. Death came out of nowhere, and it came fast.

I was at a stoplight when a hawk suddenly flew past my windshield. It scooped up what looked like a mouse from the grass on the other side of the road and then flew away. That field mouse never saw it coming. The bird just swooped down and *whoosh!*—life for that mouse was suddenly over.

Job says, "That's my life; that's how fast it's going. It is literally flying away."

This was the message of James to the scattered Jewish believers: "Your life is like a vapor; a wisp of smoke; steam from a kettle—it's here for a moment, but then it vanishes away."[6]

In the spring of 2007, Lee Roberson, the founder of Tennessee Temple University, died days before the commencement exercises of the university he founded. This former pastor and educator was 97 years old when his body was laid to rest.

I was on the campus a couple of days later; the president of the university told me that Dr. Roberson's son had said to his father that they needed to plan his funeral. He had responded to his son by saying, "You know, I'm disappointed—I thought I'd have a few more years to preach."

Dr. Roberson had preached nearly every week for seventy years. To him, it was like being in a reed boat speeding across the water; it was like an eagle suddenly swooping down out of nowhere and carrying him away.

Frankly, it's the same for all of us. This is a part of the Gospel. We don't have much time here on planet Earth. So where do you stand with God?

THE GOSPEL DECLARES TO MANKIND THE INCARNATION OF GOD THE SON

> ***"For He*** [God] ***is not a man as I am that I may answer Him, that we may go to court together"*** (Job 9:32).

Job laments, "God is not a man like I am. He can't communicate with me. I can't see Him to talk to Him and answer Him. I can't take Him to court and state my case."

To Job, it appeared that God was distant, transcendent and, evidently, not too concerned about suffering humans.

However, God, through Christ, became human just like we are. He humbled Himself, taking the form of a servant, and was made in the likeness of men *(Philippians 2:7).*

Jesus Christ came to seek and to save those who are lost *(Luke 19:10)* He is willing to redeem His bride *(Ephesians 5:25–27).*

Jesus Christ, being fully God, was able to pay through His death and resurrection the eternal penalty of our sin against the character of an eternally just and holy God.

Jesus Christ was fully God but fully man—having been born into the human race, He became a relative of humanity and thus qualified to purchase His bride *(1 Peter 1:18–19).*

Oh, the irony of Job's longing for God to become a man so that they could commune together. The Gospel declares the incarnation of God the Son. Job didn't know what we know . . . God the Son became a man.

THE GOSPEL ANNOUNCES TO MANKIND THE ADVOCACY OF JESUS CHRIST

> ***"There is no umpire between us, who may lay his hand upon us both. Let Him remove His rod from me, and let not dread of Him terrify me"*** (Job 9:33–34).

Job cries, "I need someone to be a mediator between God and me; someone to remove the rod of God's judgment and save me from the terror of God's holiness. Is there no arbiter; no umpire to lay his hand upon us both?"

Job was referring to the custom of the ancient court which used a daysman to act as an arbitrator between two parties to negotiate a settlement. It was the custom of the daysman to put his hands on the heads of the two disputing parties to remind them that he was the one with the authority to settle the question.[7]

"Is there *anyone* who can come between me and God and speak for us both and negotiate some sort of settlement?"

With prophetic longing, Job asks the question that Paul answers as the Gospel is completed in the coming of Jesus Christ.

> *For there is one God, and one mediator also between God and men, the man Christ Jesus, who gave Himself as a ransom for all* . . . (1 Timothy 2:5–6).

Is there someone who can speak for me? Yes! It is Christ, our Redeemer.

Is there someone who can remove the rod of God and the terror of His judgment? Yes! It is Christ, our Savior.

Job's ultimate hope was not in some reason; it was in a relationship. It was in the settlement of reconciliation between himself and God.

We know fully what Job did not know. The mediator he longed for is not only alive—He is available and ready to step in on our behalf.[8]

This Mediator is capable of laying His hand on God the Father and on us. Being the Son of God, He is fully aware of the claims of righteous deity. Being the Son of man, He fully empathizes with the needs of humanity.

He has bridged the gap and He alone is capable of providing an everlasting settlement.

We do not take God to court, but we can take Him into our heart.

We do not sue God, but we can settle with God through faith in Jesus Christ, *the* Mediator between God and man.

"But man dies and lies prostrate. Man expires, and where is he?"

–Job 14:10

"If a man dies, will he live again? All the days of my struggle I will wait until my change comes."

–Job 14:14

CHAPTER THIRTEEN

THE DAY AFTER YOU DIE

Job 11–14

We have been discovering that Job's friends were making his last days miserable. Now the last of his three counselors rises to speak. We will examine their discussion before diving more deeply into Job's questions about life after death.

ZOPHAR REBUKES JOB

Zophar is assumed to be the youngest of Job's friends because he speaks last.

> ***Then Zophar the Naamathite answered, "Shall a multitude of words go unanswered, and a talkative man be acquitted?"*** (Job 11:1–2).
>
> ***"But would that God might speak, and open His lips against you"*** (Job 11:5).

Zophar obviously lacks the courtesy of Eliphaz which prompted him to apologize before speaking. At the same time he doesn't have the cowardice of Bildad who hides behind his traditions.[1]

Zophar is a pugnacious fighter . . . with him, it's an all out frontal attack. There are no punches pulled by Zophar *the Zealot*. He is convinced, as are the other men, that Job is suffering because he has sinned against God.

Frankly we are all a little more like Zophar, Eliphaz, and Bildad than we'd like to admit. No matter how wise and good a person may have been in the past, when misfortune strikes, we tend to wonder if it was due to hidden sin or some error on their part:

- A child runs away and we assume that the parents must have been a little less committed in the home, behind the scenes, than they appeared in public.
- A man has a heart attack and we assume he was working too hard and maybe even took time away from his family.
- A neighbor goes bankrupt and we assume he had it coming through financial misjudgments.[2]

We naturally assume some kind of error, failure, or even sin is the reason for the suffering in someone's life.

Zophar doesn't beat around the bush for one minute as he comes out swinging. He even suggests that God has not punished Job for *all* his sins. He says,

> ***"Know then that God forgets a part of your iniquity"*** (Job 11:6*c*).

In other words, "Job, you're actually getting off light."

Then Zophar reminds Job that he is no match for God. He delivers this condescending speech about the fact that God is "higher, deeper, longer, and broader" than anything we can imagine. Note what he reminds Job:

> ***"For He knows false men, and He sees iniquity without investigating"*** (Job 11:11).

"Well, Job, God knows you're a hypocrite; He *knows*!"

Then Zophar delivers this insult:

> ***"An idiot will become intelligent when the foal of a wild donkey is born a man"*** (Job 11:12).

The Hebrew word translated ***idiot*** refers to someone who is morally hollow; empty—a man of no reason or sense. In our colloquialism, we would call him a blockhead or an airhead. It could be expanded to give the full brutality of this insult by amplifying the translation to read, "Job, an empty airheaded idiot like you will no more get wisdom than a wild donkey will give birth to a human being."[3]

Let this rebuke sink in. Try to imagine yourself in Job's place, sitting on the ash heap at the town dump. You have lost nearly everything. You haven't been able to eat or sleep for days, your skin is itching uncontrollably, and you're running a high fever. You are devastated and nearly delirious over the loss of your children—your family—your finances—even your closest friends have turned against you.

Warren Wiersbe writes insightfully, "How sad it is when people who should share *ministry* end up creating *misery.*"[4]

Zophar says, "Repent, Job; come clean and confess your sin. If you do, you'll get your life back" ***(Job 11:13–14*** paraphrase***)***.

"If you don't," he warns Job, ***"the eyes of the wicked will fail, and there will be no escape for them; and their hope is to breathe their last"*** (Job 11:20).

With these final words, Zophar just sucks the wind out of Job's sails. He condemns him to die without hope of escape unless Job follows his advice and repents of his secret sins.

This has to be the lowest point in Job's life. All three friends have now spoken. One by one they have taken Job farther and farther away from hope.

JOB'S RESPONSE

Job responds to all three of his counselors with sarcasm:

> ***"Truly then you are the people, and with you wisdom will die!"*** (Job 12:2).

"You men evidently have all the wisdom in the world and when you die, there won't be any left on the planet."

Then Job fights back:

> ***"But I have intelligence as well as you; I am not inferior to you"*** (Job 12:3).

"Go ahead and smirk," Job says, "go ahead and call me names. I'm not ***inferior*** to you!

> ***"I am a joke to my friends, the one who called on God and He answered him; the just and blameless man is a joke"*** (Job 12:4).

"I'm not an empty-headed idiot." Job continues, "I know I'm a ***joke*** to you now. You're laughing up your sleeve at my attempt to stand for the integrity of my character. But I *do* know as much about God as you!"

He then launches into an amazing description of God's character and power:

> ***"With Him are wisdom and might; to Him belong counsel and understanding. Behold, He tears down, and it cannot be rebuilt; He imprisons a man, and there can be no release. Behold, He restrains the waters, and they dry up; and He sends them out, and they inundate the earth. With Him are strength and sound wisdom, the misled and the misleader belong to Him. He makes counselors walk barefoot and makes fools of judges. He loosens the bond of kings and binds their loins with a girdle. He makes priests walk barefoot and overthrows the secure ones. He deprives the trusted ones of speech and takes away the discernment of the elders. He pours contempt on nobles and loosens the belt of the strong. He reveals mysteries from the darkness and brings the deep darkness into light"*** (Job 12:13–22).

Job says, "I know all this . . . ***my eye has seen all this, my ear has heard and understood it"*** (Job 13:1).

He repeats his earlier statement: ***"What you know I also know; I am not inferior to you"*** (Job 13:2).

This is not new stuff to Job.

Job calls them all ***worthless physicians*** (Job 13:4). "You are using treatment that doesn't help. You are prescribing medicines for the soul that are only making things worse. But no matter how bad it gets, no matter what God does to me—in fact, if He were to put me to death—I would still claim Him as my God and I would still hope in Him."

Wow!

This is the amazing declaration of Job 13:15: ***"Though He slay me, I will hope in Him."***

This is the verse many people recall when they think of the perseverance of Job. At this point, I am now even more amazed at his response.

Yes, Job has passed the test! At his lowest moment, Job refuses to curse God.

We can also pass the test! If Job can, we can!

- There *can* be unconditional trust in God.
- There *can* be obedience without any guarantees.
- There *can* be faith without healing or prosperity.
- There *can* be trust even in the most difficult trial.

LIFE AFTER DEATH

Understand that even though Job passes this test, he is still overwhelmed with the belief that his life will soon end. He frankly doesn't know if God *will* slay him. He asks of God, **"[H]*ide me in Sheol . . . until Your wrath returns to You*"** [until Your anger against me subsides] (Job 14:13).

Job wonders aloud, "If God were to put me in Sheol—if I were to die—what happens next?"

With this question, Job raises the question of the ages: What will happen to me one moment after I die?!

ALL PREPARE TO DIE

The older a person grows, the more they think about the brevity of life.

Christianity Today carried excerpts of interviews with very elderly people. Jeanne Calment, at 120 years of age, was verified as being the oldest living human being at the time. She still had plenty of spunk, too. When asked to describe her vision for the future, she answered, "Very brief."

Another woman interviewed was asked to give some of the benefits of living to the age of 102. After thinking for a moment, she smiled and said, "Well, for one, there's no more peer pressure."

I really like the determination of another: she had never married and told her pastor, John Fetterman, to make sure there were no pallbearers at her funeral. He asked, "Why would you request that?"

She responded, "They wouldn't take me out while I was alive; I'm not going to let them take me out when I'm dead."

Frankly, for most people, the talk of dying is not a laughing matter, is it? A growing number of people, in fact, are convinced that they will be able to cheat death. This interesting article verifies the idea:

> It is reported that at least twelve American multimillionaires are now planning to come back to life better than ever. They are so confident in the progress of science and modern medicine that they have arranged for their bodies to be frozen at a cryogenic suspension plant.
>
> They have even set up "personal revival trusts" which are designed to not only ensure but expand their wealth so that it will be waiting for them at the bank when they have been medically resurrected in 100–200 years.
>
> David Pizer, a 64-year-old millionaire, was interviewed and said that the ten million dollars he left to himself—after all the compound interest had been added over the years—would make him the richest man in the world when he woke up.[5]

I really don't blame this unbeliever. There is something in the heart of mankind that believes this life is not the end.

Randy Alcorn writes in his book entitled *Heaven* about that innate, intuitive sense we all have that we will live somewhere forever.

Australian aborigines pictured heaven as a distant island beyond the western horizon. The ancient Mexicans, Peruvians, and Polynesians believed they would go to the sun or the moon after death. Native Americans believed that in the afterlife, their spirits would hunt the spirits of buffalo. The ancient Babylonian legend called the Gilgamesh Epic refers to a resting place of heroes and even hints of a tree of life. Romans believed that the righteous would picnic in the beautiful meadows of Elysia, while their horses grazed nearby.

It is true, as God's Word says that [God] *set eternity in their heart.* (Ecclesiastes 3:11).

Throughout history, one of the unifying themes of the human heart is the inherent curiosity over life after death. The question is not so much,

"*Will* we live forever?" but, "*Where* will we live forever?" Stated otherwise, "What's going to happen to us the day after we die?"

While your family is planning your funeral service, what will you be experiencing?

These are the very same questions posed in the oldest book in the biblical record—Job asked about life after death. He was driven to these questions because of one very obvious dilemma: he thought his life would soon end.

Even though Job will later declare his faith in his living Redeemer, at this point in his pain, Job is deeply unsettled and from his lips come two penetrating questions that mankind has been asking ever since.

WHERE DO WE GO WHEN WE DIE?

> ***"But man dies and lies prostrate. Man expires, and where is he?"*** (Job 14:10).

Job wants to know where he will be the day after he dies. He is not concerned about the transition; he wants to know about the *destination.*

Even to the Old Testament believer, death was murky and the grave was unsettling. Job did not have the completed record of Scripture that we have today. He could not pull up his Bible software and do a word search on death and the afterlife. He could not pull out his *Strong's Concordance* to cross reference anything, much less open a commentary that offered insights or crack open a lexicon to do word studies.

We not only have a completed record of Scripture today, we have volume after volume of detailed explanations and commentary.

In Job's day, there were more questions than answers. Job is asking in total sincerity, "Where do we go when we die?"[6]

Job himself mentions a place called ***Sheol (Job 14:13)***. Perhaps Job's question has less to do with the destination than it does with the *details* about that destination.

This Hebrew word Sheol appears nearly seventy times in the Old Testament. Much of the confusion about it comes from the fact that, at times, it is translated "hell," and other times, "the grave."

Sheol is not hell, and though the word can refer to the grave, it is not the grave, either. Sheol is a holding place where departed spirits await their final judgment.

The prophet wrote,

> *Sheol from beneath is excited over you to meet you when you come; it arouses for you the spirits of the dead, all the leaders of the earth; it raises all the kings of the nations from their thrones* (Isaiah 14:9).

We need to understand a few things about this place.

Sheol and the Grave Are Two Separate Places

The grave is the place where the body is laid. Sheol is the place where the spirit of the deceased is living—as alive as ever.

In the Old Testament, it is clearly taught that both the righteous and the unrighteous went to Sheol after dying. David, in fact, had further revelation about death and the future life of those who died:

> *As sheep they are appointed for Sheol; death shall be their shepherd . . . But God will redeem my soul from the power of Sheol, for He will receive me* (Psalm 49:14–15).

David expected to go to Sheol when he died, but he did not expect to stay there forever.

Throughout the Old Testament, the term Sheol is used for the region of departed spirits. B. B. Warfield, a scholar from a past generation, commented,

> Israel from the beginning of its recorded history had the most settled conviction of the persistence of the soul in life after death; the body is laid in the grave and the soul departed for Sheol.[7]

Before Jesus Christ appeared on the planet as the suffering Savior, the Old Testament had been translated into the Greek language. It was called the Septuagint (or the LXX: seventy), in reference to its supposed seventy translators. The Lord quoted from it, as did the apostles. Whenever the word Sheol appeared, it was translated as the Greek word Hades. In fact, later, whenever the New Testament Greek text was quoting a Hebrew passage, the word Sheol was always translated Hades.

Hades and Sheol are the *same* place. Again, Hades was not a reference to the grave but to the place of departed spirits.

Sheol Is Comprised of Two Different Regions

The mystery of Sheol and Hades is cleared up by the preaching of Jesus Christ. He revealed an actual event in the lives of two deceased men whose spirits went to Hades. Luke's Gospel records the deaths of a rich unbeliever and a poor believer.

In this account, Christ confirms the two-region view of Sheol and Hades:

> *"Now the poor man died and was carried away by the angels to Abraham's bosom; and the rich man also died and was buried. In Hades, he* [the rich man] *lifted up his eyes, being in torment, and saw Abraham far away and Lazarus in his bosom. And he cried out and said, 'Father Abraham, have mercy on me, and send Lazarus so that he may dip the tip of his finger in water and cool off my tongue, for I am in agony in this flame.' But Abraham said, 'Child, remember that during your life you received your good things, and likewise Lazarus bad things; but now he is being comforted here, and you are in agony. And besides all this, between us and you there is a great chasm fixed, so that those who wish to come over from here to you will not be able, and that none may cross over from there to us'"* (Luke 16:22–26).

Don't misunderstand—the rich man did not end up in Hades because he was rich but because he had not followed after God. He had not demonstrated that relationship by the repentance of his sin; he will admit as much later in this same passage. And Lazarus did not get into the comfort region (Abraham's bosom) because he was poor but because he had trusted in the God of Abraham.

- **Jesus authenticates the two-region construction of Hades.** One region is a place of physical suffering and the other is a place of comfort—referred to as Paradise.

- **Jesus teaches that Hades is a place of fully operative physical senses.** The unbelieving man cries out, "I just want a drop of water; I am in agony in this flame" *(Luke 16:24).* There is evidently some form of intermediate body given to those who have died, otherwise they would be ghost-like without any sensory perception. They would not need to eat or drink, and they would not be affected by the flames. The evidence from Christ's message that Hades is a place of physical, conscious experience cannot be denied without accusing Christ of error.

- **Jesus teaches that those who are in Hades know they deserve the compartment they are in.** One author states that this man never complained of injustice. He never said, "I shouldn't be here!" Instead, he complained about the pain.[8]

Hades Is a Place of Memory and Emotion

The rich man demonstrates great passion for the lost. He has brothers who are heading down the same path.

> *"And he said, 'Then I beg you, father, that you send* [Lazarus] *to my father's house—for I have five brothers—in order that he may warn them, so that they will not also come to this place of torment.' But Abraham said, 'They have Moses and the Prophets; let them hear them.' But he said, 'No, father Abraham, but if someone goes to them from the dead, they will repent!'"* (Luke 16:27–30).

This man is immediately concerned with sending the truth to his lost family members. This deceased unbeliever has more concern for the lost than many living believers.

Hades Is Not a Figment of Someone's Imagination

Every unbeliever who dies goes to Hades and then, after the final judgment, is consigned to the lake of fire forever. According to *Revelation 20*, Hades will empty its inhabitants before the Great White Throne Judgment of God, where they will be condemned and sent to the lake of fire that we know as hell.

For now, the souls of all those who die without faith in God through Christ go to Hades, where they suffer torment and await their final judgment.

No wonder this man wanted his five brothers to escape. Hades was no longer a faraway imagined place—it was real.

And he's still there to this day.

Understand that this place of torment—Hades now and, eventually, hell forever—is not something the Church came up with to try to make people act nice to each another or to scare people into being good. It is not something that we could concoct on our own, apart from the record of divine inspiration.

Hell, like Hades, is a literal place. At this point, Hades is the holding place for those marked for judgment. Hell is the final, eternal place of judgment and torment *(2 Peter 2:9)*.

Hell is not a ghetto . . . rush hour . . . a bad relationship . . . a tough assignment . . . poverty . . . cancer. There is no such thing as "hell on earth." No matter how bad it gets on earth, it will never compare to this literal, eternal place of torment.

The question really demands an answer: where will you be the day after you die?

The Apostle Paul said of those who believe the Gospel,

> *We are confident, I say . . .* [that] *to be absent from the body* [is] *to be present with the Lord* (2 Corinthians 5:8).

Believers also are given some form of intermediate body. These bodies will allow us to enjoy the presence of Christ. We will have lips to speak and sing. We will have emotions and all the physical senses, like Lazarus of old.

Paul told the Thessalonian church that those believers who had died and were already with God will be with Christ when He comes in the clouds to rapture the Church. Their resurrected bodies from the grave will be reunited with their spirits that have been with Christ; they will then be robed with a permanent glorified body, along with all those who are alive and raptured—taken up—to meet our Lord in the air *(1 Thessalonians 4:13–18)*.

So what happens to those who, along with Lazarus, went to Hades—the comfort side of Paradise? How is it that those who *now* die go to heaven and not Hades?

John wrote in *Revelation 20* that the inhabitants of Hades will be poured out into hell after the final judgment—so there cannot be any Old Testament or New Testament believers in there.

So, what happened to them?

Paul writes that,

> *"When He* [Christ] *ascended on high, He led captivity captive"* (Ephesians 4:8 NKJV).

In other words, Christ led these Old Testament (pre-cross) believers out of Hades and into heaven, which had been prepared by His word in an instant.

Paul goes further to say,

> *(Now this expression, "He ascended," what does it mean except that He also had descended into the lower parts of the earth? He who descended is Himself also He who ascended far above all the heavens, so that He might complete all things)* (Ephesians 4:9–10).

Paul hints at this historic event when Christ descended into Hades, not to suffer in some form of hell, but for a purpose: to deliver the news of his triumph over Satan and to make *a public display of them, having triumphed over them through Him* (Colossians 2:15).

Hades is no longer a holding place for *believers*—they are in heaven and everyone who dies in Christ immediately goes to heaven, as well.

WILL WE LIVE AGAIN AFTER WE DIE?

> ***"If a man dies, will he live again?"*** (Job 14:14).

The answer is, "Yes . . . *forever*!"

Jesus Christ gave the answer to Job's poignant question—a question bound up in the heart of mankind—when He said,

> *"I am the resurrection and the life; he who believes in Me will live even if he dies"* (John 11:25).

Those who place their faith in Christ will have this future—everlasting life in a new heaven and a new earth as their eternal home *(Revelation 21–22).*

Again, the critical question is not, "*Will* we live forever?" but "*Where* will we live forever?"

There is life after death! Job knew it intuitively, and so do we.

This is not philosophical speculation . . . religious mythology . . . a fabrication to make people act nicer or feel better. It is the answer from God. This is the word from the Creator. And His word is totally reliable and entirely credible and eternally true. Period.[9]

Where will you be the day after you die?

You will be fully conscious—fully aware. You will be *you*, more alive than ever, clothed in a temporary body, either suffering in Hades, awaiting an eternal sentence in hell, or enjoying the presence and worship of Jesus Christ.

For those who believe the Gospel, you will experience an end to the struggles of life that Job longed to escape. You will be free—for death will have released you to everlasting life.

Then Eliphaz the Temanite responded, [2]"Should a wise man answer with windy knowledge and fill himself with the east wind? [3]Should he argue with useless talk, or with words which are not profitable?"

–Job 15:1-3

Then Job answered, [2]"I have heard many such things; sorry comforters are you all. [3]Is there no limit to windy words? Or what plagues you that you answer? [4]I too could speak like you, if I were in your place. I could compose words against you and shake my head at you."

–Job 16:2

"My spirit is broken, my days are extinguished, the grave is ready for me. [2]Surely mockers are with me, and my eye gazes on their provocation."

–Job 17:1–2

CHAPTER FOURTEEN

WHEN FAIRYTALES HAVE THE WRONG ENDING

I watched the Disney animated movie "Happily N'Ever After" with one of my daughters. It had a rather unpredictable story line that kept us guessing. An old wizard in a tall tower ran everything in Fairytale Land. He had a set of scales representing good and evil by which he balanced all events. He did such an excellent job that the fairytales always came true and everyone *always* lived happily ever after:

- Cinderella could wear the glass slipper and marry the prince.
- Sleeping Beauty always woke up and married the prince.
- Rapunzel let her hair down for the prince to climb up and rescue her.
- Little Red Riding Hood was always saved and the woodsman always killed the wolf.

The wizard made sure the scripts were followed and everyone kept to the storyline.

Unfortunately disaster struck after the wizard left for a golf vacation in Scotland. His two bumbling assistants managed to mess everything up, allowing the scales to get out of balance. That's when life in Fairytale Land turned upside down:

- Cinderella's mean stepmother became the ruler of the universe.
- Sleeping Beauty's handsome prince bent down and kissed her, then fell asleep, too.
- Rapunzel's long hair caused her to lose her balance, fall out of the tower, and crush the prince below.
- Little Red Riding Hood was eaten by the wolf.

Fairytales weren't going the way they were supposed to go!

Imagine your own script going awry:

> You're driving home from work after a terrible day at the office. In bumper-to-bumper traffic, the guy behind you smashes into you, forcing you to hit the car in front of you, and it happens to be a brand-new Porsche. You finally get everything documented by the police, but the Porsche owner is so angry he promises to sue you. When you finally arrive home, you forgot the milk; the dog's hungry and gnawing on the kitchen cabinets; your kids are misbehaving and gnawing on each other; the pile of mail is overdue bills and your checkbook balance is zilch; your wife tells you the doctor wants both of you to come to his office first thing in the morning. About then, you think *Lord, what is going on?! And while I'm at it, where are You?* And no answer comes. And tomorrow is worse than today. You are about to lose your job, your wife is sick, and the guy in the Porsche files suit.[1]

Frankly, many people imagine God like that Disney wizard: it's His job to keep the scales of good and evil perfectly balanced and everybody on script. And it's His job to keep us from hitting Porsches. If He should ever take a vacation or take His hand off the scales, everything would get fouled up and the expected ending to everyone's daily fairytale wouldn't come true.

I fear that many Christians have the unspoken belief that if you follow the script and keep your nose clean, your shoes polished, and your pants pressed, life will deliver the right ending to every chapter and everyone will live happily ever after.

When it doesn't happen, God gets the blame.

By the time we arrive at ***Job 15***, Job's trials are growing more terrible. And it isn't an accident with an angry driver—it's a series of accidents brought about by God.

Job's spirit is crushed; his eyes are red from perpetual tears; he's more exhausted than ever, and those who've shown up to encourage him only make things worse.

But the one Person who *doesn't* ever show up—the One who is noticeably absent—is God.

Keep in mind that Job has followed the script . . . he has memorized his lines . . . he has acted his role with passion. But his fairytale seems to be turned upside down; it's as if the wizard in charge of the scales has left on vacation.

Job 15 begins the second round of speeches between Job and his misguided counselors.

In the first round, Eliphaz, Bildad, and Zophar delivered speeches that basically said Job was in need of repentance. In this second round, all three counselors will speak again . . . and simply turn up the heat.

When Eliphaz spoke the first time he was discreet—and diplomatic. Not this time. Now he drops the pretense and comes out swinging. He's not happy Job discounted his earlier counsel.

> ***Then Eliphaz the Temanite responded, "Should a wise man answer with windy knowledge and fill himself with the east wind? Should he argue with useless talk, or with words which are not profitable? Indeed, you do away with reverence and hinder meditation before God"*** (Job 15:1–4).

How dare Job ignore such sage, experienced wisdom! It's as if Eliphaz is saying, "Job, you're ruining my walk with God by hanging around this trash dump, trying to talk sense into you."

In the opening salvo of this chapter, we have a graceless man offering counsel to a grieving man. He will only deepen Job's wounds.

Donald Grey Barnhouse wrote that ***Job 15*** reveals the sad fact that the tongues of professing Christians are often all too busy doing the devil's work.[2]

The counsel of Eliphaz begins with:

- offended **pride** ***(Job 15:2)***;

- **insults *(Job 15:3)***;
- pious **condescension *(Job 15:4)***;
- a big dose of **condemnation**:

> ***"For your guilt teaches your mouth, and you choose the language of the crafty. Your own mouth condemns you, and not I; and your own lips testify against you"*** (Job 15:5–6).

In other words, "Job, every time you open your mouth, you dig the hole that much deeper." Besides, he implies, "Who do you think you are?"

Eliphaz now resorts to **sarcasm**:

> ***"Were you the first man to be born, or were you brought forth before the hills? Do you hear the secret counsel of God, and limit wisdom to yourself? What do you know that we do not know? What do you understand that we do not? Both the gray-haired and the aged are among us, older than your father"*** (Job 15:7–10).

"We're the veterans here, Job. Look at our gray hair . . . we're older than your father . . . we are the original wise men from the East."

And they are obviously not about to change their position on Job's pain.

It is critically important to these three counselors that they *win* the argument; that their diagnosis is correct. In fact, the diagnosis has now become more important than the patient.

Why? If Job is *not* a sinner being punished by God, then their understanding of God is all wrong. What's worse, they have no protection against suffering *themselves*. If obedience was not a guarantee of health and wealth, then what happened to Job just might happen to *them*.[3]

No wonder it was so critically important that Job confess. No wonder they so adamantly claimed that they'd figured out the role of the wizard: they knew how the scales of justice *worked*.

They were insistent that Job's fairytale ending wasn't working out simply because he hadn't followed the script:

> ***"Why does your heart carry you away . . . that you should turn your spirit against God?"*** (Job 15:12*a*, 13*a*).

Job just *can't* be a righteous man . . . this *has* to be his fault!

And this brings us to some observations about Eliphaz's counsel—and about wrong counsel, in general.

FOR THOSE OFFERING COUNSEL

Wrong Counsel Supports Its Case More than It Offers Comfort

An unwise, short-sighted, or self-centered counselor is more interested in his perspective than in resolving your pain. And he *must* win the argument. Eliphaz didn't want to be a help to Job as much as he wanted to be right.

When a counselor's perspective outpaces biblical support, they tend to commit the error of Eliphaz: they repeat themselves—only louder.

Wrong Counsel Ultimately Is Self-Serving and Self-Promoting

Eliphaz is actually constructing a profile for God that makes God the servant of man. In his mind, religion isn't worth the effort; besides, what motive could there possibly be for serving God if God never paid you back . . . and then some?

Eliphaz is actually repeating the exact same argument Satan brought up in ***Job 1*** when he told God, "Take away Job's family and his health and his fortune, and he'll curse you to your face."

In other words, keep his relationship from paying off—take away his fortune and watch him resign his faith.

Every believer faces this same twofold challenge: How do you respond when Christianity doesn't seem to pay? How do you respond when obedience creates conflict and/or discomfort?

We'd like to believe that whenever we do the right thing, good things will happen. After all, fairytales should always have happy endings.

One day, a simple illustration happened right in front of me. I was leaving a store parking lot and there was just enough room for me to pull in front of a lady waiting for the light to change. I needed a couple of inches to get into the lane and she graciously waved me in with a smile, put her SUV in reverse . . . and backed into the car behind her.

It just so happened to be a brand-new Jaguar. I've noticed that people who drive Jaguars are really picky . . . about dents and stuff like that.

I felt so bad for this woman who had been kind and polite to me, doing a good deed. She was doing the right thing, but it made life for her suddenly uncomfortable.

Ultimately, our motive in doing the right thing is not so good things happen but so God will be glorified.

Jesus Christ challenged His disciples in Matthew 5:16, *"Let your light shine before men in such a way that they may see your good works*" . . . and give you a raise . . . elect you to the board . . . put you on first string . . . give you an "A" for Good Conduct.

Not even close. The text ends, *"so that they might see your good works and glorify your Father who is in heaven."*

If counselors do not ultimately point you away from yourself and toward the glory and honor of God, chances are you might just be following the self-serving, self-promoting, comfort-seeking, compromise-allowing, self-assuring counsel of Eliphaz.

Through the remainder of this chapter, Eliphaz continues to deliver his own experience, another reminder of poor counsel; he opines:

> ***"I will tell you, listen to me; and what I have seen I will also declare"*** (Job 15:17):

- The wicked are in pain all their lives ***(Job 15:20)***.
- The wicked are riddled with anxiety ***(Job 15:22)***.
- The wicked are terrified of death ***(Job 15:23)***.
- The wicked regard themselves as invincible ***(Job 15:25)***.
- The wicked's wealth won't last ***(Job 15:28–29)***.
- The wicked will lose everything ***(Job 15:30)***.
- The wicked will not leave an inheritance/legacy ***(Job 15:31–33)***.
- The wicked's doom is certain ***(Job 15:34–35)***.

Eliphaz is obviously talking about Job and he barely camouflages his condemnation. In his view, everything that has happened to Job is *proof positive* of his perspective: "There it is, Job . . . *bad* people don't enjoy a fairytale life.

No wonder Job responds,

> ***"I have heard many such things; sorry comforters are you all"*** (Job 16:2).

The word ***sorry*** can be translated *burdensome*. Job continues,

> ***"I too could speak like you, if I were in your place. I could compose words against you and shake my head at you"*** (Job 16:4).

In other words, "Let's trade places, Eliphaz, and then see how easy it is for you to swallow what you're ladling out."

It would do some counselors good to hear, "*You* climb into this hospital bed; *you* stand in this unemployment line; *you* sit in this bankruptcy courtroom; *you* change places with me and see how easy it is to come up with obvious answers and simplistic reasons for trials and tribulations."

One author said that sometimes we have to experience misunderstanding from unsympathetic friends in order to learn how to minister to others.[4]

If that's true—and it is—Job will one day be a first-class giver of comfort! But for now, he's not sure he'll make it out of intensive care.

He laments regarding his **emotional** pain:

> ***"If I speak, my pain is not lessened, and if I hold back, what has left me?"*** (Job 16:6).

He refers to his **physical** state:

> ***"He*** [God] ***has exhausted me"*** (Job 16:7*a*).

He has become a desolate island, **socially**:

> ***"You have laid waste all my company"*** (Job 16:7*b*).

He is at his wit's end, **spiritually**:

> ***"My spirit is broken, my days are extinguished, the grave is ready for me"*** (Job 17:1).

There's just no way out . . . there's no hope left.

C.S. Lewis, in his book *A Grief Observed*, wrote about his spiritual and emotional struggles after the death of his wife. He wrote with openness and candor, like Job in this response.

> Where is God? This is one of the most disquieting symptoms. When you are happy, so happy that you have no sense of needing Him you will be, or so it feels, welcomed with open arms. But go to Him when your need is desperate, when all other help is vain, and what do you find? A door slammed in your face; a sound of bolting and double bolting on the inside . . . after that, silence.[5]

No wonder Lewis had rich lessons to teach when he eventually emerged from his grief; the silence of God can be an amazing tutor for significant truths.

Those who suffer acutely tend to see more clearly. Perhaps that's because, in times of greatest desperation, your mind is alert to greater observations from the Word of God; your heart most tender to the Spirit of God; your life most available to the will of God.

You have benefited from the bittersweet fruit of sorrow.

Earlier, Job made an incredible resolution:

> ***"Though He slay me, yet will I trust Him"*** (Job 13:15 KJV).

How Satan hated to hear such words of undying loyalty—even when the fairytale ending had disappeared from Job's sight.

In an article written by Jill Briscoe, the wife of Stuart Briscoe who pastored for many years, she recounted the story of David, their young elementary-aged son:

> David was going to be taken for a doctor's appointment and he was told by his father, "You're not going to go to school on Monday; you're going to come with me to get an x-ray." That was the length of their conversation on Friday. Monday came and David got into the car, face white and drawn, eyes wide with fear. Stuart said, "David, you're not afraid, are you?" to which his son replied, "Of course I'm afraid, Daddy!" "Why?" asked his father. Little David responded, "'Cause I know what an execution is!" "Son, I said an *x-ray*, not an *execution*." Jill concluded with this thought: the amazing thing was that he actually showed up—and got into the car. Why? Because he truly trusted his father.[6]

With that kind of childlike resolve, Job was willing to get in the car and buckle up. For one thing, his determination is still bound to a clear conscience. He laments,

> ***"My face is flushed from weeping, and deep darkness is on my eyelids, although there is no violence in my hands, and my prayer is pure"*** (Job 16:16–17).

Job makes these comments, even though his prayers don't seem to be paying off.

Later, another amazing resolve is voiced by Job:

> ***"Nevertheless, the righteous will hold to his way, and he who has clean hands will grow stronger and stronger"*** (Job 17:9).

That's another way of saying, "I'm not giving up on my character. I'm not cashing in my faith. I'm going to stay buckled into my seat, no matter where this journey leads . . . even though life doesn't seem to be working out in my favor at the moment."

With incredible faith, Job clings to God:

> ***"Even now, behold, my witness is in heaven, and my advocate is on high"*** (Job 16:19).

Amazing.

But should we commit to anything less? Frankly, we have clearer and fuller revelation of Who our advocate is:

> *He* [Jesus Christ] *always lives to make intercession for* [His people] (Hebrews 7:25).

The great Scottish missionary and pastor Robert Murray McCheyne wrote,

> If I could hear Christ praying for me in the next room, I would not fear a million enemies. Yet the distance makes no difference. He is indeed praying for me.[7]

The writer of Hebrews asks us to make the resolve of Job our own:

> *Therefore, since we have a great high priest who has passed through the heavens, Jesus the Son of God, let us hold fast our confession. For we do not have a high priest who cannot sympathize with our weaknesses, but One who has been tempted in all*

> *things as we are, yet without sin. Therefore let us draw near with confidence to the throne of grace, so that we may receive mercy and find grace to help in time of need* (Hebrews 4:14–16).

Paul challenged Titus to hold *fast the faithful word which is in accordance with the* [apostles'] *teaching . . . to exhort in sound doctrine and to refuse those who contradict* (Titus 1:9).

Spiritual disciplines are not called spiritual delights. Although they produce spiritual delight, they come by way of spiritual discipline. Prayer doesn't get easier—it gets harder. The spiritual battle for purity doesn't ease up—it heats up.

It's an entirely different study, but I can't help but smell the fragrance of Good Friday as I read of Job's struggle throughout ***Job 16–17***. His lonely exile reminds me of the suffering of Christ centuries later. Notice the crucifixion in these statements:

> ***"They have gaped at me with their mouth, they have slapped me on the cheek with contempt; they have massed themselves against me. God hands me over to ruffians and tosses me into the hands of the wicked"*** (Job 16:10).
>
> ***"Surely mockers are with me, and my eye gazes on their provocation"*** (Job 17:2).

Judas is spotted in the shadows of Job's comment here:

> ***"He who informs against friends for a share of the spoil"*** (Job 17:5).

We can see the Lord standing before His own nation as Job laments,

> ***"But He has made me a byword of the people, and I am one at whom men spit*** [literally: in whose face people spit]***"*** (Job 17:6).

Job had no idea that his own suffering would mirror, in some ways, the suffering of our Lord. Job would fellowship in the sufferings of Christ—and also, as Christ came to liberate him from Paradise, become a partaker in the victory of Christ over death and Sheol.

Before we leave this chapter in Job's life, we have some timeless truths to clarify.

FOR THOSE EXPERIENCING CRITICISM

Remain Open

There may be truth buried underneath harsh words and unkind thoughts. Learn as much from your critics as you can. And then grow wiser because of them.

Keep Alert

People love to sell you their critical spirit about anything and everything. Just make sure you don't buy into that critical spirit just because they're offering it to you at half-price.

Stay alert. There is a reason that Satan, your enemy has been nicknamed *the Accuser of our Brethren* (Revelation 12:10).

Stay Focused

Don't get sidetracked by cynics who counsel. Job held tightly to the anchor of his faith. And he persisted in his belief that life will eventually vindicate him as having walked with God.

Don't lose sight of the path. The devil will just as readily distract you from the truth as he will attempt to destroy the truth.

Remain open . . . keep alert . . . stay focused.

FOR THOSE OFFERING COMFORT

This episode between Eliphaz and Job is a good reminder that comfort is not dispensed in convenient doses. Encouragement and wisdom are not cough medicine. How many opportunities do we pass by? We are truly surrounded by people who silently—desperately—need an encouraging word.[8]

For several months before my mother-in-law passed away, she went through weekly dialysis treatments. I picked her up from the clinic one afternoon and she began telling me about all the people who come into that clinic to be hooked up to those machines three days a week . . . several hours at a time. The patients come in all sizes, ages, races, and personalities. There was an 85-year-old who waved at everybody when she arrived.

Among them was a middle-aged couple who had just begun treatment. There was also a 16-year-old boy with a pleasant attitude toward those around him. This young man expecially impressed my mother-in-law. Hooked up to the dialysis machine, three to four hours at a time, every Monday, Wednesday, and Friday afternoon, the young man patiently endured the treatment.

I couldn't help but wonder who knew about his condition at his high school. Did students know why he left campus and missed the afternoon ball games? I wondered how many teachers knew why his classes were arranged for early dismissal three days a week.

Who had any idea that he suffered?

A dialysis clinic is one of a thousand little worlds where people live day in and day out. Frankly, we would probably be amazed by the multitude and variety of sufferers that we greet in office corridors, Sunday school classrooms, and city streets.

Grace should always be alert. Comfort should always be on call. A kind word; a handshake; a hug; a nod of recognition; a few words may be the desperately needed demonstration of counsel, comfort, and grace.

God does not comfort us to make us comfortable but to make us comforters. In fact, God's comfort is never given; it is always loaned. God expects us to distribute it to others.[9]

People need to be reminded—perhaps you, too—that this is not the end of your fairytale. No matter how it seems to be working out, it's not over yet.

The truth is every single believer will live happily ever after. Your Prince is on His way, and He will set everything right . . . He will make everything new.

So, hang on to that resolve to follow your Redeemer. And keep looking up . . . the Prince may arrive at any moment.

"As for me, I know that my Redeemer lives, and at the last He will take His stand on the earth. Even after my skin is destroyed, yet from my flesh I shall see God; Whom I myself shall behold, and whom my eyes will see."

–Job 19:25–27*a*

CHAPTER FIFTEEN

THE MAGNUM OPUS OF FAITH

Job 18–19

The sky over Germany in 1941 was as blue as it had ever been. Spring had come, but for thousands of Jews laboring and suffering in Nazi concentration camps, hope had become little more than a thread to which they desperately clung.

> In one particular camp, according to the journal entries of other prisoners, a group of Jewish men were assigned to carry stones from one end of the camp to the other. It was rumored that they were going to construct a building. Others whispered that the stones were part of a road project. Day after day, the men hauled stones, their backs aching, their bodies groaning under the load. Finally, weeks after they had begun this monumental task, they finished the job. The stones had been piled in an enormous mass, ready for use. That night the men stretched out on their bunks with a slight sense of accomplishment and anticipation.
>
> The next day the men were ordered into the camp yard as usual. Their new assignment was announced: they were to simply carry the stones back to the other side of the camp where they had been. With crushed spirits they began the task. And so, the stones were moved back and forth, without

> purpose or plan. It was then, as the men realized that they were engaged in meaningless activity, they began to waver and, eventually, one by one, die.[1]

Hardship without meaning is simply too heavy a burden to bear. Pain without purpose is a penalty most unbearable.

Something similar happened to an entire town—only in a different context.

> The powers-that-be had planned to build a hydroelectric dam across a valley in Maine where a small town had been situated for generations. The people were to be relocated before the town was literally submerged under the water of a new reservoir. During the time between the decision to begin the project and the completion of the dam, this well-kept town with clean sidewalks, tidy houses, and manicured lawns began to fall into disrepair. One resident explained it this way: "Where there is no hope for the future, there is no need to work in the present."[2]

When the prospects of a future are destroyed, the drive to accomplish, work, advance, repair—or even endure—is abandoned.

Why? Without a future and a purpose, despair—like the tendrils of a vine—wraps itself around the heart and chokes off hope.

As far as Job is concerned, God has assigned him to carry heavy boulders from one end of his imprisoned life to the other. There is no apparent purpose in the project . . . no sense to his suffering.

And to make matters worse, Bildad *the Black and White* has decided to deliver yet another message of guilt and condemnation. In fact, he, like Eliphaz in his second speech, merely turns up the heat. In order to bring out a confession of sin, Bildad begins to describe for Job the terrible, fearful death of sinners. The scenes are true portraits for those who die without a Redeemer; the problem is they're being painted for the wrong person.

THE PIT OF FEAR AND ANXIETY

A Darkened Tent

Bildad begins his portrait:

"Indeed, the light of the wicked goes out and the flame of his fire gives no light. The light in his tent is darkened, and his lamp goes out above him" (Job 18:5–6).

This scene painted for Job is a ***lamp*** hanging in a tent. Suddenly the ***lamp*** smolders for a moment or two, the wick glowing red, and then is snuffed out, leaving the ***tent*** in darkness.

For many people, it is the darkness of death—the mystery surrounding death—that makes it the king of terrors. And it will happen to us all. There's no need to ignore the truth; you can't avoid death. The statistics are unrelenting: one out of every one person dies.

In the last century, the American newspaper tycoon William Randolph Hearst would never permit anybody to mention death in his presence. He never allowed the subject to come up—ever. But it didn't matter; he himself eventually became the subject of newsprint when his own newspapers printed his obituary.[3]

Bildad points his finger at Job and says, in effect, "Job, you're ignoring the obvious; the light of your life is about to go out and you will be left in the darkness of God's judgment."

A Trapped Animal

"A snare seizes him by the heel, and a trap snaps shut on him. A noose for him is hidden in the ground, and a trap for him on the path" (Job 18:9–10).

"You're already trapped! Come clean, Job . . . before death catches you for good."

A Pursued Victim

"All around terrors frighten him, and harry [dog] ***him at every step. His strength is famished, and calamity is ready at his side"*** (Job 18:11–12).

"There's no escape! Surrender, Job . . . there's no way out!"

An Unmarked Grave

"Memory of him perishes from the earth, and he has no name abroad" (Job 18:17).

The Message paraphrases Bildad's words:

> "Their lives go up in smoke;
> acid rain soaks their ruins.
> Their roots rot
> and their branches wither.
> They'll never again be remembered—
> nameless in unmarked graves.
> They are plunged from light into darkness,
> banished from the world.
> And they leave empty-handed—not one single child—
> nothing to show for their life on this earth.
> Westerners are aghast at their fate,
> easterners are horrified:
> 'Oh, no! So this is what happens to perverse people.
> This is how those [ignorant of] God end up!'"

Again—Bildad is preaching the truth about the wicked dying . . . he's just preaching to the wrong man. Thanks again, Bildad *the Blusterer*.

He is doing nothing more than adding more locks and bolts to the cell door of Job's pit—a pit of growing anxiety.

Bildad opened with the words ***"How long will you hunt for words?"*** (Job 18:2*a*).

And now Job begins his response: ***"How long will you torment and crush me with words?"*** (Job 19:2).

This conversation began with Bildad asking, "Job, how long are you gonna *excuse* yourself with words?" And Job responds, "How long are you gonna *execute* me with words?"

While Bildad described the terrors of *death*—and they are truly terrible apart from God—Job responds by describing the troubles of *life* . . . and they are truly troubling.

You can't help but notice, by way of contrast, the perspective of these two men on what was truly lost.

Bildad considered Job's losses to be:

- loss of physical strength ***(Job 18:12)***;
- loss of finances ***(Job 18:15)***;

- loss of fame and reputation ***(Job 18:17)***.

Job considered these things to be true losses, but what bothered him most were the following losses:

- loss of justice ***(Job 19:7)***;
- loss of direction for his life ***(Job 19:8)***;
- loss of credibility and honor ***(Job 19:9)***;
- loss of hope ***(Job 19:10)***;
- loss of intimacy with God ***(Job 19:11)***.

In the next few verses, Job catalogs losses in his relationships with others:

- ***"my acquaintances are completely estranged from me"*** (Job 19:13);
- ***"my relatives have failed"*** [fallen away] (Job 19:14*a*);
- ***"my intimate friends have forgotten me"*** (Job 19:14*b*);
- ***"my maids consider me a stranger . . . I call to my servant, but he does not answer"*** (Job 19:15*a*, 16*a*);
- ***"my breath is offensive to my wife"*** (Job 19:17*a*);
- ***"I am loathsome to my own brothers"*** (Job 19:17*b*);
- ***"Even young children despise me"*** (Job 19:18*a*);
- ***"All my associates abhor me and those I love have turned against me"*** (Job 19:19).

The loss of fellowship with God and friendship with others were far greater losses to Job than fame and fortune.

Don't miss the difference between Bildad and Job. Bildad thought losing fame and fortune were great losses. Job *never* mentions them. Instead, Job considered the loss of intimacy with God and his broken relationships with family and friends to be the real losses.

What do we consider true losses in life?

There was a humorous reminder of this issue several years ago when we were constructing the church buildings we now occupy. We held our Sunday morning service on the land before our building project got underway, which meant our then-current location was left vacant while we met on our new property.

That same Sunday morning, the co-worker of one of our church members drove by our empty church parking lot. He was heading to the office to get in some extra work. When he realized that he'd be traveling the road in front of our church, he looked at his watch and thought, *Oh no, I'm gonna be stuck in that church traffic jam for ten minutes.* As he got closer, there was no traffic line-up . . . no cars waiting to be directed into the overstuffed parking lot. He wondered why. When he drove past our church building and saw the parking lot was empty, he grew afraid. An unbeliever, he immediately thought, *It's the rapture!* It definitely made him think about his future! Maybe churches ought to do something like that once a year.

Would your testimony as a church be one that so closely associates with Jesus Christ that people would be filled with terror at the thought of future judgment if you didn't gather? If you didn't show up at work for a few days, would anybody wonder the same thing?

That kind of reputation is built by living life for what really matters.

For Bildad, it meant fame, riches, and *stuff.* He assumed that because Job had lost his wealth—his position among the powerbrokers of southern Arabia—he would find life unbearable.

For Job, what really mattered were things that never show up on a bank statement or stock portfolio.

What would you consider your greater losses? Your house; retirement fund; job; boat; health . . . *or* your integrity in the business world; your testimony for Christ; your relationships; your fellowship with God.

What losses would keep you up at night?

Read over what Bildad thought were Job's true losses and you soon learn that he would have fit right in with the average person on the street. Today he would be selling books on management, finance, and self-improvement:

- *How to Stay in Top Form Physically and Mentally*
- *How to Avoid Financial Ruin*
- *How to Expand Your Reputation in the Community*
- *How to Climb the Corporate Ladder*
- *How to Shatter the Glass Ceiling*
- *How to Move and Shake Your World*

Job could honestly say, "I had all that! And now that I've lost it all, what matters most is my fellowship with the Lord, my integrity, and my relationships with extended family and friends."

I received an email from a couple in our church who are living out some of Job's experience. They have lost their business, their financial health, their home, and currently are facing bankruptcy. Yet, they wrote in their email about their ultiamte values—their faith and trust in the purposes of God; their relationship with their sovereign Lord. From the pit of fear, they were climbing to the pinnacle of faith.

RISING TO THE PINNACLE

Would you believe that in the midst of Job's experience—from the depths of the pit—you hear nothing less than one of Scripture's highest pronouncement of faith:

> ***"Oh that my words were written! Oh that they were inscribed in a book!"*** (Job 19:23).

They will be, Job! People have been able to read them for some four thousand years now!

And what was it that Job wanted to be read long after his ordeal was over?

> ***"As for me, I know that my Redeemer lives, and at the last He will take His stand on the earth. Even after my skin is destroyed, yet from my flesh I shall see God; Whom I myself shall behold, and whom my eyes will see"*** (Job 19:25–27*a*).

Talk about a pinnacle of faith and assurance—***"I know that my Redeemer lives!"***

Amazing.

One of the world's most famous oratorios is *Messiah* by George Frideric Handel. It is considered his Magnum Opus—*greatest work or most renowned achievement.*

I found it interesting that Handel's Magnum Opus was written under difficult circumstances. He had suffered a stroke but recovered in six weeks, was quite portly in girth, and had bouts of depression. He ended his career despondent and discouraged.

> In April 1741, he gave what he considered his farewell concert and felt forced to retire from public activities at age 56. However, a wealthy friend, Charles Jennings, gave Handel a libretto [text of a dramatic musical work] based on the life of Christ, taken entirely from passages in the Bible. He also received a commission from a charity to compose a work for a benefit performance.
>
> Handel set to composing on August 22, 1741, in his little house on Brook Street in London. He grew so absorbed in the work that he rarely left his room, hardly stopping to eat. Within six days Part One was complete. In nine more days, he had finished Part Two, and in another six, Part Three. The orchestration was completed in another two days. In all, 260 pages of manuscript were filled in the remarkably short time of 24 days. A friend who visited him as he composed found him sobbing with intense emotion. Later, as Handel groped for words to describe what he had experienced, he quoted the Apostle Paul, saying, "Whether I was in the body or out of my body when I wrote it I know not."
>
> Sir Newman Flower, one of Handel's many biographers, summed up the consensus of history: "Considering the immensity of the work and the short time involved, it will remain, perhaps forever, the greatest feat in the whole history of music composition." Soon after this, Handel's fortunes began to increase dramatically, and his hard-won popularity remained constant until his death. He personally conducted more than thirty performances of *Messiah*. Many of these concerts were benefits for the Foundling Hospital, of which Handel was a major benefactor.[4]

It was indeed his Magnum Opus. From the depths of anxiety—an incredible declaration of assurance; from the pit of fear—this pinnacle of faith.

It was Handel's declaration of the triumphant Gospel of Jesus Christ—Messiah—and to this day, *Messiah* is sung all over the globe. One of the texts which he incorporated into his work is this declaration of Job. Before it was part of Handel's Magnum Opus, it had been the Magnum Opus of Job.

This is perhaps the crowning achievement of Job's faith: "I am in the pit, but ***as for me, I know that my Redeemer lives"*** (Job 19:25*a*).

FEATURES OF THE MAGNUM OPUS OF FAITH

Certainty of Faith

***"As for me, I* know."** I would agree with Spurgeon who preached from this text that you would expect Job to be certain of nothing. Nothing seemed to be certain with Job but uncertainty. [But this he knew]. The Messiah lives. The winds may rage and the tempests roar, but they cannot shake this rock—I know . . . I know.[5]

Not, "I hope so" . . . "I think so" . . . not "Maybe so" or "It could be so." Job *knew*.

If Job could speak with this type of conviction, with what little revelation he had been given—and none of it yet in written form—how much more should we who carry around with us the completed infallible Word of God believe.

The Apostle John wrote of this assurance:

> *These things I have written unto you that believe in the name of the Son of God, that you may know that you have eternal life* (1 John 5:13).

Possession of Faith

***"I know that* my . . ."** Notice that Job did *not* say, "I know that my wife's Redeemer lives . . . my parents' Redeemer lives . . . my grandfather's Redeemer lives . . . my Sunday school teacher's Redeemer lives."

The faith of Job was personal . . . it belonged to *him.*

Martin Luther used to say that the meat of the Gospel was found in the pronouns.

Well said . . . and Job would echo its truth: **"MY *Redeemer lives."***

Concentration of Faith

"I know that my* Redeemer . . ."** Where did Job get this word ***Redeemer? It's the Hebrew *go'el* for Kinsman Redeemer. He must have received it from the Holy Spirit's revealing ministry.

And what a precious revelation it was:

- The go'el was someone who could buy a relative out of slavery.
- The go'el had the right to defend a relative in court.
- The go'el could marry the widow of a near relative and give her a future and a hope.

Long before Boaz fell in love with the widow Ruth and became her go'el (her kinsman redeemer), long before Boaz had purchased the right to redeem her estate and take Ruth as his bride, Job understood that there was *a* Kinsman Redeemer who could buy *him* out of slavery, defend *him* in court, and give *him* a future and a hope.

There in the pit of his despair, Job was holding out, by means of revelation, for His coming Redeemer.

Foundation of Faith

***"I know that my Redeemer* lives!"** Were it not for the resurrection, our faith would be meaningless, Paul wrote *(1 Corinthians 15:14).*

Job didn't say, "I know that my Redeemer will live *someday*" or, "I know that my Redeemer used to be alive." Oh, no. This is the foundation of Job's Magnum Opus: his Redeemer *is* alive.

Applying this text to his audience, Charles Spurgeon preached,

> Spring on this rock, man! If you are struggling in the sea just now, and waves of sin and doubt beat over you, leap on to this rock—Jesus *is* alive.[6]

Expectation of Faith

"And at the last He will take His stand on the earth!" (Job 19:25*b*). Frankly, Job is revealing more than he fully understood. He's certainly delivering more truth about Christ than he could ever begin to explain.

From the pit of despair came this powerful declaration of prophetic truth.

In fact, we are even now joining Job in looking forward to that victorious day when Christ will personally, literally stand upon the earth, *For "He has put all things under His feet"* (I Corinthians 15:27*a*).

Job refers to a ***Redeemer*** who ***stands***, a picture of conquest and victory and triumph. This is the expectation of Job's faith . . . and ours!

Motivation of Faith

"Even after my skin is destroyed, yet from my flesh I shall see God" (Job 19:26). Not only is the Redeemer going to reign triumphantly on the earth—not only will there be a future with God and man fellowshipping together as they once did in the garden—Job exults, "I'm going to be there, too."

"I shall see God." No wonder critics and skeptics try to tear this verse from the lips of Job or distort its clear and simple, yet profound prophetic truth.

In this prophetic paragraph, you have the doctrines of the incarnation, atonement, resurrection, and coronation, along with a future physical resurrection for those who follow after God.

What a declaration.

In his Magnum Opus of faith, Job literally delivers the Gospel that still echoes throughout the ages. We are heading for a kingdom. Not death—but deliverance . . . full and final triumph in the company of our Kinsman Redeemer, Jesus Christ.

> Henry Morrison and his wife were faithful missionaries on the continent of Africa during the mid-to-late 1800s. They had served on the mission field for forty years. In fact, they had never returned to the States until this particular voyage which signaled the end of their fruitful and dedicated missionary service. As the steamer headed into New York Harbor they had wondered if anyone would remember them or come to greet them.
>
> Henry and his wife stepped to the railing of the ship's upper deck and were astounded to see hundreds of people lining the dock, waving banners that announced WELCOME HOME! There were ribbons and banners and balloons everywhere as smiling people waved and cheered while the ship was towed to the dock. Henry's heart almost leaped out of his chest and he turned to his wife and said, "Sweetheart, the believers have remembered us . . . so many have come to welcome us home."
>
> Unknown to them, sequestered in private quarters hidden from the rest of the passengers' knowledge, Teddy Roosevelt was

> onboard. He had been on a big game safari in Africa and was returning to the States. The banners and balloons were for him. The press had leaked the news; the waving, cheering crowd was there to welcome home the President of the United States.
>
> Henry and his wife, along with all the other passengers, were detained from disembarking until the president and his entourage left the steamer, all the while the Marine Corps Band blaring, "Hail to the Chief."
>
> Henry Morrison said, "It just doesn't seem right that we've served the Lord so faithfully for these forty years. We've served in anonymity, but we've been faithful to God. Teddy Roosevelt goes to Africa to shoot some elephants and the whole world welcomes him home. It just doesn't seem right that we come home and there is no one to even greet us."
>
> Henry's wife looked up at him and gave that now famous response: "But Henry, we're not home yet. We're not *home*."[7]

One author wrote,

> If we were given all we wanted here, our hearts would settle for this world rather than the next. God is forever luring us up and away from this one, wooing us to Himself and His kingdom where we will certainly find what we so keenly longed for.[8]

Home is not here . . . it's over there.

And keep in mind that while you're heading for home, you're not just moving heavy rocks from one place to another, undergoing pain without purpose—struggle without sense or meaning.

You're building a life which is nothing less than a magnum opus of faith in the provision of Christ now—and the visible presence of Christ to come.

So keep singing the lyrics of your own personal song of faith in Christ. There is indeed a Redeemer who *is* alive, and you will see Him one day and reign with Him in triumphant glory.

These are the lyrics to the Magnum Opus of your faith—*your faith*—in *your* Redeemer, your soon-coming King.

Hal-lelujah! Hal-lelujah! Hallelujah! Hallelujah! Hal-le-lu-jah![9]

*Then Zophar the Naamathite answered, [2]"Therefore my disquieting thoughts
make me respond, even because of my inward agitation. [3]I listened to the reproof
which insults me, and the spirit of my understanding makes me answer. [4]Do
you know this from of old, from the establishment of man on earth, [5]that the
triumphing of the wicked is short, and the joy of the godless momentary?"*

–Job 20:1–5

(Continued on next page)

(Continued)

Then Job answered, 2"Listen carefully to my speech, and let this be your way of consolation. 3Bear with me that I may speak; then after I have spoken, you may mock. 4As for me, is my complaint to man? And why should I not be impatient? 5Look at me, and be astonished, and put your hand over your mouth. 6Even when I remember, I am disturbed, and horror takes hold of my flesh. 7Why do the wicked still live, continue on, also become very powerful? 8Their descendants are established with them in their sight, and their offspring before their eyes, 9Their houses are safe from fear, and the rod of God is not on them. 10His ox mates without fail; his cow calves and does not abort. 11They send forth their little ones like the flock, and their children skip about. 12They sing to the timbrel and harp and rejoice at the sound of the flute. 13They spend their days in prosperity, and suddenly they go down to Sheol. 14They say to God, 'Depart from us! We do not even desire the knowledge of Your ways. 15Who is the Almighty, that we should serve Him, and what would we gain if we entreat Him?' 16Behold, their prosperity is not in their hand; the counsel of the wicked is far from me. 17How often is the lamp of the wicked put out, or does their calamity fall on them? Does God apportion destruction in His anger? 18Are they as straw before the wind, and like chaff which the storm carries away? 19You say, 'God stores away a man's iniquity for his sons.' Let God repay him so that he may know it. 20Let his own eyes see his decay, and let him drink of the wrath of the Almighty. 21For what does he care for his household after him, when the number of his months is cut off? 22Can anyone teach God knowledge, in that He judges those on high? 23One dies in his full strength, being wholly at ease and satisfied; 24His sides are filled out with fat, and the marrow of his bones is moist, 25While another dies with a bitter soul, never even tasting anything good. 26Together they lie down in the dust, and worms cover them. 27Behold, I know your thoughts, and the plans by which you would wrong me. 28For you say, 'Where is the house of the nobleman, and where is the tent, the dwelling places of the wicked?' 29Have you not asked wayfaring men, and do you not recognize their witness? 30For the wicked is reserved for the day of calamity; they will be led forth at the day of fury. 31Who will confront him with his actions, and who will repay him for what he has done? 32While he is carried to the grave, men will keep watch over his tomb. 33The clods of the valley will gently cover him; moreover, all men will follow after him, while countless ones go before him. 34How then will you vainly comfort me, for your answers remain full of falsehood?"

Job 21:1–34

CHAPTER SIXTEEN

WHAT CHRISTIANS WANT TO KNOW BUT ARE AFRAID TO ASK

Job 20–21

A young Midwestern lawyer suffered such deep depression that his friends actually thought it best to keep all knives and razors out of his personal possession. At age 22, his business venture failed. He ran for the state legislature and suffered defeat. Another attempt at business failed shortly thereafter. Then, when he was 26, the sweetheart he had hoped to marry died unexpectedly, crushing his heart. A year later, he suffered what most believe today to have been a nervous breakdown.

When he ran for Congress some years later, he was defeated. Trying again at age 39, he was defeated once more. At age 46, he lost a bid for a seat in the Senate, and a year later lost in an attempt to become Vice President. He suffered another devastating loss for a Senate seat at age 49. It was during this time that he had another breakdown and wrote in his private journal, "I am now the most miserable man living. Whether I shall ever be better, I cannot tell."[1]

This is not exactly the kind of thinking we would expect the future President of the United States to have, but Abraham Lincoln was immersed in grief. He did recover. In fact, he was perfectly suited to lead our country during one of our darkest hours. Abraham Lincoln had been prepared for heroic endurance as a future leader.

John Henry Jowett (1787–1855) was considered to be one of the most influential pastors/authors/teachers in the English-speaking world. Yet he confided to a close friend on one occasion,

> I wish you wouldn't think I am such a saint. You seem to imagine that I have no ups and downs, but just a level and lofty stretch of spiritual attainment with unbroken joy. By no means! I am often perfectly wretched, and everything appears most murky.[2]

F. B. Meyer, a best-selling author and Bible teacher of the late 1800s, was a man who was as well-read by his generation as any Christian author of our generation. However, in his private journal he poured out to God in great frustration this prayer, "Lord, why is Your hand always on the other person?"

This is not a spiritual-sounding question, but it is an honest one. Perhaps you've struggled with the same question, asking, "Lord, why have You opened the windows of blessing on everyone *except* me?"

This is one of the primary questions racing through the mind and heart of Job.

HONEST QUESTIONS

Job's questioning is similar to Asaph's admission in Psalm 73:

> *I was envious of the arrogant as I saw the prosperity of the wicked* (Psalm 73:3).

It is David's honest lament in his prayer journal:

> *How long, O LORD? Will You forget me forever?* (Psalm 13:1*a*).

Believers aren't supposed to talk this way; good Christians don't ask questions like these—or do they?

Job will ask eight questions that every Christians has thought about or wanted to ask, but were too afraid for others to know they asked them . . . much less thought them.

Why Does God Treat Unbelievers Better than He Treats Me?

Job laments,

> ***"Why do the wicked still live, continue on, also become very powerful? . . . Their houses are safe from fear, and the rod of God is not on them"*** (Job 21:7, 9).

In other words, "Why do I suffer discipline and heartache, while my unbelieving neighbors and co-workers seem to have the blessing of a God they don't even believe in?"

Why Do Unbelievers Prosper Financially and I Don't?

> ***"His ox mates without fail; His cow calves and does not abort. . . . They spend their days in prosperity"*** (Job 21:10, 13*a*).

Job is honestly asking, "Lord, why is it that the one who never bows his knee to You; who never sees the inside of an altar; who never acknowledges You is getting multiplied herds and flocks from You, while I've faithfully sacrificed to You—and look what I get? My herds have been stolen and all my financial resources are gone!"

Perhaps you, too, like Job, have questioned the fairness of God.

Why Do Unbelievers Have Numerous Children and I Don't?

> ***"They send forth their little ones like the flock, and their children skip about"*** (Job 21:11).

The unbelievers are surrounded by kids that are as plentiful as their flocks of sheep.

> ***"Their descendants are established with them in their sight, and their offspring before their eyes"*** (Job 21:8).

Not only do unbelievers have children, but they seem to enjoy all their children in their immediate presence. The text says ***in their sight***. There are no goodbyes; no long-distance calls; no long trips during Christmas. Unbelievers have their children in their sight—***their offspring are before their eyes***.

As believers, *we* are the ones who know that children are a gift from God. We praise the Creator who ordains conception and establishes the home. Yet Job asks, "Why were my children taken, while unbelievers around me are enjoying family feasts?"

If you think only unspiritual Christians dare to ask these questions, think again.

Why Do Unbelievers Enjoy Better Health than I?

> ***"They spend their days in prosperity, and suddenly they go down to Sheol"*** (Job 21:13).

Job laments, "Unbelievers die without extended illness or trouble."

This is not a reference to some sort of quick judgment from God, but to a long life and then, sudden death that leaves no room for suffering or anguish or trouble. The wicked seem to live in one long progression of good health until they suddenly die.

> ***"One dies in his full strength, being wholly at ease and satisfied"*** (Job 21:23).

Job complains that the ungodly seem to enjoy better health than the godly and enjoy their health to the very day they die.

In other words, how come unbelievers seem physically strong; have great check-ups; run with ease on the treadmill; have no need for One-A-Day vitamins, a high fiber diet or bifocals?

People deserving perdition are reveling in prosperity. People without faith are in perfect health. Why? Job is actually willing to ask this question out loud.

Why Do Unbelievers Seem to Live a Carefree Life?

> ***"They sing to the timbrel and harp and rejoice at the sound of the flute"*** (Job 21:12).

"Here I am suffering," Job says, "and I am the God-fearer."

Unbelievers are the ones playing their music nonstop. Their lives are nothing but fun and games.

> ***"They say to God, 'Depart from us! We do not even desire the knowledge of Your ways. Who is the Almighty, that we should serve Him, and what would we gain if we entreat***

> ***Him?' Behold, their prosperity is not in their hand"*** (Job 21:14–16*a*).

Job implies, "God is the sovereign who allows unbelievers to have their prosperity. Why doesn't He cut it off?"

Asaph struggled as well when he said,

> *They* [the wicked] *are not in trouble as other men, nor are they plagued like mankind* (Psalm 73:5).

In other words, they seem trouble-free; carefree; burden-free. Life seems so easy for the unbeliever, while the believer is weighed down with a myriad of struggles and trials. Why are the scales of justice reversed?

Charles Spurgeon, preaching on this text, said,

> The prosperous wicked escape the killing toils which afflict the mass of mankind. They have no need to ask, "Where shall we get bread for our children or clothing for our little ones." Ordinary domestic and personal troubles do not appear to molest them. Fierce trials do not seem to arise to assail them. The unspiritual man is worse than other men, yet he is better off. He deserves the hottest hell, and yet he has the warmest nest.[3]

Job asks, "Why is it that people who don't follow God seem to enjoy the most good?" Many Christians dare not ask the same but wonder still.

Why Do Unbelievers Get Promotions and I Am Ignored?

> ***"How often is the lamp of the wicked put out, or does their calamity fall on them? . . . Are they as straw before the wind, and like chaff which the storm carries away?"*** (Job 21:17*a*–18).

Why do the ungodly get the media attention? Why are the paparazzi not chasing missionaries around the globe or taking shots of people exiting church?

Asaph expressed it this way,

> *Surely in vain I have kept my heart pure and washed my hands in innocence* (Psalm 73:13).

We live for God and the other guy gets the promotion. We walk with Christ and all our friends get married and move away.

Sincerity doesn't seem to bring success. Purity doen't seem to be rewarded with a promotion.

Why Doesn't God Judge Sinners so Their Children Will Be Warned?

> ***"You*** [Zophar] ***say, 'God stores away a man's iniquity for his sons.'*** [I, Job, say] ***Let God repay him so that he may know it. Let his own eyes see his decay, and let him drink of the wrath of the Almighty. For what does he care for his household after him, when the number of his months is cut off?"*** (Job 21:19–21).

Did you catch the inference of this text? Why not judge the unbelieving father who is content with sin, since by his own actions he really doesn't care about his children anyway? Why not judge him so that his children will be warned not to follow in his footsteps?

The best thing children could see is their father's sin judged—right? That would be the strongest deterrent to sin.

In early American history, thieves were publicly flogged. You can still visit places where criminals were placed in stocks in Williamsburg, Virginia. You can step up to the stocks, put your head through the yoke, your hands and feet through the holes, and then stand there to get a sense of what it must have been like to be publically shamed and punished.

I'm not suggesting we go back to public stocks. However, the absence of judgment on sin—the public silence, the public endorsement and approval and applause of the sinner—only paves the way for the next generation to take sin even further.

King Solomon wrote,

> *Because the sentence against an evil deed is not executed quickly, therefore the hearts of the sons of men among them are given fully to do evil* (Ecclesiastes 8:11).

Sinners get away with their sin, boast of their sin, pursue their sin, flaunt their sin, thus communicating to the next generation that sin, evidently, pays!

God must not see what's happening, and if He does, He must not really care.

Why Doesn't God Make Believers Unique in the Eyes of the World?

When we go to the local elementary school play, as soon as the kid comes on stage dressed in his elephant costume or a big sunflower costume, a camera flashes and hands wave; it's obvious who the parents are. They beam, "That's our child. We are so proud of little Aidan that, even though he looks absolutely hilarious in his costume, we're taking 300 pictures."

We are the sons and daughters of God! We have stepped out onto the stage of life and . . . *hello*—there is no camera; no special introduction; no obvious endorsement; there is not even protection from the school bully who tells us how dumb we looked as a sunflower.

Job says, "I don't understand why God doesn't make it absolutely clear that the godly are special and unique and that the *rest* of the world is unimportant."

> ***"One dies in his full strength, being wholly at ease and satisfied; his sides are filled out with fat, and the marrow of his bones is moist, while another*** [possibly even a godly man] ***dies with a bitter soul, never even tasting anything good. Together they lie down in the dust, and worms cover them"*** (Job 21:23–26).

According to Job's words, there seems to be no difference whatsoever in the end. Believer and unbeliever, spiritual and pagan are all lumped together in the graveyard at the end of life. The undertaker is the great equalizer. In the end, there is no distinction.

Ah, but the funeral is not the end, is it?

> ***"For the wicked is reserved for the day of calamity; they will be led forth at the day of fury"*** (Job 21:30).

Unbelievers may have had trouble-free years on earth, but eternity will be filled with fury.

HUMBLE TRUTHS

There are some fascinating truths we can observe about God through Job's questions:

- God is neither defeated nor disrupted by the unbelief of sinners.
- God is neither embarrassed nor embittered by the questions of believers.

These are true even when we privately wonder, *Why is the hand of God always on someone else?*

Isn't this what asking for wisdom is all about? Perhaps this is the reason James promised us that when we go to God and ask for wisdom, we will not be reproached or rebuked *(James 1:5).*

So often our requests for wisdom are preceded by questions about why and how God is operating His world and our lives.

Perhaps you noticed that as Job began to pour out his heart in asking questions we would never expect a godly person to ask—or even admit to having thought—he began with the word ***why***:

> ***"Why do the wicked still live*** [while most of my family is dead]***, continue on, also become very powerful?"*** (Job 21:7).

These are honest questions from a grieving man.

I have been enjoying a commentary on the life of Job by Chuck Swindoll, for many years the chancellor of my alma mater. He tells the story of a couple who lived in the same married couples apartment complex near the seminary in which he and his wife lived. Chuck and Dennis were students at Dallas Seminary in the early 1960s. Dennis and his wife Lucy became good friends with the Swindolls as they made their way through seminary.

> During that time, Dennis and Lucy had a baby boy, whom Dennis absolutely adored. After he graduated, they moved to Los Angeles where he furthered his education, with the goal of helping people who struggled through difficult childhoods to move on and enjoy productive lives. In the midst of his PhD studies, their little boy stumbled into a swimming pool in a neighbor's back yard and drowned. They lost their precious son, devastating Dennis.

> Years later, Dennis admitted to me the way he had responded to this loss: "I got in my car, having just lost my boy, and grabbed the steering wheel and drove almost every freeway in Los Angeles. During those hours, I screamed out to God, expressing all the grief and anger and sadness and confusion from deep within my soul. I said things to Him in that car that I'd never said to anybody before. I yelled it out and it wasn't very nice. I just vomited it out to God."
>
> Near dawn, Dennis pulled into the driveway of their small home, his shirt dripping wet with sweat. He turned the key and dropped his head onto the steering wheel still gripped by his hands, sobbing with giant heaves. He said "I was comforted with this thought: God can handle it! He can handle everything I said."[4]

What a great thought . . . and a humbling truth of God's condescending grace toward His own.

I am not condoning blasphemy and I am not suggesting taking it out on your best friend. However, when you finally ask questions—even when you scream them at the top of your lungs—God is listening. He is listening when you ask those forbidden questions that Christians are not supposed to ask, much less think.

At the end of ***Job 21***, we do not find God wielding a club and saying, "Okay, Job, now you've gone too far." No, God can handle Job. God can handle Job's questions. He will remain steady, even while His children are suffering and confused.

Let me encourage you to ask questions you once thought off-limits. In the meantime, keep these timely truths close to your heart.

TIMELY ENCOURAGEMENTS

Stop Comparing Your Life with That of Unbelievers

Stop comparing the number of children or grandchildren; the tools and gadgets (including the cars) in the garage; the work title; the price of furniture; the yearly salary and benefit package; clothing brands; report cards; achievements.

In light of eternity, these things are truly unimportant.

Stop Competing with Other Believers

The church was never intended as a place of competition, but cooperation. It's not about who teaches the largest class; who gets the featured solo; who was elected deacon; who was asked to give their testimony at the couples conference.

Most often we are competing for temporal, self-centered stuff anway; ignoring our shared, eternal, unending, never-corroding or rusting or perishing inheritance.

Start Cherishing What You Have Today

Job's world didn't change, but *Job* will change. So often we go to God and demand that He change our circumstances. However, God uses circumstances to change us.

Unanswered questions that are honest and open have a way of developing character and trust more than quick answers and worn-out clichés ever will.

Later in this biography, God will recall for Job everything he had that he had overlooked.

In the meantime, for us all,

> [We must keep] *our eyes on Jesus, the author and perfecter of* [our] *faith, who for the joy set before Him endured the cross, despising the shame, and has sat down at the right hand of the throne of God. For consider Him who has endured such hostility by sinners against Himself, so that you will not grow weary and lose heart* (Hebrews 12:2–3).

Stop comparing and competing . . . start encouraging and cherishing all that we *do* have because of the lavish grace of God.

Then Eliphaz the Temanite responded, 2"Can a vigorous man be of use to God,
or a wise man be useful to himself? 3Is there any pleasure to the Almighty if you
are righteous, or profit if you make your ways perfect? 4Is it because of your rever-
ence that He reproves you, that He enters into judgment against you? 5Is not your
wickedness great, and your iniquities without end? 6For you have taken pledges
of your brothers without cause, and stripped men naked. 7To the weary you have
given no water to drink, and from the hungry you have withheld bread. 8But
the earth belongs to the mighty man, and the honorable man dwells in it. 9You
have sent widows away empty, and the strength of the orphans has been crushed."

–Job 22:1–9

(Continued on next page)

(Continued)

21 *"Yield now and be at peace with Him; thereby good will come to you.* 22 *Please receive instruction from His mouth and establish His words in your heart.* 23 *If you return to the Almighty, you will be restored; if you remove unrighteousness far from your tent,* 24 *and place your gold in the dust, and the gold of Ophir among the stones of the brooks,* 25 *then the Almighty will be your gold and choice silver to you.* 26 *For then you will delight in the Almighty and lift up your face to God.* 27 *You will pray to Him, and He will hear you; and you will pay your vows.* 28 *You will also decree a thing, and it will be established for you; and light will shine on your ways."*

–Job 22:21–28

Then Job replied, 2 *"Even today my complaint is rebellion; His hand is heavy despite my groaning.* 3 *Oh that I knew where I might find Him, that I might come to His seat!* 4 *I would present my case before Him and fill my mouth with arguments.* 5 *I would learn the words which He would answer, and perceive what He would say to me.* 6 *Would He contend with me by the greatness of His power? No, surely He would pay attention to me.* 7 *There the upright would reason with Him; and I would be delivered forever from my Judge.* 8 *Behold, I go forward but He is not there, and backward, but I cannot perceive Him;* 9 *when He acts on the left, I cannot behold Him; He turns on the right, I cannot see Him.* 10 *But He knows the way I take; when He has tried me, I shall come forth as gold.* 11 *My foot has held fast to His path; I have kept His way and not turned aside."*

–Job 23:1–11

CHAPTER SEVENTEEN

SAINTS IN THE HANDS OF AN ANGRY COUNSELOR

Job 22–24

A Texan, a New Yorker, and a North Carolinian were drinking their favorite beverage one afternoon at a local pub. The Texan drained his glass of tequila, threw the half-empty bottle in the air, drew and fired his six-shooter, shattering the bottle. The other two were shocked; the Texan simply announced, "Where I come from, we have plenty of that already."

The New Yorker, not to be outdone, finished his glass of wine and threw his half-empty bottle into the air, drew and fired his derringer, also shattering his bottle. Looking over at the other two with an air of superiority, he announced, "Back in Manhattan, we have more than enough of that already."

The North Carolina resident drained his mug of sweet tea—which is the only drink in this story I'm recommending—threw it into the air, drew his handgun and shot the New Yorker. Catching the mug on its way down, he looked over at the Texan and said, "Where I come from, we have enough of them already."

It's a joke that's especially popular here in my hometown of Cary, where the acronym CARY has been called "Concentrated Area of Relocated Yankees."[1] And I'm one of them!

What do you say to someone who actually doesn't like people from your state . . . or your country, for that matter?

Have you ever met people who didn't like politicians or wealthy people or those in authority? People who seem happiest when riding their hobby horse into the ground.

But what if they took out their frustration on *you*? What if they didn't *like* you . . . and it was no laughing matter?

How would you respond to hateful slurs? How do you react to personal criticism? I'm not talking about the constructive kind—I'm talking about criticism that demeans you and discredits you.

What if you're the latest news on the grapevine and gossip mill, and you discover your words have been twisted or your actions have been given the worst possible interpretation?

How do you react when critics want to harm rather than help you and before you have a chance to respond, the damage is done.

Take heart, as you begin to read the third and final round of speeches from Job's counselors; this is exactly where you find this battered, weary believer.

To top it off, Job has endured for some time the confusing hush of heaven. God hasn't spoken a word, while Job's counselors have said *too* much.

And frankly, it's beginning to get ugly.

By the time you reach ***Job 22***, you discover that his counselors don't want to help him at all; the the gloves are off and they simply want to knock him out. At this point in the narrative, I like to think of Job as a saint in the hands of angry counselors.

Maybe you're already identifying with him as he endures unfair, untrue, unkind condemnation.

Perhaps you're there right now:

- your actions have been misinterpreted;
- your words have been misquoted;
- your motives have been misunderstood.

Some critic is having a field day at your place of work or inside your family circle—perhaps even at your church. If you're wondering what to do, this chapter is especially for you.

In Charles Swindoll's commentary on the Book of Job, he entitles his chapter that takes the student through Job 22–24 *How to Handle Criticism with Class*. He opens his chapter with this illustration:

> Our nation's sixteenth president was a magnificent model of handling personal assaults on his character. Public criticism against him intensified. One of his biographers said that Abraham Lincoln was slandered, libeled, and hated perhaps more intensely than any man ever to run for the nation's highest office. He was publicly called just about every name imaginable by the press of his day, including a baboon, a third-rate country lawyer, a vulgar jokester, a dictator, an ape, and a buffoon. Severe and unjust criticism did not subside . . . and as his enemies increased, so did the criticism against him. But Lincoln, his biographer wrote, handled it all with a patience, forbearance, and determination uncommon of most men.[2]

Lincoln survived his critics and has since been vindicated by history as one of the greatest presidents the United States ever elected to office. He modeled grace under pressure.

Perhaps nowhere in the biography of Job will you see the modeling of grace under pressure more than in these next few chapters. Not only will we discover how to respond to unjust and harmful criticism, we are going to get another good lesson on how to avoid becoming a *bad* counselor.

HOW TO COUNSEL THE WRONG WAY

Eliphaz will commit five blunders—five missteps that we definitely want to avoid as we attempt to counsel and encourage others. I want these five errors to serve as an outline as we unpack Eliphaz's final, angry speech to Job.

Keep in mind that this will be the last time Eliphaz speaks before he is chastised by God and commanded to ask Job to pray for *him*!

God Himself, in just a few chapters, will vindicate the character of Job. In the meantime, there are lessons to be learned on how to counsel someone the wrong way.

Condemn before Taking Time to Identify the Context

> ***Then Eliphaz the Temanite responded, "Can a vigorous man be of use to God, or a wise man be useful to himself? Is there any pleasure to the Almighty if you are righteous, or profit if you make your ways perfect?"*** (Job 22:1–3).

These words drip with sarcastic condescension. "Job, do you think you are any benefit to God? Do you think God cares about your claim to be ***righteous***? Look around you . . . where is God's reassurance that you even matter to Him?"

What Eliphaz can't imagine is that Job is, indeed, under the careful watch of Almighty God. God and Satan—and no doubt the hosts of heaven—were entirely attentive to this unfolding drama down at the trash dump. In fact, God is about to intervene with incredible reassurance on Job's behalf.

Eliphaz didn't know the context from which Job's suffering had come; nor did Job, for that matter. The point for a counselor to learn is that it is absolutely commendable to admit you don't know everything; that you could speak too soon; that you might deliver an opinion too quickly.

Much of the failure in this counseling encounter stems from the fact that Eliphaz is convinced that Job has attempted to hide sin from God, and sinners like Job get punishment by God as proof that He knows.

We're reminded all over again of the utter callousness of Eliphaz to the condition of this grieving man who has lost nearly everything. The truth is Eliphaz really doesn't care about Job. At this point, Job no longer matters. What *matters* is that Job's counselor is acknowleged as right. And the fact that Job won't admit that Eliphaz is right has made Eliphaz all the angrier . . . which leads to yet another blunder.

Make Judgments Based on Outward Appearances

> ***"Is not your wickedness great, and your iniquities without end?"*** (Job 22:5).

He says Job's list of sins is, literally, ***endless***. And how does Eliphaz know? Because this obvious judgment from God seems endless. In other words, Job's hidden sins are great because the punishment of God is great.

Eliphaz implies, "It's clear from your diseases and losses you are not the wisest man in the East—you must be the greatest sinner in the East."

People often make the same blunder that Eliphaz has made. How quickly we judge the losses and diseases of others as proof of God's discipline.

But the truth is shocking; we happen to know something that neither Eliphaz nor Job knows: God has allowed Satan to test Job by introducing him as ***"a blameless and upright man, fearing God and turning away from evil"*** (Job 1:8*b*).

The trials of Job were not put upon him because he was living an ungodly life but because he was *not.* Job wasn't perfect, but he passionately hated sin and loved God. His trials weren't proof that he was in trouble with God—they were proof that he could be *trusted* by God.

Eliphaz is drawing his angry and condemning verdict from the outward evidences of what looked like God's correction, when they were, in fact, evidences of God's confidence. God has chosen to hold Job out as a living testimony to Satan and the hosts of heaven and hell and all humanity: it is possible in the midst of great suffering to not only bring God praise but to become an individual who fulfills God's purpose.

People who only look on the surface of things will miss this deeper, richer truth. Their shallow view of God depends on the weather . . . the stock market . . . the career path . . . their good health . . . smooth sailing. That's Eliphaz the Temanite. He appears to be wise, but in the end *he* is shallow and worldly.

Eliphaz is now going to make the same blunder made by all who counsel after the flesh.

Assume the Role of the Holy Spirit

Since Job won't confess, Eliphaz is literally going to start drafting a list of sins; without witnesses or substantiated evidence, he will accuse Job of things he didn't do.

Unbridled Greed

> ***"For you have taken pledges of your brothers without cause, and stripped men naked"*** (Job 22:6).

This was a serious accusation. In Job's day, common decency dictated that if a man were forced to give his outer garment as a pledge that he'll pay his debt to a creditor, the creditor would normally return it to him for the cold night because their cloak also served as their blanket.[3]

Eliphaz effectively says to Job, "Not only do you not return the coat to the debtor, you take the rest of the man's clothes so that he is ***stripped naked*** and left to the harsh elements without any covering or warmth. Job, you are a heartless, crass, greedy man."

If you're expecting Job to jump up and shout, "You're a liar! I've done no such thing," you won't read that verse in the text. By now, Job is too crushed to respond or even interrupt.

Heartless Disinterest in the Needy

> ***"To the weary you have given no water to drink, and from the hungry you have withheld bread. But the earth belongs to the mighty man, and the honorable man dwells in it"*** (Job 22:7–8).

His words contain ridicule: "Even though the whole earth belongs to you—you, who are supposedly honorable—you're really heartless and selfish and bereft of any modicum of concern for anybody. Job, you've let people starve when you could have helped."

Again, you expect Job to counter, "That's not true—I've got plenty of people who can testify to my generosity." Still no word from this saint in the hands of an angry, accusing, unkind, self-centered, condemning counselor.

Refusal to Care for Widows and Orphans

This action respresents the epitome of false religion . . . the lowest crime of all. Eliphaz insists,

> ***"You have sent widows away empty, and the strength of the orphans has been crushed"*** (Job 22:9).

Nothing could be further from the truth. Job's entire life reflected that he had shown concern for those around him. God himself characterized Job as a man who was the prime example of godly living on earth.

Where does Eliphaz come up with this stuff? Had he heard it from others? Were enemies of Job delivering little bits and pieces of rumors from people who had envied him . . . resented his purity . . . felt convicted by his close walk with God?

We're not told, but Eliphaz is convinced. His next blunder is yet another temptation to all who counsel others.

Press for a Quick Confession

Eljphaz offers,

> ***"Yield now and be at peace with Him; thereby good will come to you"*** (Job 22:21).

He promises further,

> ***"You will pray to Him, and He will hear you; and you will pay your vows"*** (Job 22:27).

The truth is Eliphaz is actually working for the Enemy rather than God. He has made false charges and now demands that Job confess to the accusations. Then, with false sincerity, he offers Job the promise that God will take note of his confession.

Revelation 12 tells us that Satan is the accuser of our brethren. In other words, Satan delights in bringing the believer under a cloud of guilt and a sense of permanent displeasure from God. He simply wants us to throw in the towel.

Steven Lawson wrote these perceptive words regarding this scene between Eliphaz and Job:

> We must carefully distinguish between the conviction of the Spirit and the accusation of Satan. There is a difference. The Holy Spirit convicts us of specific sin. He will do so until we confess it. Then He will no longer convict us about that specific sin because it is forgiven. On the other hand, Satan is a grave digger. He uncovers all kinds of dirt from our past and throws a barrage of sins at us. Sins we have committed but not confessed (to be sure). Sins we have committed but already confessed. Even sins we haven't committed; anything to heap guilt upon our heads. He majors on sin that does not need our attention. And even after we confess our sin, Satan still haunts us with guilt. He's like a dishonest car mechanic. Even if he can't find something that needs fixing, he'll tell us

> something does. So we end up paying for things to be fixed in our lives that aren't even broken. The difference between Holy Spirit conviction and Satanic accusation is the difference between a rifle and a shotgun. The Spirit directly targets areas that need confessing; He is clear, specific, and true. Satan uses a shotgun approach, firing buckshot at anything and everything. He is vague, generic, and false.[4]

HOW TO COUNSEL THE RIGHT WAY

The truth is we all have an Eliphaz or two in our lives. Either the unseen enemy or perhaps someone who reminds us of our failures . . . someone who loves to pile on the guilt and bury us.

As spouses, unfortunately, we can play that role, too; as parents we can refuse to add grace to our standards; as teachers and colleagues, business partners and classmates, we too easily withhold words of approval, commendation, and praise.

Like Eliphaz, we can be more concerned about *being right* than we are in *bringing hope.*

Eliphaz takes aim and fires one final round of buckshot.

Promise Quick Solutions and Ignore Deeper Problems

> ***"If you return to the Almighty, you will be restored; if you remove unrighteousness far from your tent"*** (Job 22:23).

> ***"Then the Almighty will be your gold and choice silver to you. For then you will delight in the Almighty and lift up your face to God"*** (Job 22:25–26).

"Job, just do as I say and all your problems will vanish."

> ***"You will decree a thing, and it will be established for you; and light will shine on your ways"*** (Job 22:28).

Are you kidding? Job can actually have anything he wants? He can name it and claim it?! That's what Eliphaz is promising: "Job, you follow my counsel and ***light*** is just going to bathe your path from here on out—you'll never be in the dark again!"

There's an ancient Hebrew word for these shallow promises: it's pronounced *ba-lon-ey*.

Never mind ten graves. Never mind the physical affects that Job will carry with him to his own grave. Never mind rebuilding his business and home from scratch. Never mind the memories . . . never mind the questions . . . and never mind the tears. *Seriously*?

Just follow the counsel of Eliphaz and you, Job, can have a brand-new life.

Frankly, Job doesn't want a brand-new life. He wants his old life back. That life was just fine. But he will never return to the joys of yesterday. For Job there is only today—painful and cruel—and there is tomorrow . . . bleak . . . lonely . . . confusing.

Unwise counsel is typically filled with superficial promises. It doesn't provide the steel of truth to brace someone's crumbling world; it doesn't provide the strength of the Spirit they'll need to rebuild or to start over.

Job has endured the pain of unfounded accusations and now endures superficial promises that trivialize the life he lost.

Yet, not once has Job interrupted Eliphaz with angry words or condemnation. Not once does Job retort, "Who do you think you are?!" In fact, Job never even attempts to set the record straight or defend himself against these new, sensational sins created by the selfish imagination of Eliphaz.

Not once does Job strike back.

One revered Scottish author who died in the middle of the nineteenth century wrote a number of commentaries that are in my library. In his spiritual autobiography, he told of the tragedy of losing his 21-year-old daughter and her fiancé who were drowned in a boating accident:

> It was a tragedy heard around the civilized world. He received an anonymous letter a few weeks later, saying, "I know why God killed your daughter—it was to keep her from the corruption of your heresies." This man of God would later write, "God did not stop that accident at sea, but He did still the storm in my own heart so that somehow my wife and I came through that terrible time still standing on our own two feet."[5]

I have always admired the Apostle Paul for staying on course, even though near the end of his ministry his accusers had largely won the day and Paul was virtually alone. They accused him of false motives, ineffective ministry, lacking necessary skill, manufacturing his office as an apostle; loafing and living off handouts from others—all of which were untrue.

For most of my life, I would have thought that Paul was the leading model for staying the course in the face of ridicule and accusation, with Nehemiah coming in a close second.

Until I studied this chapter in Job.

He has become a new example for me; one that just might take a leading role, at least joining an elite list of choice servants of God who suffered greatly at the hands of others, yet stayed in the race to the final lap.

Job is now virtually deserted. And he doesn't really know why. He's no longer certain of his purpose in life; one by one his friends turn against him and now, in this encounter, he is accused of lacking integrity and character and purity that he had effectively lived his entire life modeling.

It will take *years* to finally vindicate his character. In fact, it will take the intervention of God.

For most of us who've read the biographies of Abraham Lincoln, perhaps more than anything else, it was his refusal to retaliate and his willingness to bear up under the strain of his role which ultimately led history to rewrite its opinion of him with respect and admiration.

> Lincoln's biographers said that he had developed four ways of responding to the criticism of his enemies:
>
> 1. Ignore it and consider much of it too petty to deserve a response.
> 2. Reply only when it would truly make a difference.
> 3. Write lengthy letters in defense of your integrity, fully venting all your emotions; then tear them up, never to be mailed.
> 4. Focus on the better side of life and maintain a good sense of humor.[6]

I can't think of a better way to maintain *grace under pressure.*

In the hands of angry counselors, Job has endured accusations we cannot imagine, all within sight of ten fresh graves, a grieving wife, and his own body covered with oozing sores.

In the next two chapters, Job will respond to Eliphaz the Temanite. Had I been there, my first words would have been to call him Eliphaz *the Termite*. At least that would make me feel better.

COUNSELORS IN THE HANDS OF A GODLY SAINT

There's a lesson or two for all of us in Job's response. Of course, the remarkable thing is that Job never technically responds to Eliphaz at all . . . at least, not directly. He will ignore the insults and innuendoes.

What he *does* is begin to deliver an open, public prayer. I have summarized his prayer in two categorical statements which we will examine.

The Heavens Are Silent, but I Will Trust the Heart of God

Job laments,

> ***"Oh that I knew where I might find Him, that I might come to His seat! I would present my case before Him and fill my mouth with arguments*** [legal jargon: "evidence"]***"*** (Job 23:3–4).

> ***"I go forward but He is not there, and backward, but I cannot perceive Him; when He acts on the left, I cannot behold Him; He turns on the right, I cannot see Him"*** (Job 23:8).

Have you ever felt like that? The pressure's on and challenges are raining down thick and fast and you'd appreciate some sign from heaven—some message that God knows what's happening and that He cares.

This is exactly what Job is lamenting—the heavens are silent!

However, notice this profound statement of trust as Job continues:

> ***"But He knows the way I take; when He has tried me, I shall come forth as gold"*** (Job 23:10).

Wow.

Job has just effectively cried out that he doesn't know which way to turn; he doesn't know which path to take; he doesn't know which way God is going or the way God wants him to turn—but at the end of the trial, he will be refined as gold, heated in the furnace of affliction.

You can't miss the irony between Job's statement and the trivial promise of Eliphaz: "Job, if you submit to God, He will be gold to you."

Job says, "I have surrendered to God, and when He's finished with me, *I* will be gold to Him."

In this prayer you detect the subtle hint that even though Job has lost all his possessions, he is declaring his faith when he says, "God may not give me more gold, but He will make *me* like gold."

Refined by the furnace . . . purified by the heat.

This is a tremendous statement of faith:

- God *knows* what's happening to me (***He knows the way that I take***).
- God has *planned* what's happening to me (***When He has tried me***).
- God has a purifying *purpose* in mind for me (***I shall come forth as gold***).

This text was the inspiration behind John Rippon's great hymn "How Firm a Foundation":

When through fiery trials thy pathway shall lie,
My grace, all sufficient, shall be thy supply:
The flame shall not hurt thee; I only design
Thy dross to consume and thy gold to refine.[7]

Although the heavens are silent, I will trust in the heart of God.

Evil Surrounds Me, but I Will Trust the Hand of God

In other words, God is sovereign no matter what. ***Job 24*** is simply the cataloguing of sins and evils that surround us; unregenerate mankind refuses to control its own actions:

- Greed and theft ***(Job 24:2)***
- Oppression ***(Job 24:3)***

- Murder ***(Job 24:14)***
- Adultery ***(Job 24:15)***

And more . . .

This is actually a subtle answer to Eliphaz who has said that Job was obviously guilty of great sin because he was being punished. Job cleverly implies that if God always punished people because of their great sin, why are so many sinners going unpunished?

The point that follows is simply this truth: even though it seems God is not in control, He is, and sin will *ultimately* be judged.

The sinner who refuses to repent makes the arrogant assumption that God must not be looking . . . He doesn't seem to be anywhere nearby. But He is.

The saint who loses heart assumes that God doesn't seem to be noticing; He doesn't seem to be close at hand. But He is. God hasn't abandoned His sovereign post . . . God has not abandoned you.

William Frey was an undergraduate at the University of Colorado in 1951. He spent a couple of hours a week reading to John, a fellow student who was blind. William writes:

> One day I asked John how he lost his sight. He told me of an accident when he was a teenager and how he had simply given up on life. "When the accident happened and I knew that I would never see again, I felt that life had ended, as far as I was concerned. I was bitter and angry with God for letting this happen, and I took my anger out on everyone around me. I felt that since I had no future, I wouldn't lift a finger on my own behalf. Let others wait on me. I shut my bedroom door and refused to come out except for meals."
>
> The young man I knew was an eager student, so I asked what had changed his attitude. John responded by telling of a life-changing event. "One day, my father came into my room and began lecturing me. He said he was tired of my feeling sorry for myself. He said winter was coming, and it had always been my job to put up the storm windows, and I was

to get those windows up by suppertime, or else! He slammed the door on the way out. Well, that made me so angry that I resolved to do it. Muttering to myself, I groped my way out to the garage, found the windows, a stepladder, all the necessary tools, and I went to work. *They'll be sorry when I fall off the ladder and break my neck*, I thought, but instead, little by little, groping my way around the house, I got the job done."

Then he stopped talking and his sightless eyes misted over as he told me, "I later discovered that at no time during that afternoon had my father ever been more than a few feet from my side. I didn't know it until later, but all the while I was climbing up and down that ladder, muttering, fumbling with the tools, and sweating my way through that horrendous project in the darkness of my blindness, my father had been beside me all the way."[8]

The same is true for Job . . . the same is true for you. As you grope through the darkness of suffering, your Father is never more than a few feet away. John Rippon's great hymn text will go on to assure us:

Fear not, I am with thee; O be not dismayed,
For I am thy God, and will still give thee aid;
I'll strengthen thee, help thee, and cause thee to stand,
Upheld by My righteous, omnipotent hand.

The soul that on Jesus hath leaned for repose
I will not, I will not desert to its foes;
That soul, though all hell should endeavor to shake,
I'll never, no, never, no, never forsake![7]

How wonderully true.

Even when the heavens are silent . . .

Even when the earth is filled with evil . . .

Even when you're in the dark . . .

Even when you don't know which way to turn . . .

Even when you're in the hands of angry counselors . . .

You are always in the hands of an all-wise, ever-near Heavenly Father.

[3]*"For as long as life is in me, and the breath of God is in my nostrils,* [4]*my lips certainly will not speak unjustly, nor will my tongue mutter deceit."*

–Job 27:3–4

[2]*"Oh that I were as in months gone by, as in the days when God watched over me;* [3]*when His lamp shone over my head, and by His light I walked through darkness."*

–Job 29:2–3

[27]*"I am seething within and cannot relax; days of affliction confront me.* [28]*I go about mourning without comfort; I stand up in the assembly and cry out for help.* [29]*I have become a brother to jackals and a companion of ostriches.* [30]*My skin turns black on me, and my bones burn with fever.* [31]*Therefore my harp is turned to mourning, and my flute to the sound of those who weep."*

–Job 30: 27–31

[5]*"If I have walked with falsehood, and my foot has hastened after deceit,* [6]*let Him weigh me with accurate scales, and let God know my integrity."*

–Job 31:5–6

CHAPTER EIGHTEEN

THE LAST STAND OF A DESPERATE MAN

Job 25–31

The last stand of the Spartans created an enduring legend. Thermopylae (literally *hot gates*) was a pass the Greeks tried to defend in battle against Xerxes, who led 100,000 Persians in the spring of 480 BC. They were met by 300 Spartans and several thousand allies. The Greeks needed to detain the Persians long enough for the rest of their allies to gather their forces. They knew it would be suicide. Led by King Leonidas, the Spartans heroically held the Persians at bay for nearly a week until—outnumbered, betrayed, and outflanked—they were finally defeated.[1]

In the Battle at Thermopylae, Dieneces was the most honored Spartan. According to Spartan scholar Paul Cartledge, Dieneces was so loyal that when told there were so many Persian archers that the sky would grow dark with their flying arrows, he replied: "So much the better—we shall fight them in the shade."[2]

What a rare and self-denying spirit.

As brave as it might sound to fight off warriors under the shade of a sky blackened by arrows, nothing compares in courage to standing alone for the truth of the Gospel.

I have stood in the sanctuary of John Knox and gazed at his pulpit, elevated and attached to a massive column. From that pulpit he was the lone voice preaching against the atrocities of his queen against believers. He had no compatriots to cheer him on.

I have stood in John Wesley's Chapel and imagined what it must have been like to preach with great courage; to be one of the lone voices against slavery and have the congregation respond by rioting and breaking pews to pieces.

I would love to have visited the courtroom in Worms, Germany, where Martin Luther, in 1521, was placed on trial for being a heretic. There, before the highest religious and political leaders of his day, he stood alone and said, "My conscience is bound to the Word of God. I cannot and I will not recant. Here I stand. I can do none other."

It's one thing to face trouble and anguish and, perhaps, even death when you are surrounded by friends and admirers. It's quite another to face death alone.

John the Baptist stood alone when he pointed his finger at Herod and told him he was an adulterer for marrying his brother's wife.

Jeremiah the prophet stood alone when he told the disturbing truth to his nation and, as a result, was thrown into an abandoned well where he sank in the mud until he was rescued from certain death.

The chief example of standing alone would be our faithful Lord, who endured the cruelest of deaths, experiencing the hatred of the people He had come to save. He suffered the abandonment of His Father, as the sky grew dark with divine judgment, all the while abandoned by those who had followed Him. No one has ever been as alone as Jesus Christ.

There is something especially courageous and admirable—and rare—about someone who stands alone for the honor and truth of God.

Perhaps even now you are in this position in your dormitory or in the neighborhood or in your family where Jesus Christ is a curse word. You know what it's like to stand alone.

We are about to watch the lonely stand of Job as the final flurry of arrows darken the sky against him . . . as he refuses to surrender his integrity.

Job is about to deliver his last and longest speech. Afterwards, Elihu will condemn him, immediately followed by God's long awaited response.

The hush of heaven is almost over.

If there are any lingering doubts about Job's integrity and trust in God —albeit confused and pained and challenged—these chapters will settle the score . . . once and for all.

Satan will lose his wager. Job will not blaspheme God; in fact, instead of cursing God, Job begins to describe the greatness of God.

JOB'S SOLILOQUY

Job's long speech will echo five questions about which mankind still wonders. To some of these, he will provide answers; to others, he will simply continue lamenting his grief and agony.

Who Can Understand the Greatness of God?

Job invites us to travel to the depths of the underworld—the place of the grave; to go down as deeply into the earth as possible, but then to travel northward, straight up and beyond earth's atmosphere into the spaces of our universe—and learn that God is sovereign over it all. From the lowest point of imagination to the highest pinnacle, God is over all.

Job declares;

"Behold, these are the fringes of His ways" (Job 26:14*a*)

What a great thought this is. No matter how deep we travel or how high we ascend, we have only reached the outer ***fringes***; the outer edges of ***God's ways***. We are nowhere near the core of His hidden glory and power. We can only see the ***fringes*** and hear the whispers of His greatness.

Job effectively says, "Do you think you have God figured out? You haven't even gone past the ***fringes*** of His greatness. Who can understand Him? Your worship of God is way too limited because your view of God is way too small!"[3]

A.W. Tozer gives us a warning in his powerful little book entitled *The Knowledge of the Holy*. He writes,

> So necessary to the church is a lofty concept of God that when that concept in any measure declines, the church with her worship and her moral standards declines along with it. The first step down for any church is taken when it surrenders its high opinion of God. We do the greatest service to the next generation of Christians by passing on to them undimmed and undiminished that noble concept of God.[4]

Relief comes from trusting, following, and obeying a great, unexplainable, majestic, and mysterious Lord.

Another author explains,

> Whenever there are sores on your body and they are running with pus and the fever will not go down, the perspective of Job is where you need to be. "I don't understand . . . but I have a sovereign God of the universe who does. And He does all things well. He is in charge. I am the clay; He is the Potter. I am the disciple; He is the Lord. I am the sheep; He is the Shepherd. I am the servant; He is the Master.[5]

Let suffering return you to a high view of this majestic and mysterious God who acts without explanation and moves beyond our understanding. All we can grasp of this majestic Lord are the ***fringes*** of His activity.

Job's response to God's greatness demands a recommitment to holiness.

> ***"For as long as life is in me, and the breath of God is in my nostrils, my lips certainly will not speak unjustly, nor will my tongue mutter deceit"*** (Job 27:3–4).

This is the last stand of a desperate man. Job says, "I will *not* be moved. I don't understand, but I'm not abandoning my character or my trust in God."

What follows is the next logical question of Job.

Why Does Mankind Ignore the Coming Judgment of God?

> ***"For what is the hope of the godless when he is cut off, when God requires his life?"*** (Job 27:8).

In other words, how tragic it is for mankind to ignore its conscience and run from God, assuming they can actually run *away.*

> ***"The east wind carries him away, and he is gone, for it whirls him away from his place. For it will hurl at him without sparing; he will surely try to flee from its power"*** (Job 27:21–22).

What a dangerous way to live and think: "I can get away with my unbelief—God will not judge *me.*"

As Job takes his stand, he also wonders—as everyone who suffers wonders, *Where can I find wisdom to handle my life?*

Where Can We Find True Wisdom?

In this third question, Job actually gives a longer answer than James. The first thing Job says is that we cannot dig wisdom out of the earth.

> ***"Man does not know its value, nor is it found in the land of the living. The deep says, 'It is not in me'; and the sea says, 'It is not with me'"*** (Job 28:13–14).

Not only can we not mine wisdom from the earth, but we also cannot buy wisdom from other people.

> ***"Pure gold cannot be given in exchange for it, nor can silver be weighed as its price"*** (Job 28:15).

There is no half-price special for wisdom—supermarkets don't sell it and warehouse clubs can't stock it.

So where do we get wisdom? Job and James answer.

James tells us, in light of being surrounded by various trials:

> *If any of you lacks wisdom, let him ask of God who will give generously* (James 1:5).

James could have correctly added, "little by little—and just in time!"

Job expands and underscores;

> ***"God understands its way, and He knows its place. . . . And to man He said, 'Behold, the fear of the LORD, that is wisdom; and to depart from evil is understanding'"*** (Job 28:23, 28).

Don't miss this key principle to finding wisdom: wisdom is a byproduct we gain while pacticing these two activities:

1. *Worshipping God in total reverence.* This is Job's meaning when he speaks of ***the fear of the LORD***. It simply means we take God seriously.
2. *Walking with God in transparent obedience.* When we take God seriously, we'll consider our lives seriously—***we'll depart from evil***, living life for His glory.

Simply put, wisdom is the byproduct that comes to those who worship God and walk with Him. When there is surrender and submission to God, wisdom becomes our companion.

How Do We Define True Happiness?

I find it fascinating that Job sort of leans back on his elbows and begins to talk about the good old days. This is not unlike people who suffer. They are actually encouraged as they reflect on better days and happier moments. They often enjoy taking a stroll down memory lane.

As you follow Job down this lane, he actually defines true happiness. We can pull from his words five ingredients of contented, happy living.

1. An Awareness of God's Presence and Care

> ***"Oh that I were as in months gone by, as in the days when God watched over me; when His lamp shone over my head, and by His light I walked through darkness"*** (Job 29:2–3).

There are plenty of texts that inform us that Job believes God is still aware of his needs, but in the good old days it was *obvious*. In fact, what made the good old days so genuinly *good* was the sense that God was close at hand:

> ***"As I was in the prime of my days, when the friendship of God was over my tent"*** (Job 29:4).

2. An Appreciation for Whatever God Gives

> ***"And my children were around me; when my steps were bathed in butter, and the rock poured out for me streams of oil!"*** (Job 29:5*b*–6).

In other words, "Man, life was blessed; my steps were bathed in butter—a delicious delicacy surrounded me."

This is like going to a wedding reception and discovering a table with fresh strawberries and a chocolate fountain—you park there. Chunks of pineapple and banana are available, too. You can stand there and dip until your reputation is virtually destroyed . . . or until your wife says, "Honey, there's a long line of angry people behind us."

That's what I call a *good* wedding reception.

Job pulls out a food item from his culture and exaggerates it to suggest how good life used to be: ***my steps were bathed in butter.***

A member of our recent church membership class brought me two dozen doughnuts slathered with chocolate icing. Some teachers like apples. Not me. Those doughnuts had been freshly made that day at a local bakery. Happiness, obviously to me, is a dozen of them. To Job, it was butter.

But he goes deeper than food.

3. An Occasion to Influence Others

> ***"When I went out to the gate of the city, when I took my seat in the square, the young men saw me and hid themselves, and the old men arose and stood. The princes stopped talking and put their hands on their mouths. The voice of the nobles was hushed, and their tongue stuck to their palate. For when the ear heard, it called me blessed, and when the eye saw, it gave witness of me"*** (Job 29:7–11).

Job's recollection of good days included the opportunity to represent truth and integrity and justice among his peers. He seemed more *useful* then.

4. An Opportunity to Be Generous and Compassionate toward the Needy

> ***"Because I delivered the poor who cried for help, and the orphan who had no helper. The blessing of the one ready to perish came upon me, and I made the widow's heart sing for joy. I put on righteousness, and it clothed me; my justice was like a robe and a turban. I was eyes to the blind and feet to the lame. I was a father to the needy, and I investigated the case which I did not know. I broke the jaws of the wicked and snatched the prey from his teeth. Then I thought, 'I shall die in my nest, and I shall multiply my days as the sand. My root is spread out to the waters, and dew lies all night on my branch. My glory is ever new with me, and my bow is renewed in my hand'"*** (Job 29:12–20).

To Job, and to us today, true happiness comes from helping those who cannot help themselves . . . who cannot pay us back.

5. A Respect Earned by Giving Godly Counsel

> ***"To me they listened and waited, and kept silent for my counsel. After my words they did not speak again, and my speech dropped on them. They waited for me as for the rain, and opened their mouth as for the spring rain. I smiled on them when they did not believe, and the light of my face they did not cast down. I chose a way for them and sat as chief, and dwelt as a king among the troops, as one who comforted the mourners"*** (Job 29:21–25).

These were the ingredients of true happiness. These were the elements that made up the good old days of Job's yesteryear.

In the next chapter, Job moves on to recount the many ways in which his happy circumstances turned sour and bitter.

Job 30 will catalogue the catastrophic changes in his life—everything he enjoyed in the previous chapter is now reversed.

At the end of the list, Job summarizes with these somber words:

> ***"I am seething within and cannot relax; days of affliction confront me. I go about mourning without comfort; I stand up in the assembly and cry out for help. I have become a brother to jackals and a companion of ostriches. My skin turns black on me, and my bones burn with fever. Therefore my harp is turned to mourning, and my flute to the sound of those who weep"*** (Job 30: 27–31).

This is the point at which we would expect Job to finally throw in the towel. He has stood alone . . . long enough. Now it's too much to bear.

Perhaps you've been at this point, too; maybe you're there right now.

You remember the good days—when butter was plentiful; when your children were around you; when God seemed near and you seemed useful. Yes, *those* were the good old days.

But now, it's different. *These* are the days of affliction; pain; suffering; loss; disease; debt; abandonment—a ***harp*** that now mourns and a ***flute*** that can only play in the minor key.

Instead of stepping down in surrender, Job digs in his heels and makes new commitments to God. He basically says, "I will *not* give up my integrity. I will *not* throw away my character. I will *not* give up."

This is truly amazing . . . and convicting.

In the following chapter ***(31)***, Job defines for us the answer to a fifth and final question.

How Can We Develop a Life of Integrity?

There are ten resolutions made by Job that answer this question.

1. Determine Pure Boundaries

> ***"I have made a covenant with my eyes; how then could I gaze at a virgin?"*** (Job 31:1–2).

Integrity is developed by determining ahead of time what we will and will not look at. For us today, that would include media and internet sources of immorality.

At the outset of these ten ways to develop integrity, make this mental note: *integrity does not happen by accident.* Integrity must be pursued, developed, and deeply desired by those willing to stand alone.

2. Develop Honesty

> ***"If I have walked with falsehood, and my foot has hastened after deceit, let Him weigh me with accurate scales, and let God know my integrity"*** (Job 31:5–6).

Integrity and honesty are synonymous. So tell the truth.

3. Disallow Moral Compromises

Job talks candidly about resisting the enticement of a woman and hanging around a neighbor's house for the wrong reasons. He candidly warns against pursuing a single woman, and equally refuses to be available to a married woman.

Job allows no compromise or excuses for being ***enticed by a woman*** or ***lurking at my neighbor's door*** (Job 31:9). In other words, stay away. Don't hand out your business card or phone number that might open a door for moral sin to enter.

We need to recognize, especially in light of our culture where men and women work together every day, that there is no such thing as innocent flirting; there is no room for moral compromises of any sort—no excuses, such as, "Oh, it's nothing dangerous." I have pastored long enough to see marriages destroyed by couples who were in the same Bible study become involved with one another, and couples who counseled each other leave their spouses for one another.

Make no allowances for moral compromise—guard the gate . . . guard your heart!

4. Defend the Disadvantaged

Job's words can be turned into a positive definition of integrity; a reference for someone who does not take advantage of his power and position to mistreat an employee. He takes care to see that complaints against him are handled with kindness and fairness ***(Job 31:13–15)***.

5. Distribute to the Needy

Job describes a man of integrity who will distribute to the ***poor***, the ***widow***, the ***orphan***, and the ***needy (Job 31:16–23)***.

Eliphaz condemned him earlier for not caring for the orphan or the widow ***(Job 22:9)***; Job now replies,

> ***"If I have lifted up my hand against the orphan, because I saw I had support in the gate, let my shoulder fall from the socket, and my arm be broken off at the elbow"*** (Job 31:21–22).

In other words, "If I've mistreated a widow or an orphan, let me be come physically disabled."

6. Deplore Materialism

Job declares that a man or a woman of integrity does not put their trust and ***confidence in gold*** (Job 31:24–25).

7. Denounce Spiritual Compromises

It was the custom of the ancients to blow kisses toward the temples and shrines of their gods to show allegiance. Job declares,

> ***"If I have looked at the sun when it shone or the moon going in splendor, and my heart became secretly enticed, and my hand threw a kiss from my mouth, that too would have been an iniquity calling for judgment, for I would have denied God above"*** (Job 31: 26–28).

Developing integrity demands that we denounce spiritual or doctrinal compromises.

8. Display Compassion toward Others

> ***"Have I rejoiced at the extinction of my enemy, or exulted when evil befell him? No, I have not allowed my mouth to sin by asking for his life in a curse. Have the men of my tent not said, 'Who can find one who has not been satisfied with his meat'? The alien has not lodged outside, for I have opened my doors to the traveler"*** (Job 31:29–32).

Integrity is displayed through showing compassion toward everyone—even enemies.

9. Despise Hypocrisy in All Things

Job asks,

> ***"Have I covered my transgressions like Adam, by hiding my iniquity in my bosom?"*** (Job 31:33).

In other words, "I have not acted like Adam, who attempted to mask his disobedience with fig leaves."

People of integrity will refuse to play the hypocrite. They are real and genuine. There's no hidden agenda.

10. Deny Any Excuse for Greed

Job sums it up by saying that integrity demands that we deny any excuse for greed.

What Job has done is take his stand upon a foundation of personal integrity. Before his fellow man and his sovereign Lord, he reveals his heart—not so much his perfection in life, but his *direction* in life.

He courageously announces,

> ***Behold, here is my signature; let the Almighty answer me! And the indictment which my adversary has written*** (Job 31:35).

Job says, in effect:

I have determined pure boundaries.

I have developed honesty.

I have disallowed moral compromises.

I have defended the disadvantaged.

I have distributed to the needy.

I have deplored materialism and never trusted in money.

I have denounced any spiritual compromise.

I have displayed compassion toward others.

I have declined hypocrisy in all things.

I have denied any excuse for greed.

If you didn't notice, Job has covered every area of life. His integrity has saturated his:

- thoughts
- ethics
- work
- home
- community
- finances
- testimony
- relationships
- stewardship[6]

We have been fed the lie that it is possible to be a person of integrity in public, while being dishonest or immoral in private. The truth is a lack of integrity in *any* area is to surrender integrity.

Job says, "Take a good look anywhere in my life. Go through my files. Check my internet sites. Interview my employees. Look at my expense accounts. Sift through my bank records. Look at my giving record at church and other charities. Interview my wife. Talk to my neighbors. Ask my business associates. Talk to my closest friends. You will find the intention, direction, and resolve of my heart is to be a person of integrity. It's not something I would *like* to be; it is what I *must* be."

Job took his stand . . . how about you?

Job experiences suffering from God and the silence of God, but he never discards his integrity—even in desperate times and difficult days.

You can hear the integrity and resolve of Job in the words of John Wesley, one of the pioneer leaders in the First Great Awakening (1730s–1770s), who prayed,

I am no longer my own, but Thine.
Put me to what Thou wilt, rank me with whom Thou wilt.
Put me to doing, put me to suffering.
Let me be employed by Thee or laid aside for Thee,
Exalted for Thee or brought low for Thee.
Let me be full, let me be empty.
Let me have all things, let me have nothing.
I freely and heartily yield all things to Thy pleasure and disposal.
And now, O glorious and blessed God, Father, Son, and Holy Spirit,
Thou art mine, and I am Thine.
Amen.

Then these three men ceased answering Job, because he was righteous in his own
eyes. 2*But the anger of Elihu the son of Barachel the Buzite, of the family of*
Ram burned; against Job his anger burned because he justified himself before
God. 3*And his anger burned against his three friends because they had found*
no answer, and yet had condemned Job. 4*Now Elihu had waited to speak to Job*
because they were years older than he. 5*And when Elihu saw that there was no*
answer in the mouth of the three men his anger burned. 6*So Elihu the son of*
Barachel the Buzite spoke out.

–Job 32:1–6

CHAPTER NINETEEN

THE LEARNING CURVE OF LIFE

Job 32–37

A *learning curve* is a reference to certain times in life when changes and challenges take on new twists and turns—most often suddenly. A new job has a steep learning curve where you need to learn a lot of new information in a short period of time. A freshman in college finds himself on a steep learning curve.

This expression was first coined in 1885, in the field of the psychology of learning. Later, in 1936, an engineer used it to estimate the cost and efforts of airplane assembly. His application of the *learning curve* was simply this: the more you repeat a series of operations, the less time and effort will be expended in order to achieve the same result.

My roommate in college once encouraged me to take up golf lessons. He explained how difficult it was to hit a golf ball. I said, "C'mon, it can't be that hard." He said, "Let me show you."

I should have walked away.

Instead, we went to the front yard of our dormitory, golf clubs in hand. He gave me several instructions and I immediately felt I'd entered a game of Twister.

Then, to add insult to injury, he put an orange down on the ground and said, "Okay . . . hit it." I smirked and swung hard . . . and missed. He said, "Keep your head down"—like that would help. I swung again . . . and again. That orange remained completely unscathed . . . mocking me all the while. I finally hit it—but only because I swung the club *down* like an axe. That orange never left the ground.

And to think I now pay $25 for the opportunity to do the same thing to golf balls . . . with equal exasperation.

Do you remember the learning curve of driving a car? I learned on a Volkswagen Bug . . . baby blue, with four on the floor. My parents let me practice in front of our house. With a stick shift, you had to remember several things at once—like golf—how to let the clutch out slowly until it engages, being careful not to pop it too quickly and stall, all while accelerating and changing gears. I learned fairly quickly. No one got hurt—the neighbors stayed indoors.

I arrived at my first Driver's Ed class and was thrilled to see that the car I would be learning to drive was a Volkswagen Bug, with four on the floor. I knew I was already way down the road, so to speak.

I slipped into the driver's seat, my instructor sat in the seat next to me. I pressed in the clutch, started the engine, put the car in first gear, pressed the gas pedal, eased off the clutch, and away we sped. Suddenly the car screeched to a halt. I looked over and discovered that my instructor had a set of brakes on his side of the car—something my wife has wanted for years.

He looked at me and said, "Son, you're here to learn, not race."

So much for *that* learning curve.

What about the learning curve of marriage? I know you probably had premarital counseling: four sessions and a notebook. You wondered to yourself, *How hard can this be? What more is there to learn?* Actually, the learning curve of marriage doesn't really *begin* until the wedding ceremony is over.

One author said marriage is like getting on a plane heading for the Bahamas. You've got all your shorts and Hawaiian shirts packed, along with plenty of sunscreen; you've even got a new snorkel and a pair of fins. Then the plane lands and you discover you're at the North Pole. Instead of a breeze, it's a blizzard. You need a fur coat, not a swim suit. Your fins and snorkel should be snowshoes and a ski mask.

Talk about a learning curve. And about the time you catch up on the learning curve of marriage, you find yourself buried in diapers.

And there's nothing quite like the learning curve of parenting.

You soon discover the euphoria when you finally get the babies bathed, powdered, diapered, and snuggled into their pj's with little footies attached.

They've just finished their bottle of milk laced with NyQuil . . . *just kidding* . . . and the nursery lights are turned out at last.

You tiptoe out . . . don't breathe . . . *Please, Lord, let this be a deep sleep—like hibernation—and let it last three months.* I prayed that often over our newborn twins. It never worked.

Maybe your learning curve was a major move to another city . . . or forced retirement . . . or the loss of a business.

No matter who we are, there is at least one learning curve which is common to *all* of us—old or young; married or single; children or none; rich or poor; employed or jobless.

You never know when this curve's coming . . . and you are *never* fully prepared.

It's the learning curve of suffering.

David speaks to this unique curriculum as he writes,

> *It is good for me that I was afflicted, that I may learn Your statues* (Psalm 119:71).

David is clear: suffering places you on a learning curve which ultimately teaches wise and godly living. Trouble is a tutor who assigns an unbearable amount of homework.

If affliction introduces the believer to a learning curve, then Job has been riding one of the fastest curves you can imagine. He's been on it for months now; maybe as long as a year or two.

By now, we're all ready for the curve to level out; we're anticipating the hush of heaven to be broken by the voice of God.

Job has actually just spoken his final words. He appealed directly to God and is now waiting for Him to respond. But instead of God, a brand-new voice suddenly echoes over the ash heap.

A young man named Elihu steps forward to deliver a speech that will take up the next six chapters of the narrative. He will actually introduce some new concepts that are much closer to the truth than was the counsel of Eliphaz, Bildad, and Zophar.

In fact, Elihu will introduce the idea that God might have sent Job this suffering—not because he had sinned but to *keep* him from sinning. That thought certainly hadn't been bantered around the town dump.

Elihu actually suggests to Job that God might have been protecting him from greater sin by sending affliction—which, by the way, was the testimony of the Apostle Paul:

> *Because of the surpassing greatness of the revelations, for this reason, to keep me from exalting myself, there was given me a thorn in the flesh a messenger of Satan to torment me—to keep me from exalting myself!* (2 Corinthians 12:7).

Suffering kept Paul spiritually minded.

Elihu suggests this possibility to Job, which would have been tremendously encouraging. He also suggests another new concept: suffering not only keeps people from sin, it causes them to learn the ways of God.

As Elihu begins to speak in ***Job 32***, he basically spends the entire chapter introducing the fact that he's going to offer counsel . . . and why.

He admits that he's angry. At first you think, *Uh-oh, join the crowd; what good can come from angry counselor?* However, you soon discover that Elihu is angry for the right reason:

> **[A]*gainst Job his anger burned because he justified himself before God*** (Job 32:2*b*).

In other words, Job was leaning dangerously toward self-righteousness.

Elihu is also angry with Job's three friends:

> ***And his anger burned against his three friends because they had found no answer, and yet had condemned Job*** (Job 32:3).

He's evidently listened while the other three men, without any objective evidence, determined that Job's sufferings had resulted from secret sin.

Elihu was righteously angry. Aristotle wrote that righteous anger was, "to be angry with the right person to the right extent at the right time with the right motive and for the right reason." That is not easy, and not everyone can do it.[1]

Elihu was, for the most part, a wonderful counselor who not only challenged Job's wrong attitudes but encouraged him with new insights. In fact, Elihu's speech offers what every wise counselor will provide: he prepared Job to hear from God.

While he was president, a former political leader loved to tell this story:

> A young country boy had just finished Bible college but had never preached a sermon. When he arrived at the rural church where he had been scheduled to preach, he walked in and, to his disappointment, there was only one man present. The young preacher walked over to him, shook his hand, and asked, "Well, what do you think I oughta do?" The old rancher said, "Well, I don't rightly know, son; I'm just a cowpoke. But if I went out in my field and found only one steer, I'd feed it." That's all the young preacher needed. He delivered a sermon that went on and on and on . . . and on. Over an hour later, he finally ended his marathon message. He walked back to the rancher and asked, "What'd you think?" The old cowhand replied, "I don't rightly know, son, but I'll tell you this: if I went out in my field and found only one steer, I wouldn't feed him the whole load."[2]

Elihu is about to back up the wagon and dump the entire load. It'll be a marathon message. Frankly, Job will savor every morsel.

Elihu begins his counsel in ***Job 33***.

Now in order for you to hang your Stetson on some obvious pegs of truth, let's track his speech along four major points.

WHEN LIFE IS CONFUSING, GOD IS STILL COMMUNICATING

"Job, God is speaking! Not like you wanted . . . not through channels you expected . . . but He is, indeed, communicating."

Through Dreams

Elihu makes the point that God speaks . . . through dreams and visions in the night ***(Job 33:13–15)***.

In Job's day, the Bible was incomplete. In fact, many scholars believe the Scriptures had yet to begin. If, indeed, Job was the first book ever compiled and edited by Moses—as many Old Testament scholars believe—God communicated to His choice servants through dreams and visions.

That practice will actually continue through the completion of the New Testament scriptures *(Hebrews 1:1-2; Revelation 22:18–19)*.

For us today, God does not deliver revelation through dreams; we're not waiting for Him to speak . . . He has already spoken. He has already revealed His Word through the prophets and apostles who composed the Book you treasure most.

The trouble with the average Christian is boredom over the revealed Word of God. No wonder confusion abounds. For many, attempting to discern hidden spiritual truth from a dream does nothing more than open a subjective door to spiritual danger.

Even in the Old Testament, the prophet Isaiah challenged the nation Israel to stay close to the revealed Word through God's prophets:

> *To the law and the testimony! If they do not speak according to this word, it is because they have no dawn* [light in them] (Isaiah 8:20).

Today, dreams are not intended to communicate *new* revelation from God. They are nothing more than our subconscious minds at work—perhaps working through truths or situations that have impacted us. Dreams can certainly impress us, even when we're asleep.

But if they distract us from the revealed truth of God's Word, they are to be discarded as soon as we awaken; if our dreams support the truth of God's Word, then we're really not following a dream, are we? We are remaining committed and surrendered to the revealed Word of God.

I was an unsaved seventeen-year-old, rebelling against God, living the life of a hypocrite, dutifully joining my family in church every Sunday morning and Sunday night, yet refusing repentance and defying the demands of following Christ. I knew that the Gospel meant absolute surrender of my life to the leadership of Christ.

One night I dreamed that I was suffering in the flames of eternal hell. My dream was in vivid full-color imagery. When I woke up I was covered in sweat, terrified over what I'd just "seen."

Frankly, what I had seen was the imagery of scriptural descriptions of hell; it was the truth of God's Word already implanted in my heart. In other words, conviction and guilt actually invaded my subconscious mind while I slept.

It so powerfully impacted me that I got out of bed and onto my knees, surrendering my life to Jesus Christ.

My dream did not add to or contradict the Word of God; it merely reinforced what I already knew.

One of the troubling fads within the Church is the penchant for traveling outside the revealed Word of God into areas where "new information" is delivered via dreams and visions. Dreams often end up creating nothing less than distractions and diversions.

Keep in mind that we have:

> *All Scripture* [which] *is inspired by God and profitable for teaching, for reproof, for correction, for training in righteousness; so that the man of God may be adequate, equipped for every good work* (2 Timothy 3:16–17).

For Job, prior to the completed revelation of God's Word, God could and did speak new truths through dreams and visions.

Through Suffering

Elihu reminds Job that God was most definitely communicating to him through his personal suffering:

> ***"Man is also chastened with pain on his bed . . . then he will pray to God"*** (Job 33:19, 26).

That word translated ***chastened*** can be rendered *instructed.*

Suffering is often the doorway to deep truths and even deeper insights.

We've already considered that perceptive statement by C. S. Lewis, "Pain is His [God's] magaphone to rouse a deaf world.[3]

Elihu advises Job that God has been shouting all along through his suffering.

He also surprised Job by informing him that God has used other individuals as messengers ***(Job 33:23)*** to remind a man what is right for him.

"Job . . . even when your life has been most confusing, God has actually been communicating."

WHEN LIFE SEEMS UNFAIR, GOD IS NEVER UNJUST

Elihu will simply repeat the truth that God always does what is right, even when we can't see it.

He directly defends the character and nature of God:

> ***"Therefore, listen to me, you men of understanding, far be it from God to do wickedness, and from the Almighty to do wrong. For He pays a man according to his work, and makes him find it according to his way. Surely, God will not act wickedly, and the Almighty will not pervert justice"*** (Job 34:10–12).

When you are discouraged and life seems unfair, the best thing you can invite into your life is a friend who will counsel you to remember that God always does what is right, even though He chooses not to explain Himself.

Elihu goes on to describe certain truths about God:

- He is a just Rewarder ***(Job 34:11)***.
- He is the sovereign Authority ***(Job 34:13)***.
- He is the independent Sustainer of life ***(Job 34:14–15)***.
- He is the impartial Ruler ***(Job 34:16–20)***.

> ***"Who* [God] *shows no partiality to princes nor regards the rich above the poor, for they all are the work of His hands?"*** (Job 34:19).[4]

In other words:

- We play favorites . . . God doesn't.
- We show partiality . . . God never has.
- We skewer the scales of justice with highly paid lawyers . . . God judges one and all with the same scales of perfect justice, holiness, and judgment.

"Job . . . even if life seems unfair, God is never unjust."

But isn't it possible for someone to be just and also *unkind*?

Elihu seems to anticipate this question from Job and, without pausing to allow Job to ask, Elihu answers with another key principle.

WHEN LIFE SEEMS HARD, GOD IS NOT HEARTLESS

God is not distant when we despair.

This precious promise is sifted from the ash heap of Job's suffering, this time from the lips of Elihu:

> ***"But no one says, 'Where is God my Maker, who gives songs in the night?'"*** (Job 35:10).

Elihu continues:

> ***"'Who teaches us more than the beasts of the earth and makes us wiser than the birds of the heavens?'"*** (Job 35:11).

Imagine, our God is able to give us ***songs in the night.*** There's a big difference between whistling in the dark and a song in the night, right?

Sometimes I need to run over to the church to pick up a book when no one's around and it's late at night. The buildings are big, deserted . . . and dark. I usually whistle.

That's not bravery, it's downright cowardice.

But to be in a dark, lonely, deserted, frightening place—to endure alone whatever suffering brings—and *still* sing praise to God . . . that's incredible courage!

This is Paul and Silas singing in a jail cell *(Acts 16).*

This is our Lord who sang with His disciples in the upper room, knowing He was about to enter the Garden of Gethsemane and go on to the cross:

> *After singing a hymn, they went out to the Mount of Olives.* (Matthew 26:30).

It's one thing to sing in the sunshine . . . it's another thing to have a song in the night.

Joni Eareckson Tada and John MacArthur collaborated on a book of hymn histories and some of the theology behind these great hymn texts of the Church.

As we earlier commented, Joni broke her neck in a diving accident and has, for several decades, served Christ through a variety of ministries, although paralyzed from the neck down.

In one particular chapter, the story wasn't about Joni's suffering but the homegoing of the mother of James Dobson, founder of Focus on the Family. This is a recollection of those precious final moments:

In a few minutes we were sitting on the edge of Myrtle Dobson's bed. Suffering from Parkinson's disease, which rendered her confused, she was unable to speak more than a word or two at a time. Dr. Dobson spoke kindly to his mother, reminding her who we all were, even though we had known her very well. She just nodded and smiled. After a few minutes of small talk, Bobbie (one of the guests) spoke up, "Why don't we sing. Myrtle loves to sing." So we did.

O worship the King, all glorious above,
And gratefully sing His pow'r and His love;
Our Shield and Defender, the Ancient of Days,
Pavilioned in splendor and girded with praise.

For the first few lines of the hymn, she silently smiled back at us. Could she understand? Was she listening? We really couldn't tell. But as we sang the final verse, her mouth began to form the words; then she joined in with each unforgettable word. What was even more amazing than Myrtle's remembering the lyrics was the fact that she sang a perfect alto. The music may not have landed a record contract, but it was good enough to fill our hearts with enough gratitude and praise to last a lifetime.

Frail children of dust, and feeble as frail,
In Thee do we trust, nor find Thee to fail;
Thy mercies how tender! how firm to the end!
Our Maker, Defender, Redeemer, and Friend.

This hymn includes a powerful four-word summary of the character of our Sovereign God . . . did you catch it?

Our Maker, Defender, Redeemer, and Friend!

Think of it:

- Maker – He created us;
- Defender – the forces of evil melt at the sound of His name;

- Redeemer – the death of His Son was not a ransom too high to pay;
- Friend – a woman too weak to sit up without help could sing about Him—Someone who was, even then, reassuring her of His everlasting presence.[5]

This was their song in the night.

Part of what silences our song in the night is that we refuse to travel up that steep learning curve of suffering.

We complain it's too fast . . . too much . . . too hard . . . too long. But the learning curve of suffering:

- deepens the measure of our faith;
- educates us about the character of God;
- develops in us a longing for the things of God;
- teaches us to desire the future glorification of our bodies;
- causes us to long for the coming kingdom of Christ;
- creates in us a yearning for heaven.

It elevates our thinking from the trivialities of this temporary world to the glory of our Maker . . . Defender . . . Redeemer . . . Friend!

What seems heartless on God's part is actually helping us onward and upward.

No wonder Martin Luther the Reformer would say, "I have found affliction to be one of my best schoolmasters."[6]

"Listen, Job," Elihu counsels:

- "even when life is confusing, God is still communicating;
- even when life seems unfair, God is never unjust;
- even when life seems hard, God is not heartless."

Let's observe one additional truth discovered on the steep ascent of the learning curve.

WHEN LIFE IS UNSETTLED, GOD HAS NOT BEEN UNSEATED

In this last section of Elihu's speech, he will declare two things to Job.

God's Power over Sinners

Earlier, Elihu foretold the terrible end of those who refuse to follow after God. He reminds Job:

> ***"Judgment and justice take hold of you"*** (Job 36:17*b*).

> ***"Beware that wrath does not entice you to scoffing; and do not let the greatness of the ransom turn you aside"*** (Job 36:18).

And what is that end?

> ***"But if they do not hear, they shall perish by the sword and they will die without knowledge"*** (Job 36:12).

"Don't forget, Job . . . God will be exalted in His power over all who challenge His authority. This is the power of God over sinners. But that doesn't exhaust God's power, Job" ***(Job 36:22–23*** paraphrase*)*.

God's Power over Seasons

Warren Wiersbe's outline highlights the weather conditions mentioned here as further proof of God's sovereign and creative control over all His creation:

1. Autumn ***(Job 36:27–37:5)***
2. Winter ***(Job 37:6–10)***
3. Spring ***(Job 37:11–20)***
4. Summer ***(Job 37:14–18)***[7]

If you listed Elihu's declarations of God's control in the weather conditions of our planet, you could easily discern God's detailed control over:

- Evaporation
- Rain
- Clouds
- Thunder
- Lightning
- Flooding

- Ice
- Dew
- and more!

All these elements of nature are not haphazard—they are secondary effects used by God to fulfill His primary and ultimate purposes. This, by the way, is the only *true* comfort to Job, whose children have died in a tornado. That God had a purpose and His purposes are never overruled—not even by Satan himself—is our deepest and most encouraging confidence.

We have a family in our church who had their beautiful home in Cary struck by lightning while they were away. The lightning bolt fried the alarm system, which kept it from issuing a fire alarm. Their home and everything in it burned to the ground.

I went to their property and stood in the front yard the next day. What an eerie sight to see the columns of their front porch still standing, fireplaces at both ends of the house still erect, and a smoldering mountain of ash in the middle where the house had been.

To make matters more difficult, the lightning strike occurred while they were at the hospital with their teenage daughter who had just come out of intensive care. When they got the news that their home was on fire, there was *nothing* they could do.

A few days later, I told them that an earlier edition of my first few sermons on Job had just been printed. We had decided to call it *When Lightning Strikes*, and the cover design (which we kept for this completed commentary) was a bolt of lightning streaking from sky to earth.

Here I was writing about it . . . they were living it. I was preaching it . . . they were experiencing it.

So was Job.

The confidence of this family remains for me a wonderful testimony of trust in their sovereign Lord.

When life is unsettled, God has not been unseated.

"So, Job . . ." Elihu intimates, "stay the course."

PRACTICING WHAT WE'VE LEARNED

We can practice the truth of these four declarations in our own lives.

Is God silent?

Where is He communicating right now? Where is His encouragement being ignored . . . overlooked . . . missed?

Is Life Unfair?

Be reminded that God is never unjust. He will make everything right. That doesn't mean He'll always settle the score on planet Earth. But it does mean that ultimately everything will be made *right* in His righteous judgment preceding the new heaven and new earth *(Revelation 20:11–15)*.

We'll soon discover a fresh definition of "fairness." For if God were fair, none of us would be worthy of experiencing the glory of His coming kingdom.

Is Life Hard?

Even when life is hard, God is not heartless. He's writing new songs for nighttime seasons. The question is not, "Lord, do you have a song for me?" but, "Lord, I am willing to sing the song. Which one will praise You best?"

Is Life Unsettled?

God is still enthroned.

For years I greeted a widow every Sunday morning with, "How are you doing today?" And she always responded, "He is *still* on the throne."

Life may be unsettled, but God has not been unseated.

His is the Kingdom forever and ever; and even now He is seated upon the pinnacle of His universe where He reigns supreme.

Frail children of dust, and feeble as frail,
In Thee do we trust, nor find Thee to fail;
Thy mercies how tender! how firm to the end!
Our Maker, Defender, Redeemer, and Friend.[8]

Then the LORD answered Job out of the whirlwind and said, [2] *"Who is this that darkens counsel by words without knowledge?* [3] *Now gird up your loins like a man, and I will ask you, and you instruct Me!* [4] *Where were you when I laid the foundation of the earth? Tell Me, if you have understanding."*

–Job 38:1–4

CHAPTER TWENTY

FINALLY . . . A WORD FROM GOD

Job 38:1–4

On a cold January day in 1962, a Croatian music teacher named Frane Selak was traveling from Sarajevo to Dubrovnik. The train jumped the tracks and plunged into an icy river, killing seventeen passengers. Selak managed to swim to shore, suffering from hypothermia, a broken arm, shock, and bruises, but happy to be alive.

One year later, he was traveling by plane from Zagreb to Jijeka, when a door blew off and literally sucked him out of the aircraft. A few minutes later the plane crashed, killing all the passengers. Selak, however, woke up in a hospital, having landed in a haystack and sustaining only minor injuries.

In 1966, he was riding on a bus that went off the road into a river. Four people were killed—but not Selak. He suffered only cuts and bruises.

In 1970, he was driving a car that suddenly caught fire. Selak managed to stop and get out just before the fuel tank exploded and engulfed the car in flames.

In 1973, a faulty fuel pump sprayed gas all over the engine while he was driving, blowing flames through the air vents. His only injury: he lost most of his hair. After that, Selak's friends began calling him "Lucky."

In 1995, he was hit by a city bus but received only minor injuries.

In 1996, Selak was driving on a mountain road when he came around a bend and saw a truck coming straight for him. He drove the car through a guardrail, jumped out, landed in a tree—and watched as his car exploded 300 feet below.

In 2003, at the age of seventy-four, Selak bought his first lottery ticket in 40 years . . . and won over a million dollars.

He had become somewhat famous for his narrow escapes, and in 2004, he was hired to star in an Australian television commercial for Doritos. He accepted, but then changed his mind and refused to fly to Sydney for filming. His reason? He said he didn't want to test his luck.[1]

If you lived in ancient times—perhaps no more than 300 years after the flood had covered the earth, creating a new landscape and creating an amazing fossil record that registered worldwide this sudden and traumatic catastrophe—you would have met a man named Job. His nickname would have been anything but "Lucky." In fact, he became a byword for the most unfortunate man alive.

This lack of good fortune was made even more surprising since Job was a righteous, devout follower of God. His worship of God was faithful and sincere.

However, unknown to Job, Satan challenged Job's motive for worship. In fact, Lucifer claimed that mankind would only worship God if He paid them off with good things. So God effectively said, "Take away the good in Job's life and you will see genuine faith."

This began a series of severe trials. Job made no miraculous escapes; he had no soft haystack on which to land or tree to keep him from falling. It took thirty-nine seconds for messengers to deliver the shocking news to Job that he had lost his children, his businesses, and his cattle.

Soon after, Job lost the encouragement of his wife, then his own health to a host of diseases and infirmities that included constant fever, pain, boils, diarrhea, vomiting, itching, loss of appetite and sleep; along with these came deep, unrelenting grief.

Throughout the course of Job's suffering, the heavens have been silent. There has been no word from God.

Some of Job's close friends arrived from afar and sat with him for a week in stunned silence. They then rose, one after the other, to condemn him in speech after speech.

Job endured it all. And while his perspective and patience with God ebbed and flowed, his faith in God remained intact.

Finally, in this dramatic conflict of suffering amid God's silence, the condemning speeches ended. All the men sat quietly, as if utterly exhausted.

It was at this moment that everything changed; for it was then that God spoke.

GOD SPEAKS TO JOB THROUGH CREATION

We have been waiting for this moment for nearly thirty-eight chapters. Job has been waiting for an eternity. *Finally* . . . a word from God:

> ***Then the LORD answered Job*** (Job 38:1*a*).

This speech given by the Lord is the longest that is recorded in Scripture. He will deliver amazing words of comfort but nothing like we would expect. In fact, His speech will entirely surprise the average Christian who has come to expect pat answers and simple solutions.

Note how the voice of God arrives on the scene:

> ***Then the LORD answered Job out of the whirlwind*** (Job 38:1*b*).

What irony that God's voice would come from within the very same thing that took the lives of Job's children. Was it a subtle message that even the devastating effects of natural disasters are not absent the control of God? I believe so, even though God does not call attention to the vehicle of His revelation.

> ***"Now gird up your loins like a man"*** (Job 38:3*a*).

In Job's day, when a man began a difficult physical task or began to run or to fight, he pulled the bottom of his robe between his legs and tucked it into his belt. The Lord is effectively telling Job to get ready for a difficult and challenging task . . . a test.

God says, "I want you to instruct Me, Job; I want you to give *Me* some answers! This will be the toughest pop quiz of your life."

And here's the first question:

"Where were you when I laid the foundation of the earth? Tell Me, if you have understanding" (Job 38:4).

What God is about to do over the course of two speeches is ask Job seventy-seven questions—all about creation.

Before we go any further, I want you to understand what God does *not* do:

- He does not condemn Job.
- He does not apologize for anything that has happened.
- He does not justify His allowances.
- He does not offer an explanation for Job to consider.
- He does not offer one word of sympathy to this grieving man.
- He does not answer the question of suffering in the world.
- He does not explain Satan's accusation or direct involvement in Job's losses.
- He does not explain why bad things happen to good people and why good things happen to bad people.
- He does not provide an explanation—God just points to creation.

Beginning in ***Job 38***, when God begins to speak comfort to Job, He does not answer any questions—He only asks questions. After the first round, Job responds by saying, basically, "I'm not saying anything—because I don't know" ***(Job 40:3–4)***.

This is total humility before God.

Have you ever had a quiz and knew none of the answers? It was not exactly your greatest moment in school, was it?

I had the opportunity some time ago to eat dinner with Dr. Dwight Pentecost, one of my favorite seminary professors.

He laughed when I told him about a moment that I still remember from the time I was in his class The Life of Christ. We used the book he had written entitled *The Words and Works of Jesus Christ*. Dr. Pentecost never used any notes—simply his Bible and his roll book. He had all his lessons memorized.

It was his custom to look at his roll book, call out a random name, and quiz the student on the spot. This was highly intimidating in a class of forty students; we never knew on whom he would call.

One day, Dr. Pentecost looked at his red roll book and said, "Mr. Davey."

I answered, "Yes, sir."

"Would you tell us the significance of Christ's answer to the Pharisees in our text today?"

I didn't know the answer and with Dr. Pentecost, I knew not to bluff. I replied, "I'm sorry, Dr. Pentecost, I don't know the answer."

Without blinking an eye or even looking up, he said, "If you had read your assignment for today, you would have seen the answer on page 278."

This was not exactly a highlight of my seminary career.

Job is going to be taken to school—to a class where he is the only student—and he has just been asked to stand and recite the answers to the Teacher's questions . . . all seventy-seven of them.

God's quiz will cover cosmology, oceanography, meteorology, astronomy, and zoology.

God will ask Job about the depths of the ocean, the measurement of the earth, the origin of and division of light, and the hydrological cycles and atmospheric elements of snow, hail, wind, rain, dew, ice, and frost.

God will question Job about the constellations of Orion and the Pleiades and their movements.

He will ask Job to explain the ways of animals like the lion, horse, raven, deer, wild donkey, ostrich, hawk, and eagle.

God will describe Behemoth and Leviathan and then ask Job if he knows how to control their power.

Job will respond, "Lord, I don't know *any* of the answers."

Is God trying to humiliate Job? No. He is actually attempting to develop in Job greater trust and faith in His power, sovereignty, creative care, and grace.

Think about the fact that here sits a man, devastated and diseased. He has lost his children, his health, his family, and his finances. He is bankrupt, bereaved, and on the edge of irreparable bitterness. And God wants him to think about an ostrich? He wants to take him to the zoo? What kind of help will that give? What kind of answer is *that*?

CREATIONISM AND CHRISTIANITY

God's creation is not an incidental paragraph in a creed but a vital part of Christianity. It is absolutely necessary to our relationship with Christ and our sense of hope when in the midst of trials. Creationism is not a secondary viewpoint—it is a foundational piece of our salvation.

If this sounds like an exaggeration, it is only because the Church has bowed to the pressure of evolution and the disregard of Scripture.

I received an email from a man in our church, and I kept it to illustrate this very point. He wrote,

> My wife especially appreciates Colonial when she has to be away on a Sunday. Yesterday was such a Sunday. She was in Charleston, South Carolina, for the weekend and chose to attend a Congregational church nearby. As it happened, yesterday was "Transfiguration and Evolution Sunday" for that church. You may have read in the newspaper that churches across the country are having "Evolution Sunday" in honor of Charles Darwin's birthday.

This man said in his e-mail that the clergyman actually preached that Jesus' transfiguration was just another step in evolution. He said his wife ended up getting up and walking out during the sermon. Good for her!

The reason the average person is surprised to discover God's comfort through His creative handiwork is because they don't believe God created anything. They believe it all just evolved with enough time and chance, or that God somehow jump-started everything and allowed billions of years for everything to evolve.

Frankly, there is nothing more pivotal than *Genesis 1*. It is against that chapter that Satan has launched his fiercest attack. Theory after theory abound. In fact, by 1808 there were catalogued no less than 80 theories of origins.

Now, even those who claim to be evangelicals are holding to an old earth belief known as "framework hypothesis." This is the belief that the days of creation are overlapping stages of a long evolutionary process. Dr. Meredith Kline of Westminster Theological Seminary has propagated this view in more recent years. The view basically states that some of the "days" of creation in *Genesis 1* are symbolic expressions that have nothing to do with time; it is just poetry. The formation of the earth took billions of years and the record of Scripture is a metaphorical framework that would overlay our scientific understanding of creation. God simply guided the process of evolution.[2]

If *Genesis 1* can be written off as a metaphor because it is too fantastic to take literally, then why believe in the Flood or the Tower of Babel or any other biblical miracle? How outlandish is the Virgin Birth and the Atonement of Christ for sin on a cross?

Defending Creationism is not a secondary issue; it is a vital issue for the believer . . . it's fascinating that creation happens to be the very *first* issue we are exposed to in the Bible.

Without a Literal Six-Day Creation, We Have No Scripture to Trust

One of the best ways to interpret Scripture is to allow Scripture to interpret itself. What does the rest of Scripture say?

The Scriptures repeat the integrity of God's creation of Adam and Eve. The Scriptures do not speak of amoebas that eventually came to be a man and a woman but of the creation of a literal, historical man and his wife.

Jesus Christ Himself said,

> *"But from the beginning of creation, God made them male and female"* (Mark 10:6).

Paul wrote to Timothy,

> *For it was Adam who was first created, and then Eve* (1 Timothy 2:13).

John Wesley wrote, "He created all there is and He didn't even half try."

Every passage of Scripture referring to the Genesis account of creation treats it as a historical, literal event. God is the author of Scripture and He was the only *eyewitness* who saw the first of creation brought out of nothing into existence.

John wrote,

> *In the beginning was the Word, and the Word was with God, and the Word was God. He was in the beginning with God. All things came into being through Him, and apart from Him nothing came into being that has come into being* (John 1:1–3).

Every time the New Testament refers to creation, it always refers to a past, completed event—an immediate work of God, not an ongoing, still-occurring process of evolution.

The entire Old Testament system of Sabbath worship hinged upon a literal understanding of six-day creation.

> *For in six days the LORD made the heavens and the earth, the sea and all that is in them, and rested on the seventh day* (Exodus 20:11*a*).

Without a literal creation, we have no Scripture to fully trust.

Without a Literal Creation, We Have No Gospel to Preach

The apostles preached to the evolutionary pantheists of their day: the Buddhists. Buddhism had already reached the Mediterranean world by the time of Christ. They also preached to the Stoics and Gnostics who believed neither in one supreme personal God nor in a special creation. These were the scholars of their generation.

In one encounter, Paul cried out to these philosophers and scholars, saying,

> "[We] *preach the gospel to you that you should turn from these vain things to a living God, who made the heaven and the earth and the sea and all that is in them*" (Acts 14:15).

In Athens, creationism is part of the Gospel message, as Paul preached,

> [This unknown God is] *the God who made the world and all things in it, since He is Lord of heaven and earth . . . He Himself gives to all people life and breath and all things; and He made from one man every nation of mankind to live on all the face of the earth, having determined their appointed times and the boundaries of their habitation* (Acts 17:24–26).

The intellectual establishment of nearly every nation has repudiated creationism and some theory of evolutionism reigns supreme. The myths of evolution dominate Hinduism, Buddhism, Taoism, Shintoism, and animism. It even creeps into Islam, Judaism, and liberal Christianity.[3]

It is no surprise that Satan would attack the Word of God in this because, without creation, the reliability of Scripture is shattered and our Gospel is rendered powerless.

Without creation, there is no Gospel message.

Consider the fact that if *Genesis 1–3* is not a literal account of origins and Adam really was not the first man and the forefather of the human race, then the Bible's explanation of how sin entered the world is only a myth.

Worse yet, if we did not fall in Adam (our representative), we cannot be redeemed in Christ (the Representative of the redeemed), for Christ is considered the head of a new redeemed race, just as Adam is considered the head of the fallen race.

> *For as in Adam all die, so also in Christ all will be made alive* (1 Corinthians 15:22).

Paul cannot stress this enough as he writes,

> *Therefore, just as through one man sin entered into the world, and death through sin . . . much more did the grace of God and the gift by the grace of the one Man, Jesus Christ, abound to the many. . . . For if by the transgression of the one, death reigned . . . much more those who receive the abundance of grace and of the gift of righteousness will reign in life through the One, Jesus Christ* (Romans 5:12, 15, 17).

Without a literal creation, we have no Scripture to trust. Without a literal creation, we have no Gospel to preach.

Without a Literal Creation, We Have No Heaven to Reach

Evolution eliminates the God of Genesis, and that eliminates the God of Revelation, who comes to recreate a new heaven and a new earth. This is the world to come. The promise of a new creation is portrayed in Scripture as the result of God's powerful word, not a billion-year process.

If you believe by faith, as *Hebrews 11* says, that God created everything out of nothing, then you have no trouble believing that God can suspend the New Jerusalem in the sky above the millennial earth; you have no trouble believing that He can transform your body into an immortal, sinless one that can both eat food and fly.

Heaven is already completed. God does not have huge oysters in heaven working on the gigantic pearls that will one day become the gates of heaven. No, by the word of His mouth, they have already been created.

Christ hinted at His ability to circumvent the normal processes of time in His own miracles. When He healed the lame, they got up and walked. But this was more than just walking—some had been lame from birth. Their nerves sent no messages to their muscles whereby they could, with balance, begin to walk. But Christ not only healed this disease, He deposited instantaneously into their brains and bodies all the necessary wiring, history, muscle memory, and experience necessary to walk *(Matthew 21:14)*.

Christ's healing the blind was an amazing creative act. Inside the human eye are at least 100 million cells. Even with his limited knowledge, Charles Darwin admitted that the human eye caused him to doubt his theory more than anything else.

Approximately seven million cells are cones, each loaded to fire off a message to the brain when a photon of light crosses its path. They are responsible for color vision and work best in relatively bright light. The other cells are called rods and are almost entirely responsible for night vision.

The human brain receives millions of reports simultaneously from eye cells and absorbs, sorts, and organizes them to produce the images that we see.

Christ was demonstrating a fraction of His understanding of human anatomy and the functions that needed restoring and refashioning in order to make someone capable of seeing.

Through Christ, God created the universe, mankind, and the living creatures—all bearing maturity and the ability to function.

On another occasion, Christ revealed this same power when He attended a wedding *(John 2)*. The wine had run out; He told the servants to pour water into the water pots and then to draw some out and take it to the headwaiter. At some point between pouring and drawing, the water turned to wine. All the marks of maturity were there. Christ completely bypassed the fermentation and aging process. He made wine instantly!

In *Mark 6*, Christ invited five thousand people to sit down on a hillside. He was given five loaves of bread and two fish the size of sardines, commonly pickled and eaten with the dry bread to help give the meal some taste. He took those five loaves and two fish and fed five thousand. He did not go fishing. He did not plant wheat and wait for it to grow. He bypassed all the normal processes of time and created fish and bread ready to eat.

John MacArthur wrote,

> When God created the earth and its creatures, there were immediately eagles soaring overhead; elephants roaming around with full tusks appearing to be fifty years old; mountains, rivers, waterfalls and canyons; features that the typical geologist would surmise had been formed by several ages of wind and water and earthquake. But they were made in one day. And when Adam looked up into the heavens and saw that incredible expanse with millions of bright stars, he was seeing light from millions of light-years away—even though these stars had all been there less than four days. The light he saw was itself part of God's creation.[4]

God spoke and it was so.

Job has lost everything. And what will God say to him? "Job, let Me take you on a tour of the created order—from the heavens, to the earth, to the animals."[5]

In the amazing mind of God, He knew that a show-and-tell of creation's magnificence would help settle the heart of a grieving man because it would elevate God to supreme Creator, and Job could find security and hope in his Creator God.

Science is still catching up to the incredible demonstration of God's creative power and design.

The study of DNA has exploded our understanding of the complexity of creation. I have read that one person's DNA has enough information within it to fill six million pages, yet these strands are so small that they could all fit into one ice cube. However, if our DNA were unwound and joined together end to end, the strand would literally stretch from the earth to the sun and back again 400 times.

DNA makes us who we are; this is why we smile like we do and enjoy the taste of certain things and the touch and feel of others. This is the information that makes us unique—so unique that our fingerprints are ours alone. This is the handiwork of our Creator; it gives us all unique meaning, beauty, and purpose.

God created all . . . God knows all . . . God understands all.

Christ with His power to create, bypassing the processes of time and working all things according to His will, has already sat down at the right hand of God's authority, having completed heaven. When John saw heaven in Revelation, it was not under construction . . . the heavenly city was completed.

LESSONS FROM GOD'S SPEECH

A college student went to class to take a final exam at the end of the semester. To his amazement he did not know the answer to any of the questions. Not one! He knew that he had no possibility of passing the exam, so he attempted to win his professor's mercy with humor. Across the top of the exam page he wrote, "Only God knows the answer to these questions; Merry Christmas!" He turned in the paper and went home for the Christmas break. During the holidays, the student received in the mail his exam that had been graded by his professor. At the top, it read in big letters, "In that case, God's grade is 100 and yours is 0; Happy New Year!"[6]

Job is going to be asked seventy-seven questions—and they will reveal he has none of the answers but that God is in control of everything.

Several lessons emerge from God's pop quiz to Job.

If God Created Us, He Can Save Us

What the evolutionists destroy for themselves is the only personal God capable of taking them and, by His grace, making them a new *creation.* Instantly they would be newly born; a member of a new race—redeemed!

The God capable of fashioning us is capable of forgiving us.

If God Created the Universe, He Can Control the Universe

Job would have wondered about this, but he will be reassured.

If God Created This Existing Universe, He Can Create an Eternal Universe

What we are about to discover as God begins to speak comfort is that the solution to suffering is not a proposition; not an answer; not an explanation. Ultimately and finally, it is a Person.

> *Therefore, those also who suffer according to the will of God shall entrust their souls to a faithful Creator in doing what is right* (1 Peter 4:19).

Our hope when suffering is bound up in the truth that God is Creator. God created all there is. He controls all that He created. God synchronizes what He controls to bring about His eternal concerns.

We can trust Him. Why? Because *He* is the Creator God.

*Then the LORD answered Job out of the whirlwind and said, [2]"Who is this
that darkens counsel by words without knowledge? [3]Now gird up your loins
like a man, and I will ask you, and you instruct Me! [4]Where were you when I
laid the foundation of the earth? Tell Me, if you have understanding, [5]who set
its measurements? Since you know. Or who stretched the line on it? [6]On what
were its bases sunk? Or who laid its cornerstone, [7]when the morning stars sang
together and all the sons of God shouted for joy? [8]Or who enclosed the sea with
doors when, bursting forth, it went out from the womb; [9]when I made a cloud its
garment and thick darkness its swaddling band, [10]and I placed boundaries on it
and set a bolt and doors, [11]and I said, 'Thus far you shall come, but no farther;
and here shall your proud waves stop'? [12]Have you ever in your life commanded
the morning, and caused the dawn to know its place, [13]that it might take hold
of the ends of the earth, and the wicked be shaken out of it? [14]It is changed like
clay under the seal; and they stand forth like a garment. [15]From the wicked their
light is withheld, and the uplifted arm is broken. [16]Have you entered into the
springs of the sea or walked in the recesses of the deep? [17]Have the gates of death
been revealed to you, or have you seen the gates of deep darkness? [18]Have you
understood the expanse of the earth? Tell Me, if you know all this."*

–Job 38:1–18

CHAPTER TWENTY-ONE

WATER, EARTH, AND SKY

Job 38:1–18

Perhaps the best known scientific celebrity of the past couple of decades was Carl Sagan. He was a renowned astronomer, not to mention an antagonistic atheist who seemed bent on destroying any belief in theism and biblical creationism. He became the leading voice for naturalism: the belief that everything has a natural cause and a natural explanation.

> Sagan's tribe has increased over the years. One religious leader made an attempt to explain away the miracle of Jesus walking on water by postulating that Christ was walking on floating pieces of ice. How does anyone suggest that and keep a straight face? Instead of walking on the waves of the storm, Jesus was evidently surfing on pieces of floating ice over to the disciples' boat—and none of that is a miracle?
>
> This is naturalism. It is the twin sister of evolution: that all there is can be explained by natural processes. However, these systems of belief require faith—faith in the universe itself. It is not surprising then that Carl Sagan was led to give the universe divine attributes. These are the words he repeated on

> his show that aired on television each week: "The universe is all that is, or ever was, or ever will be."
>
> All the scientists in the world, including Carl Sagan, could never scientifically measure all that was, and all that is, and all that is to come. But it does not matter; they will take the leap of faith and attribute omniscience and omnipotence to the universe—to Mother Nature. She gives life; she orders life; she created all there is.
>
> This is nothing less than the religion of nature. This is the deification of the universe. It really does not get rid of an omniscient eternal being, it just changes who that being is.
>
> Sagan looked at the universe and came to the conclusion that nothing was greater than what he saw.[1]

If you fell asleep seventy-five years ago and woke up today to learn of our politically correct views regarding origins, the evolution of man, and the deification of nature, you would be convinced that our intelligence is not developing forward but digressing backward.

The Apostle Paul informs us that this digression, in any culture, would cast off the Creator and deify creation. So today, for people in our world to consider a tree or the sun to be self-conscious relatives of the human race is simply another step backward.

Two recent reports on National Public Radio were related to a journalistic contest that invited articles on a person's values and beliefs.

One elderly retired woman who went to a mainline Protestant church most of her life wrote:

> I am sitting on our small deck knitting and resting old legs, entertained by my spiritual sister, an equally old pine tree. She is at least as old as I am. She leans a bit; so do I. We both soak in the sun and the air and are trying our best to live lightly in our worlds. One day in the not too distant future, she will fall and fertilize the earth, and so will I. It is a consoling thought. I have lost my traditional heaven and hell beliefs . . . there

> are those who want to give my life more importance than the tree, but I don't believe them. They think there is a special place for me somewhere for eternity, but I don't believe them. I believe my tree and all other living things believe and feel in their particular living way.[2]

Another author—this one a published poet and professor at the University of New Mexico—writes in her article dated July 8, 2007:

> I believe in the sun. In the tangle of human failures of fear, greed, and forgetfulness, the sun gives me clarity. The sun is our relative and illuminates our path on this earth. Humans are vulnerable and rely on the kindnesses of the earth and the sun.
>
> One day recently, I walked out of a hotel room just off Times Square at dawn to find the sun. It was the fourth morning since the birth of my fourth granddaughter. I had bundled up the baby and carried her outside. I held her up and presented her to the sun, so she would be recognized as a relative, so that she wouldn't forget this connection, this promise, so that we all remember the sacredness of life.[3]

How tragic not to understand that to give the sun the attributes of God is to *undermine* the sacredness of life. Apart from God, mankind becomes nothing more than an animal with no more dignity than a pine tree.

Paul warned that the unbeliever *becomes futile in his speculations, and his foolish heart is darkened . . . he suppress the truth of a Creator and elevates creation* (Romans 1:21–25 paraphrase).

In 1996, Carl Sagan died. Less than three weeks before he died, he was interviewed by Ted Koppel on "Nightline."

> Sagan knew he was dying and Koppel asked him, "Dr. Sagan, do you have any pearls of wisdom that you would like to give to the human race?" To this, Sagan responded bleakly, "We live on a hunk of rock and metal circling a humdrum star that is one of 400 billion other stars in the Milky Way . . . this

> is well worth pondering. Our planet is a speck in the great enveloping cosmic dark. In our obscurity, in all this vastness, there is no hint that help will come from elsewhere to save us from ourselves."[4]

Is that his pearl of wisdom?! Yes, because the religion of naturalism, the faith bound up in evolution, and even the mystical reach of pantheism lead ultimately to the lonely insignificance of humanity. All of which then naturally lead to despair. All that we and the trees are going to do is die, fall over, and fertilize a plot of ground.

If only Carl Sagan had read Job. There *is* help! There *is* hope!

God eventually speaks to Job and the encounter we have longed for and fully expected has come to pass.

The amazing thing is that God begins by giving Job a lesson on creationism, not suffering. Instead of answering Job's questions about why bad things happen to good people and good things happen to bad people, God reveals His power and providence over all that He created.

Evidently, to the mind of God, understanding that He alone is the Creator of all that is brings a person back from the edge of despair, utter insignificance, and bitterness, and breathes new perspective and fresh faith into their heart.

These chapters of Job are for believers. They will not breathe faith into the unredeemed; they will only breathe more skepticism and more unbelief. However, for those of us who believe, this tour around God's universe will bolster our faith and give us fresh new joy in the greatness and glory of God—which then has a way of settling our fears and quieting our heart.

> *Thou wilt keep him in perfect peace, whose mind is stayed on Thee* (Isaiah 26:3 KJV).

God speaks to Job out of the whirlwind:

> ***"Where were you when I laid the foundation of the earth? Tell me, if you have understanding, who set its measurements? Since you know. Or who stretched the line on it? On what were its bases sunk? Or who laid its cornerstone, when the morning stars sang together and all the sons of God shouted for joy?"*** (Job 38:4–7).

You'll notice that God does not begin four chapters of a response by proving to Job that He was the one who created the earth. He just begins in these verses with the reminder that Job wasn't there when He did it!

God was the only eyewitness to the beginning. Because of special revelation—the inspired Scripture we hold in our hands—we have been given the only eyewitness account of the beginning of time, and it comes from the Author/Creator Himself.

It was Herbert Spencer, the philosopher and early enthusiastic advocate of Darwin, who outlined five scientific ideas that he believed categorized everything that science could investigate. These were time, force, action, space, and matter.

Spencer believed that everything that could be known could fit into one of these five categories.

> As with all naturalistic, dead-end theories, he had to give at least one of these categories eternality, since no evolutionary process could account for the origin of any of them. At least one of them must be eternal in order to spawn the other four. Even though Spencer could not account for the origin of time, force, action, space, and matter, he believed correctly that these five can categorize everything.
>
> In the opening lines of God's special revelation, *Genesis 1:1*, we actually have the origin of all five of Spencer's categories:
>
> 1. In the **beginning** – time;
> 2. In the beginning, **God** – force;
> 3. In the beginning, God **created** – action;
> 4. In the beginning, God created the **heavens** – space;
> 5. In the beginning, God created the heavens and the **earth** – matter.
>
> In these few opening words, God reveals the origin of everything.[5]

Nehemiah, the rebuilder of Jerusalem, prayed,

> *"You alone are the LORD. You made the heavens, even the highest heavens, and all their starry host, the earth and all that is on*

it, the seas and all that is in them. You give life to everything" (Nehemiah 9:6 NIV).

EARTH

"Where were you when I laid the foundation of the earth? . . . set its measurements? . . . stretched the line on it? On what were its bases [foundations] ***sunk? Or who laid its cornerstone?"*** (Job 38:4–6).

God is speaking in the language of an architect and builder. The site for the building was traced or surveyed. A measuring line was stretched out to ensure the exact measurements were followed. Who made sure the foundations were dug and the block laid correctly and the cornerstone squarely?

In other words, "Job, were you there to check My blueprints? Did I need you or anyone to make sure the precise measurements necessary for the sustaining of life were followed?"

Job had already delivered this staggering truth:

"He stretches out the north over the empty space and hangs the earth on nothing" (Job 26:7).

God did not do this on the back of a huge turtle or an elephant or on the shoulders of Atlas. He did it on nothing.

Job is revealing amazing scientific truth. The north-pointing axis of the earth is extended indefinitely beyond the boundaries of the earth's surface, pointing to the polar star and orienting both the geography of the earth and the stars in the heavens.

One believing scientist wrote,

> Job is telling us not only that the earth was suspended in space, but also that it rotates about its north projecting axis, maintained in its orbit by a mysterious force we call gravity, which could just as rationally be called *nothing*—or perhaps better yet, the will of God.[6]

Since no human being was there to see God do this, we either believe the record of God or come up with our own manmade theory.

In John MacArthur's book *Battle for the Beginning*, he writes of one popular theory known as the big bang. Scientists who hold to the big bang theory must explain how a universe full of matter appeared out of nowhere in an instant. An article in the *Los Angeles Times* reported:

> The big bang theory is looking more supernatural all the time. About twenty years ago, the late Carl Sagan famously said that big bang science would eventually show that the universe was created without any creator. Since then, the picture has changed quite a bit. Now there is a growing theory within big bang thinking called cosmic inflation, which holds that the entire universe popped out of a point with no content and no dimensions, expanding instantaneously to its current size. Now being taught at Stanford, the Massachusetts Institute of Technology, and other top schools, this explanation of the beginning of the universe bears haunting similarity to the traditional theological notion of creation "out of nothing."

This article quoted one of the world's foremost astronomers Allan Sandage of the Observatories of the Carnegie Institution in Pasadena, California, who recently proposed that the big bang could only be understood as "a miracle," in which some higher force must have played a role.[7]

Can you imagine being Carl Sagan . . . dead for less than 20 years before MIT and the Carnegie Institute effectively nullify your theory saying, "The big bang doesn't *remove* the necessity of a divine being, it *reveals* the necessity for an original cause."

The truth remains, if we want to know how the world began, we must get the information from the only source who can tell us. No human observed the process, and no human can repeat the process.[8]

Notice that there were other eyewitnesses to the details of earth's creation:

> ***"When the morning stars sang together and all the sons of God shouted for joy"*** (Job 38:7).

In ***Job 1, the sons of God*** is a reference to angels who came to present themselves to Him, and Satan was among them.

This is poetic parallelism; ***the morning stars*** are the same individuals as ***the sons of God***.

In fact, according to the account given in *Genesis 1*, the physical stars we see in the sky were not created until the fourth day.

Exodus 20 adds to the testimony of *Genesis 1* that all things were created during the six days of creation. So angels were not created eons before *Genesis 1*.

For angels to be able to rejoice over the creation of the earth on day three, according to ***Job 38***, we can safely assume—though we are not specifically told—that angels were created during the first day of creation, along with light.

This host of heaven was created fully capable and willing to sing the glories of their Creator God. In the same way that Adam and Eve were created fully grown and mature, capable of communicating, worshiping, and carrying out their God-given assignments, the angels were created fully capable and ready to sing and serve at their Creator's bidding.

John Hartley wrote in his New International Commentary on Job,

> In ancient times, the laying of a foundation stone for a public building such as a temple was a high occasion and was commemorated by a celebration with music and praise. God informs Job in chapter 38 that on the occasion of laying earth's cornerstone, the angels were assembled as an angelic chorus to sing praises to God the Creator for the glory of His world.[9]

This would also mean that at some point between day one and the temptation of Eve in the garden of Eden, Satan would try to seize the throne of God as he led an uprising which resulted in the fall of millions of angels—still led to this day by Lucifer, whose destruction is ever nearer.

SEA

God moves now from questions regarding the origin of earth to questions regarding the sea.

> ***"Or who enclosed the sea with doors when, bursting forth, it went out from the womb?"*** (Job 38:8).

Several ancient Near Eastern myths attempt to explain the origin of the sea. A few myths like the Enuma Elish from Babylon and the Baal Cycle from Ugarit recount the fierce battle in which their supreme deity won his right to rule by defeating the sea god. Epic battles took place for the gods and/or goddesses to conquer the sea.[10]

In total contrast to mythical thought, the sea in ***Job 38*** is spoken of as a newborn infant ***(v. 8)***, on which God put a diaper of darkness and pajamas made of clouds ***(v. 9)***. He then put it in a playpen designed by Himself and put up a baby gate ***(v. 10)***. He placed restrictions to which the sea immediately submitted ***(v. 11)***, for God said, ***"'Thus far you shall come, but no farther; and here shall your proud waves stop.'"***[11]

We know that our Creator has instituted all the necessary secondary causes to keep the tides consistent with His plan to care for the ecosystems of our world.

Science has discovered the amazing effect of the moon upon our ocean tides. They are caused by the moon's gravitational pull.

> The moon circles the earth and completes a full orbit around the earth every 27.3 days, traveling a distance of almost a million and a half miles each month. As the moon orbits the earth, it causes the earth to swell ever so slightly. The earth actually bulges out toward the moon, and this is what affects the water level of the oceans. As the earth rotates on its axis, these bulges move across the face of the earth creating two high and two low tides every day. Just this one characteristic of planet Earth and its bodies of water is absolutely vital to sustaining life on it. Scientists have now spent nearly twenty billion dollars trying to answer the question of how the moon evolved. The record of Scripture tells us it was accomplished by the creative power and word of God on the fourth day.[12]

Job is reminded by God ***(Job 38:8–11)*** that the movement and boundaries of bodies of water are determined and directed, even in their ebb and flow, by His creative handiwork.

God now moves from questions about the earth ***(Job 38:4–7)*** and questions about the sea ***(Job 38:8–11)*** to questions about the sky ***(Job 38:12–15)***.

SKY

> ***"Have you ever in your life commanded the morning, and caused the dawn to know its place?"*** (Job 38:12).

"Hey, Job, have you ever created a new day?"

One author provoked my thinking regarding this question by bringing up the context of Job's ancient world. On the first day of creation, God commanded the light into existence *(Genesis 1:3–5)*. Each dawn thereafter was considered a reenactment of that first day. The ancients did not view nature as a system of mechanical laws; did not consider the succession of days guaranteed, but believed that God spoke each new day into existence.[13]

God is virtually asking, "Job, can you call into existence the miracle of light? Can you create a new day?"

Of course the answer is no.

Today we understand that the heavenly bodies of light—primarily the sun—were created by God in the heavens on the fourth day, and the precise tilt of the earth's axis and the exact makeup of the sun create new dawns and dark nights.

God's perfect handiwork is an amazing thing to consider.

We've come to learn that the rotation of the earth on its axis is what determines a twenty-four hour day. The moon's orbits around the earth determine our months. And the earth's revolutions around the sun determine our years.

Even the precise tilt of the earth's axis is vital in maintaining earth's seasons. One author wrote,

> Imagine how different life would be if the earth suddenly began rotation at one-third its current speed. Days would be three times longer. We would be forced to stagger our sleep so that sometimes we would sleep during sunlight hours and remain awake during long hours of darkness. The variation in daytime and nighttime temperatures would be dramatically

> altered. Every rhythm of our lives would be overthrown. But all life on earth is perfectly suited to a twenty-four hour day, and according to Scripture, that is because the same Creator who made all living things also determined and fixed the length of our days.[14]

Charles Boyle, a brilliant thinker and devoted Christian, was fascinated with Kepler's and Newton's discoveries about planetary motion and the intricate design of the universe. Boyle hired a watchmaker to design an actual working mechanical model of the solar system that demonstrated the motion of the planets around the sun. They all moved according to the pattern of their orbit. It was an incredible display of skill and precision. On one occasion Boyle was showing the model to an atheistic scientist, who was very impressed with the clockwork model. The atheist said, "This is a very impressive model. Who made it for you?" Boyle responded with a grin, "No one made it . . . it just happened."[15]

> *By the word of the LORD the heavens were made, and by the breath of His mouth all their host* [stars and planets]. *He gathers the waters of the sea together as a heap; He lays up the deeps in storehouses. Let all the earth fear the LORD; let all the inhabitants of the world stand in awe of Him. For He spoke, and it was done; He commanded, and it stood fast. . . . The counsel of the LORD stands forever, the plans of His heart from generation to generation* (Psalm 33:6–9, 11).

Earth, water, and sky were all created by the word of the Lord and the breath of His mouth.

The response of every believer should be to stand in awe of Him!

We find our hope in Him. We find our peace and joy in Him. We find the answer to our questions in Him. We find our future securely held in His hand.

The angels who rejoiced at the creation of the earth celebrate at the conversion of every sinner and the new creation of a believer in Christ. They will also sing around the throne of God, along with all the redeemed, as we praise this Creator God who has set us free forever.

And those who do not believe? They continue in their ever-increasing panic to find an answer other than God.

One well respected physicist wrote an article published in the *Wall Street Journal*:

> The latest data from space satellites are unmistakable; the universe will eventually die. As the universe accelerates, temperatures will plunge throughout the universe. Billions of years from now, the stars will have exhausted their nuclear fuel, the oceans will freeze, the sky will become totally dark, and the universe will consist of dead neutron stars, black holes, and nuclear debris. It seems as if the iron laws of physics have issued a death warrant. But there's still one [hope]. Leave the universe itself. Do the laws of physics allow for the creation of wormholes connecting our universe to a younger, more hospitable universe? In 2021, a new space probe will be launched which may be able to prove or disprove these conjectures. There is no choice. Either we leave for another universe, or we die in this one.[16]

He has the right idea; we need to leave this universe for another one. He just doesn't know how to make the getaway.

And he's right in another way: planet Earth and the universe around us will not last forever.

Again, the revelation of God, which informs us about the origins of this world, also tells us about the *destruction* of this world. Peter writes these astonishing words that not only agree with the record of Genesis and Job, but give further revelation about the future:

> [B]*y the word of God the heavens existed long ago and the earth was formed out of water and by water, through which the world at that time was destroyed, being flooded with water. But by His word the present heavens and earth are being reserved for fire, kept for the day of judgment and destruction of ungodly men. . . . because of which the heavens will be destroyed by burning, and the elements will melt with intense heat! But according to*

> *His promise we are looking for new heavens and a new earth, in which righteousness dwells* (2 Peter 3:5–7; 12–13).

We really *do* need to leave this earth; a gateway has been built from this world to the next. However, it is a narrow gateway and not many people are willing to stoop to enter it.

Perhaps you already have entered or will today, by God's redeeming grace. When you come to God in awe of who He is and what His Son accomplished for you on the cross and through that empty tomb, you will surely leave this earth one day and inherit a new earth and a new universe. You will live with all the believers of all the ages and all the hosts of heaven and with our Creator God forever.

Make your reservation through faith in Jesus Christ, and rest assured that you will soon leave this world and enjoy a new world . . . a coming, new creation that will last forever.

19 *“Where is the way to the dwelling of light? And darkness, where is its place,*
20 *that you may take it to its territory and that you may discern the paths to its*
home? 21 *You know, for you were born then, and the number of your days is great!*
22 *Have you entered the storehouses of the snow, or have you seen the storehouses of*
the hail, 23 *which I have reserved for the time of distress, for the day of war and*
battle? 24 *Where is the way that the light is divided, or the east wind scattered on*
the earth? 25 *Who has cleft a channel for the flood, or a way for the thunderbolt,*
26 *to bring rain on a land without people, on a desert without a man in it,* 27 *to*
satisfy the waste and desolate land and to make the seeds of grass to sprout? 28 *Has*
the rain a father? Or who has begotten the drops of dew? 29 *From whose womb has*
come the ice? And the frost of heaven, who has given it birth? 30 *Water becomes*
hard like stone, and the surface of the deep is imprisoned. 31 *Can you bind the*
chains of the Pleiades, or loose the cords of Orion? 32 *Can you lead forth a constel-*
lation in its season, and guide the Bear with her satellites? 33 *Do you know the*
ordinances of the heavens, or fix their rule over the earth? 34 *Can you lift up your*
voice to the clouds, so that an abundance of water will cover you? 35 *Can you send*
forth lightnings that they may go and say to you, ‘Here we are’? 36 *Who has put*
wisdom in the innermost being or given understanding to the mind? 37 *Who can*
count the clouds by wisdom, or tip the water jars of the heavens, 38 *when the dust*
hardens into a mass and the clods stick together?”

–Job 38:19–38

CHAPTER TWENTY-TWO

LORD OF ALL THE WEATHER

Job 38:19–38

In the late 1970s, a book was published that created a phenomenal and somewhat unexpected following. In fact, to this day, the number of devotees from *Star Wars* to *Lord of the Rings* cannot come close to matching those of this particular book.

Alex Haley was the author of a fictional book entitled *Roots*, which became a record-breaking television mini-series, watched by 130 million people.

> In Haley's loosely told family history, he begins with the story of Kunta Kinte—who seven generations earlier in 1767 was kidnapped in Gambia and transported to the Province of Maryland to be sold as a slave. The novel follows the story of Kunta and succeeding generations.
>
> While doing his research, Alex Haley went to the village of Jufureh, where Kunta Kinte grew up and which is in existence to this day; he listened to a tribal historian tell the story of Kunta's capture and abduction from home. Haley also traced the records of the ship *The Lord Ligonier*, which he said carried his ancestor to America.

> The most emotional moment of Haley's life was on September 29, 1967, when he stood at the site in Annapolis, Maryland, where his ancestor had arrived two hundred years before.
>
> *Roots* has been published in thirty-seven languages and Haley won a special Pulitzer prize in 1997. There are many people—both black and white—who doubt the historicity of *Roots*. In fact, Alex Haley had to settle out of court on charges of plagiarizing another author. My point is not whether everything Haley said was true or original. My point is the remarkable response of people around the world. When the book was aired in mini-series format on television, more than 60 percent of Americans tuned in. What was the reason for this incredible interest? For starters, *Roots* emphasized that African Americans have a long history and not all of that history is lost, as many believed. But the popularity of this series obviously crossed racial divides. Why? It spoke to the human heart's desire and longing to connect with the past.[1]

One author wrote, "This man's link to his past gave a sense of meaning to us all."[2]

This is really a search for dignity and value, is it not? Our search for roots is ultimately a search for the meaning of life.

R. C. Sproul wrote,

> If our past history tells us that we have emerged from the slime, that we are only grown up germs, what difference can it possibly make whether we are black germs or white germs; whether we are free germs or enslaved germs? Who cares? We can sing of the dignity of man, but unless that dignity is rooted in that which has intrinsic value, all our songs of human rights and dignity are so much whistling in the dark. If all you have is the present—with no history—there is no dignity, only nothingness.[3]

No wonder mankind on every continent, regardless of race, nationality, or creed asks the same questions: "Who am I?"; "Where did I come from?"; "Do I really matter?"

It is no surprise to find that genealogical studies have skyrocketed in the past thirty years. There are, on average, more than a thousand hits every minute of every day on websites dealing with genealogical resources.

Tens of millions of people are involved in tracing their own roots to discover where *they* came from. It is an attempt to help discover who they are and where they might be heading.

Fortunately, we who have trusted Christ have been given the ultimate resource in genealogical studies. We know the names of our ancestors, beginning with the first ancestor who started the entire family tree—Adam. Our value is rooted in history and revealed to us by God.

What tragic confusion abounds, not only about our past but about our future, when the inspired genealogical resource is tossed aside.

I read the National Public Radio transcript of an interview with singer Mary Chapin Carpenter who had the hit song "Grand Central Station." She said in the interview that she was inspired by an iron worker who had been on the scene when the towers fell on 9/11. He worked at Ground Zero for days afterward. At the end of each shift, he felt compelled to go to the train station so that the souls of the victims could follow him. Carpenter said, "He'd find himself just going to Grand Central Station and standing on the platform and thinking whoever wanted to go home could catch the train home."[4]

This was her inspiration. How tragic. How hopeless. How meaningless.

If our past is disconnected from the revelation of God, then not only is our past meaningless, but our future is equally pointless. We are just souls floating around hoping to land someplace better than this.

God has spoken in His Word. In fact, He speaks to one of our ancestors named Job, who was wondering about the value of his life. He informs Job of his roots. He takes Job on a verbal tour of the origins of the universe, this planet, and life itself.

The tour reveals that our history has its roots in the hands of God. And our future has its hope in the hands of God.

As God speaks to Job, He continues to reveal His creative mastery over the present conditions of Job's world—and ours. He asks Job one unanswerable question after another.

> ***"Have you understood the width of the earth?"*** (Job 38:18*a*).

Job did not. We do. Planet Earth has:

- approximately 57 million square miles of land surface;
- approximately 139 million square miles of water surface;
- an equatorial circumference of 24,902 miles.

The point God is making is *not* that these questions are unanswerable by Job. It is to bring Job to the rather obvious realization that not only does he not understand all of God's creative handiwork—he can't even control what he *does* understand. He, and we, cannot control the weather.

Can we control the rain? Can anyone make the frost or bring us snow on December 24 . . . and make sure it melts two days later? The only person who could control the weather by His own power was Christ, who walked on water and allowed Peter to do the same *(Matthew 14)*. Christ could say to the raging storm, "Be still," and not only did the waves cease their churning, but the raging wind immediately became calm *(Mark 4:39)*.

God, in the remaining verses of ***Job 38***, will not only reveal His creation of origins and history but His control over the present conditions of weather. He will take Job on a verbal tour of a dozen things relative to weather conditions.

LIGHT AND DARKNESS

> ***"Where is the way to the dwelling of light? And darkness, where is its place, that you may take it to its territory and that you may discern the paths to its home?"*** (Job 38:19–20).

One author wrote,

> Perhaps nothing in all of physics is more fascinating or more mysterious than light. Light is the single most important source of energy and heat on earth. Without light, life on

> earth would be impossible for very long. Virtually all the earthly mechanisms we depend on for the transfer of energy are derived, ultimately, from light. Wind, the water cycle, and ocean waves would all cease if the earth were to remain in utter darkness for very long. The earth would quickly turn cold and all life would cease.[5]

Is it any wonder that the first creative order from God and the starting point of creation was,

> *Then God said, "Let there be light"; and there was light* (Genesis 1:3).

Now the record of Genesis informs us that the light sources of sun, moon, and stars were not created until the fourth day. So, the form of this light in the verse above, as God's early act of creation, is unknown to us. It might have been a light that emanated from a specific God-ordained place or, perhaps, it was the disclosure of His own Shekinah glory.

It should not be difficult for us to believe that the One whose glory is described as pure light can command light to appear. In fact, the Book of Revelation says that in heaven there will be no need for the sun to shine because the light will be provided, *for the glory of God has illumined it, and its lamp is the Lamb* (Revelation 21:23).

The more we discover about light and harness it, the more amazing possibilities are opened.

Light gives us the ability to heat a cup of coffee in the microwave; listen to radio waves; get burned at the beach with ultraviolet rays; get checked out by the doctor through x-rays; get held up at the airport by security scans.

We have all seen crews laying pipe along the roads through which fiber optic cables will be laid. Fiber optic messages move along tiny pulses of light at, literally, the speed of light with pinpoint precision. These pulses are basically rapidly flashing on-and-off signals, carrying everything from digitized telephone calls to video images. All of this is possible because of the marvelous properties of light.[6]

Your eyeglasses change the direction of light so precisely that you can see images better because of them.

How did this amazing thing called light come to be?

God said,

> "[I am] *the One forming light and creating darkness"* (Isaiah 45:7*a*).

Look at a rather futuristic clue about light that God revealed to Job:

> ***"Where is the way that the light is divided?"*** (Job 38:24*a*).

We now know that the different colors of light are simply varying wavelengths of light in the spectrum. In 1665, Sir Isaac Newton discovered that the prism was not coloring the light but was simply dividing the light into its varying wavelengths.

Prisms separate the colors of light because as the light passes through the prism, its direction is bent. Different color waves, moving then at different speeds, come out of the prism separated into a visible display.[7]

David writes,

> *You have prepared the light and the sun* (Psalm 74:16*b*).

> *You make the dawn and the sunset shout for joy* (Psalm 65:8*b*).

Now, we would normally take this as poetic personification. The dawn and the sunset are visual, not audible. Suerly they do not produce *literal* music?!

Could God be revealing through David something we have yet to discover—that light actually sings?

Well, if light and heat and sound are vibrations—wave and particle—the mere existence of color may have a musical harmony we have yet to hear.[8]

Would it not be fascinating to discover and hear, for the first time, this symphony of light?

"Job, you have no idea about the elements of light and darkness which I have created," God says.

Neither do we.

WATER

God mentions forms of water varied by weather conditions.

> ***"Have you entered the storehouses of the snow, or have you seen the storehouses of the hail, which I have reserved for the time of distress?"*** (Job 38:22–23*a*).

God could be referring to one of His plagues; He sent hail to devastate the land of Egypt *(Exodus 9:18–35).*

Perhaps this is a reference to the time God protected His people by sending hail upon the invading armies *(Joshua 10:11).*

It may be a reference to the final judgment of God during the tribulation period when, as John writes,

> *And huge hailstones, about one hundred pounds each, came down from heaven upon men; and men blasphemed God because of the plague of the hail, because its plague was extremely severe* (Revelation 16:21).

The production of water is one of God's marvelous creations. Without it we would not be able to live. In fact, we would not exist.

> The human body has been called a water machine, designed primarily to run on water and minerals. In just the last ten years, medical science has begun to focus more on the healing ability of our body and its dependence on water. The human body is made up of over 70 percent water. Our blood is more than 80 percent water; our brain is over 75 percent water. The function of every cell in our body is controlled by electrical signals sent through our nervous system from the brain. Our nerves, in reality, are an elaborate system of tiny waterways.[9]

This is just the beginning.

"Job, have you ever thought about water in so many different forms? What about snow, when cold temperatures turn its molecules into crystals of lovely and varied form?"

Why do snowflakes have such intricate beauty and symmetry? Why do they not all look alike?

What did Job understand when he said that God ***"imparted weight to the wind and meted out*** [weighed] ***the waters by measure"*** (Job 28:25)?

We, today, have an entire science (hydrology) devoted to water; it is the study of the occurrence and behavior of water.

We now know that the global weights of air and water must be in critical relationship to each other in order to maintain life on earth. In fact, if the weights of either air or water were much different, life as we know it could not survive. Planet Earth was uniquely designed for life.

By the way, this passage also informs us that air and wind have ***weight***. This was not confirmed until nearly four thousand years after Job spoke these words.

The study of air and its weight has developed into the science of aerodynamics, which became the basis for aerospace developments.

> "[Who brings] ***rain on a land without people, on a desert without a man in it, to satisfy the waste and desolate land and to make the seeds of grass to sprout?"*** (Job 38:26–27).

"Job, can you explain how we get rain?"

Job could not, and we cannot fully explain it. We know that water is converted by solar energy into the vapor state. Since water vapor is lighter than air, it rises and then condenses around dust particles and salt particles. We're not sure how, but water droplets bind together to form larger and larger drops, which finally become so large that their weight is greater than the wind, causing them to fall to the ground as rain or hail or snow.

Look at God's words to Job:

> ***"Who can count the clouds by wisdom"*** (Job 38:37*a*)

In other words, "I know the weight of the air and keep it balanced by My wisdom."

> "[Who can] ***tip the water jars of the heavens, when the dust hardens into a mass and the clods stick together?"*** (Job 38:37*b*–38).

God is delivering truth that will take centuries for us to discover.

There is more mystery, however, in rain than we can understand. One scientist asked, "What causes the small droplets to join with others and become large enough to do this? Some clouds—or rain—fall, while others grow dark and heavy but do not." Job gives the answer, which only the believer will appreciate: "[God] ***made a decree for the rain, and a way for the lightning of the thunder"*** (Job 28:26).[10]

In other words, God makes it rain.

Henry Morris writes,

> With the right combination of air turbulence and clouds, the complex forces generate an electrical field that produces lightning discharges and these violent electrical currents, in a complex energy exchange we do not yet fully understand, cause the small water droplets to bind together with others to form larger drops that then become too heavy to remain in the clouds and fall to the thirsty ground.[11]

God said centuries ago to Job,

> ***"Who has cleft a channel for the flood, or a way for the thunderbolt*** [literally: the lightning of thunder]***, to bring rain?"*** (Job 38:25–26*a*).

"Job, My handiwork uses everything from vapor to lightning to bring rain." I love how *The Message* paraphrases this paragraph:

> *"Have you ever traveled to where snow is made, seen the vault where hail is stockpiled, the arsenals of hail and snow that I keep in readiness for times of trouble and battle and war? Can you find your way to where lightning is launched, or to the place from which the wind blows? Who do you suppose carves canyons for the downpours of rain, and charts the route of thunderstorms that bring water to unvisited fields, deserts no one ever lays eyes on, drenching the useless wastelands so they're carpeted with wildflowers and grass? And who do you think is the father of rain and dew, the mother of ice and frost? You don't for a minute imagine these marvels of weather just happen, do you?"*

This display was intended to reveal to Job that God not only created everything, but He controls everything. He has established the laws of hydrology which water the earth and make life possible.

This is God's doing; this is His providence.

> David McKenna, the former president of Asbury Theological Seminary, recalled a television show he watched in which a panel of economists were asked a final question and supplied an interesting answer. The question was, "What is the greatest influence upon world economy?" The economists

> responded unanimously, "The weather." After all our efforts to manage money and stock markets in order to control the economy, the honest confession is that the weather—a factor completely out of human control—will determine bull markets and bear markets, prosperity and depression, deficits and surpluses.[12]

The weather is the marvelous engine created by God which brings both blessing and sorrow, joy and suffering—all of it fulfilling the plan and purposes of God.

Just as we cannot understand lightning, we cannot understand the hand behind the lightning.

It was not irony that God spoke from a whirlwind and referenced lightning. It was lightning that killed Job's flocks and his employees, and it was a whirlwind that toppled the house and killed all ten of his children.

By being given revelation about God's creation and control of nature, Job was brought to trust and worship the nature of *God*—not nature.

> When God speaks, it is done. Our answer is not in what is done, but in Who it is that speaks. The leper came to Christ, riddled with a fatal disease, and said, *"Lord, if You are willing, You can make me clean." And He stretched out His hand and touched him, saying, "I am willing; be cleansed." And immediately the leprosy left him* (Luke 5:12*c*–13). The Creator stood before the tomb of Lazarus and cried out with a loud voice, *"Lazarus, come forth." The man who had died came forth* (John 11:43).[13]

The Creator of life speaks healing and life, and the elements—both seen and unseen—obey Him.

On the day that Christ hung upon the cross, the sky suddenly grew dark and the light of the sun disappeared, as if a curtain had been drawn. The Gospels indicate that the sun—at high noon—was no longer visible. It seemingly disappeared as the sky grew dark and dangerous. All nature appeared to have hidden for three hours as the dreadful judgment against its Creator fell from God the Father. Then Jesus cried,

> *"My God, My God, why have You forsaken Me?"* (Matthew 27:46).

This is the anguish of God the man, separated in judgment from God the Father. And all of His creation seemed to agonize with Him as an earthquake shook the planet and rocks literally split open as if ripped apart in pain.

Jesus cried again, *"It is finished!"* (John 19:30).

And then He died.

It is interesting to me that the skies grew bright again, for at His death at three o'clock, the darkness lifted. The wrath of God was satisfied. It is as if nature could uncover its head and come out of hiding. The debt of sin had been paid in full.

The Creator who can command everything has everything under His command.

STARS

God gives one more visual demonstration to Job.

> ***"Can you bind the chains of the Pleiades, or loose the cords of Orion? Can you lead forth a constellation in its season, and guide the Bear with her satellites? Do you know the ordinances of the heavens, or fix their rule over the earth?"*** (Job 38:31–33).

"Look up, Job, beyond the rain clouds and the lightning. Look at the stars. Can you manage and control them?"

Of course, Job's answer is no.

While the Bible is not a handbook on astronomy, whenever it speaks to the subject, it is without error and with perfect precision.

Consider the fact that the ancients thought the moon was larger than the sun. Ordinary observation would lead to that conclusion. It is closer and seems larger.

How did Moses know that the sun was larger than the moon? He wrote,

> *And God made two great lights, the greater light to rule the day, and the lesser light to rule the night* (Genesis 1:16 KJV).

Moses did *not* know this by observation, but God's Spirit breathed His infallible word through him and the truth was given by revelation.

Today we know that the sun could gobble up 60 million moons!

And what is the comparison of the earth to the sun in size? If the sun were the size of a basketball, the earth would be the size of the head of a pin. Planet Earth is a speck in comparison to the sun.

Moses could have erred and referred to the sun as the greatest or largest object in the sky—which he did not. He said it was the greatest light in direct reference to the earth.

Now we know much more. We know that the star Antares, for example, is so large that it could hold 64 million suns. There is another constellation which includes the star Epsilon, which is 27 billion times larger than the sun.

Teddy Roosevelt used to take guests who visited the White House out onto the lawn after dark to look up at the stars. Sometimes he would even lie down on the grass and invite his guests to do the same. Then, after some time, he would get up, brush himself off, and say, "Well, I believe we are now small enough . . . let's go on to bed."

How small are we?

> *When I consider Your heavens, the work of Your fingers, the moon and the stars, which You have ordained; what is man that You take thought of him?* (Psalm 8:3–4).

Otherwise stated: "Who are we that You would take thought of us?"

This One who breathed the stars and planets into being by the word of His mouth *(Psalm 33:6)*—this transcendent Lord of the universe—condescended to become a human being, robed in flesh . . . fully man, yet still fully God. He came to our little blue speck.

He came to redeem *us.* This is how much we matter. His hand is where we have come from. His heaven is where we are going!

Then the LORD said to Job, 2 "Will the faultfinder contend with the Almighty?
Let him who reproves God answer it." 3 Then Job answered the LORD and said,
4 "Behold, I am insignificant; what can I reply to You? I lay my hand on my
mouth. 5 Once I have spoken, and I will not answer; even twice, and I will add
nothing more."

–Job 40:1–5

CHAPTER TWENTY-THREE

TO THE ZOO AND BACK

Job 38:39–40:5

It was fascinating to watch our female beagle Patches care for her puppy. She wasn't supposed to have any more and she definitely didn't ask for permission.

However, one of the neighbors in our cul-de-sac has a grey male schnauzer—obviously unconverted and definitely unsanctified. What we were afraid of happened . . . and Patches delivered one puppy. Our daughter Charity named this hyperactive ball of grey and brown fur Pixie.

It has been amazing to observe the instinctive abilities of Pixie, who somehow knows how to act like a dog—sniffing and scratching, panting and wagging. Everything about our dog is a result of DNA which was designed for her kind and implanted by Creator God.

As we've already observed, one of the most devastating discoveries to the theory of evolution is DNA. We now know that the DNA code contains the information that enables the organism to reproduce, preserve, and repair itself.

One author wrote,

> The genetic structure of every living organism limits that organism to what it is—no more, and no less . . . Charles Darwin accepted the middle 1800s theory that variations caused by the environment could be passed on and inherited

> by the young. Darwin used this theory to further postulate that one creature could change into the species of another over time. He even explained the origin of the giraffe's long neck in part: "through the inherited effects of the increased use of parts." In other words, in seasons of limited food supply, Darwin reasoned, giraffes would stretch their necks for the high leaves, supposedly resulting in longer necks being passed on to their offspring.[1]

This is the theory we hear over and over again on nature cable channels and school curriculums: animals do what they do because they have inherited, over millions of years, evolved abilities to survive. They are so much smarter now because they have been endowed with millions of years of knowledge and behavior.

This author goes on to write,

> Modern genetics has utterly disproved this hypothesis; the length of a giraffe's neck is determined by its genetic code . . . the genetic structure of every living organism limits that organism to what it is—no more and no less.[2]

All of which causes the believer to marvel at the creative ingenuity and variety of Creator God.

Creator God is the One who, on days five and six of creation, spoke and the earth and seas and skies were immediately teeming with fish and birds and creatures, large and small. All of them were functioning according to the design God had for their kind *(Genesis 1)*.

God has already taken Job on a tour of the heavens—the constellations, planets, earth, water, and sky. He now shifts and takes Job on a field trip to the zoo.

God rehearses to this suffering man His care over creation—from the small to the great. The implicit message is that if He will take care of mortal creatures, how much more will He care for immortal mankind.

"Job, you're wondering if I care about you and if I have plans for whatever happens in your life. You're wondering if I have taken note of your suffering. Let Me answer this by taking you to the zoo and back. Let Me show you one animal after another—some amazing, some ordinary. You will not only marvel over My creative designs but more deeply understand My caring devotion for you."

So, God will reintroduce Job to a host of animals: those who pounce; those who soar in the sky; others who live in mountains and deserts; those who run at high speeds; beasts of great strength.

THE CREATIVITY OF GOD

The Strong Animal

> ***"Can you hunt the prey for the lion, or satisfy the appetite of the young lions?"*** (Job 38:39).

God evidently cares about the lion's diet and has designed in them the ability to ***crouch in their dens and lie in wait in their lair*** (Job 38:40).

Pull out an "L" volume of an encyclopedia some time and look under lions. The average lion weighs up to 600 pounds and stands four feet high. I have been within a few feet of lions on an African reserve, while safely tucked inside a Jeep. They were massive as they walked by, the top of their backs reaching the bottom of my window ledge. Even though the windows were rolled up, we could hear them purring like some idling engine.

Job had no ability or desire to care for these frightening predators, but God was and is the lion tamer.

The Skittish Animal

> ***"Who prepares for the raven its nourishment when its young cry to God and wander about without food?"*** (Job 38:41).

Of all the birds God would bring to Job's attention, the first one we would have chosen wouldn't have been the raven. These large black birds with their unpleasant caw do not seem to benefit mankind on any level. They eat anything—including decomposing flesh—and have been known to hunt with wolves, eating the remains that are left.

God wanted Job to know that He even cares for the ravens and their young. He hears when they cry out, as if they are crying out to Him.

Even undesirable, unpleasant, unattractive birds are known and cared for by God's providence.

"How much more, Job, will I care for you?"

By the way, this was the message of Jesus Christ:

> *"Are not five sparrows sold for two cents? Yet not one of them is forgotten before God"* (Luke 12:6).

In other words, not even the small sacrificial sparrow is outside the providence of God.

Then Christ concluded by saying to His audience,

> "[Y]*ou are more valuable than many sparrows"* (Luke 12:7*b*).

This is a message that is lost in our culture. As the Creator is denied, animals are elevated. In our own generation, we witness animals given human rights and equal status with mankind. Confusion is at an incredible level. One of the fastest growing branches of law in America is animal law.

This is the animal kingdom which the resurrected Christ will tell Peter, "[K]*ill and eat* [and enjoy]*!"* (Acts 10:13).

This animal kingdom is now considered *more* valuable than mankind and should no longer be used to enhance and sustain human life. Today, we cannot crush the egg of an eagle without severe penalty, but we can destroy the embryo of a human being. We can kill an unborn baby and, according to most politicians, be able to use its stem cells for experimentation. What a tragic reversal of human rights.

Listen to what would be a radical message today, and it comes from the lips of Jesus Christ:

> *"Look at the birds of the air, that they do not sow, nor reap nor gather into barns, and yet your heavenly Father feeds them"* (Matthew 6:26*a*).

In other words, God cares about them. But then, Christ goes on to say,

> *"Are you not worth much more than they?"* (Matthew 6:26*b*).

Christ would not be invited to appear on Oprah's network. His message is way too radical.

Jesus' point was that the care and arrangement by the Father for the animal kingdom is intended as an encouraging illustration of the amazing care and arrangement of the Father for His highest creation—mankind.

The Shy Animal

> ***"Do you know the time the mountain goats give birth? Do you observe the calving of the deer? Can you count the months they fulfill, or do you know the time they give birth?"*** (Job 39:1–2).

The obvious answer to all of the above is no.

These animals stay hidden during the day, and they come out at night.

"Job, I see them at all times; their ways are not hidden from Me."

The Stubborn Animal

> ***"Who sent out the wild donkey free? And who loosed the bonds of the swift donkey, to whom I gave the wilderness for a home and the salt land for his dwelling place? He scorns the tumult of the city, the shoutings of the driver he does not hear. He explores the mountains for his pasture and searches after every green thing"*** (Job 39:5–7).

"Job, has the donkey ever asked you for permission to roam? Have you told it where to live?"[3]

No, the truth is we can hardly tell a donkey anything: ***"the shoutings of the driver he does not hear."***

"But I, the Creator, have determined its habitat. I have told it where to live."

What a lesson for Job . . . God not only assigned the habitat for the wild donkey, He assigns the habitat for His sons and daughters.[4]

God not only created *you* for a place in life, but He created a *place* in life for you. If He has something to say about the place where an ordinary donkey will live, He has something to say about the place where you and I live.

God is implying to Job, "I have determined your habitat, right now, and it has only come about by My permission and providence."

The Sturdy Animal

> ***"Will the wild ox consent to serve you, or will he spend the night at your manger*** [barn]***? Can you bind the wild ox in a furrow with ropes, or will he harrow the valleys after you? Will you trust him because his strength is great and leave***

> ***your labor to him? Will you have faith in him that he will return your grain and gather it from your threshing floor?"*** (Job 39:9–12).

This animal is not the oxen we might imagine in front of a prairie plow. Even though it is translated "unicorn" in the King James Version, it isn't a reference to a lovely horse with a pointed horn in the middle of its forehead.

Most Old Testament scholars believe this animal is now extinct and was the animal known as the aurochs, which inhabited the Middle East for centuries. The bull aurochs was more than six feet wide at the shoulders and had long horns pointing forward. Imagine a Texas steer the size of a rhinoceros as a good mental image. Extinct since 1627, this enormous animal was considered to be the most powerful of all hoofed beasts—hunted in the past by the Assyrians. In *Psalm 22:11–12*, David asks to be delivered from the horns of this animal.[5]

I found it interesting that the Egyptian Pharaoh Thutmose III, who reigned 1500 years before the birth of Christ, once boasted of killing seventy-five aurochs in a single hunt.[6]

Does this animal sound like some creature in a Tolkien novel? Well, it actually *is* in his novels—a fascinating, powerful creature.

These were not domesticated oxen that Job would have used in his fields. They were wild animals that could kill a man in a dozen different ways.

God asks the question, "Job, do you think you can tame an aurochs? Can you hitch him up to your plow?"

And the answer is no.

God is implying, "If I can direct the wild donkey and tame the aurochs, then I am quite capable of controling the chaos that has come into your life, too."

The Strange Animal

God stops asking questions for a moment in this trip to the zoo, and simply makes statements:

> ***"The ostriches' wings flap joyously with the pinion and plumage of love, for she abandons her eggs to the earth and warms them in the dust, and she forgets that a foot may***

> ***crush them, or that a wild beast may trample them. She treats her young cruelly, as if they were not hers; though her labor be in vain, she is unconcerned; because God has made her forget wisdom, and has not given her a share of understanding"*** (Job 39:13–17).

She wasn't the brightest animal God made on the planet!

What an odd bird. In fact, the ostrich is the largest living bird, weighing up to 300 pounds and reaching a height of eight feet. It is the only bird with eyelashes. It has wings, but it can't fly. As a result, the female builds her nest in the sand.

The comment that ***she treats her young cruelly, as if they were not hers*** is a reference to the fact that before the female ostrich buries her eggs in a shallow hole in the sand (usually dug by the male), she keeps some of the eggs out of the nest to be used as food for the chicks that hatch.

Her basic ignorance was legendary in the Middle Eastern world. In fact, Pliny, the first-century Roman naturalist and author, was among the first to write of the ostrich hiding its head and neck in a bush, thinking it was safe because it could see nothing.

But notice, however, for all her ignorance, she is exhilarating to watch as she runs:

> ***"When she lifts herself on high*** [to run]***, she laughs at the horse and his rider"*** (Job 39:18).

One thing the ostrich can do better than most animals is run. Only a handful of animals on the planet can run faster than an ostrich. Lifting her head, extending her small wings for balance, she takes off running and reaches a maximum speed of forty miles per hour—taking giant strides of up to fifteen feet while running.[7]

Pointing out the ostrich was God's way, perhaps, of saying, "I create things you'd never even conceive of creating—things that do not seem to make any sense!"

We look at an ostrich in the zoo, chuckle, and say to ourselves, *What in the world was God thinking when He created that?*

There are times when we are left wondering the same thing about our own lives. Though we fear to utter the words out loud, we wonder secretly in our hearts, *Lord, what were You thinking? What sense can I make of what You've created in my life? It doesn't add up!*

> *"For My thoughts are not your thoughts, nor are your ways My ways," declares the LORD* (Isaiah 55:8).

The Stately Animal

> ***"Do you give the horse his might? Do you clothe his neck with a mane? Do you make him leap like the locust? His majestic snorting is terrible. He paws in the valley, and rejoices in his strength; he goes out to meet the weapons. He laughs at fear and is not dismayed; and he does not turn back from the sword. The quiver rattles against him, the flashing spear and javelin. With shaking and rage he races over the ground, and he does not stand still at the voice of the trumpet. As often as the trumpet sounds he says, 'Aha!' and he scents the battle from afar, and the thunder of the captains and the war cry"*** (Job 39:19–25).

"Job, you might be able to train a battle horse, but who gave him his eagerness to fight? Who made him race into enemy forces? Who allowed him to smell war and swallow up the ground in a race to get there first?"

The horse's majesty, energy, strength, impatience for the battle, and spirit are proofs of the greatness of Him who had made him.[8]

Perhaps this is the subtle hint to Job not to run from the battle; to face the war he is in and stand firm.

Just as the horse is courageous in the face of conflict, the implication, one author wrote, was that God could also make Job confident as he faced his devastating trials.

"I have bred and mantled and infused the horse for everything it needs to face the battle. If I can do that to a horse, Job, I can strengthen you to stand the tests and battles of life."

We have been told the same. We are thoroughly equipped for every good work *(2 Timothy 3:17)*; given the full armor of God, so that we will be able to resist in the evil day and having done everything, to stand firm *(Ephesians 6:13)*; given by God's divine power everything pertaining to life and godliness *(2 Peter 1:3)*.

We are equipped, outfitted, and empowered for life.

If God would equip a regal horse for battle, how much more will He equip us who are the sons and daughters of the King?

This trip to the zoo and back is almost over. God has one more stop along the way.

The Stunning Animal

God gives Job a look at two amazing birds: the hawk, with its built-in migratory system, and the eagle—soaring above the heights . . . an amazing sight.

> ***"Is it by your understanding that the hawk soars, stretching his wings toward the south? Is it at your command that the eagle mounts up and makes his nest on high? On the cliff he dwells and lodges, upon the rocky crag, an inaccessible place. From there he spies out food; his eyes see it from afar"*** (Job 39:26–29).

I have read that an eagle's eye has eight times as many visual cells per cubic centimeter as a human eye. An eagle flying at 600 feet can watch a spider crawl across your driveway. An eagle can see fish the size of your hand jumping in a lake . . . five *miles* away.

I can barely see my computer screen five feet away.

Evolutionists would say the eagle developed this eyesight because it made its nest so high, but God gave the eagle this eyesight *because* it would make its nest so high.

THE ACCOUNTABILITY OF MANKIND

God created the ostrich to put its eggs in the sand. God created the eagle to put its eggs on the side of a mountain.

The diversity of creation shows the diversity of God's creative ability.

However, God's creative ability points toward accountability. In fact, God ends this part of the field trip with a message of pesonal accountability:

> ***Then the LORD said to Job, "Will the faultfinder contend with the Almighty? Let him who reproves God answer it"*** (Job 40:1–2).

Several times in the earlier chapters, Job wanted an audience with God. He wanted to make his case. He wanted to contend with his adversary in a court of law.

"All right, Job, this is your day in court! What do you have to say now?"

> ***Then Job answered the LORD and said, "Behold, I am insignificant; what can I reply to You? I lay my hand on my mouth"*** (Job 40:3–4).

This is an expression of reverence: "I have nothing to say. I thought I had found a legal angle to argue with You." Job's earlier arguments against God had now dissappeared. His trip to the zoo changed everything.

A lawyer thought he had found a clever way to gain an advantage in court. In fact, this true story won the Criminal Lawyers Award Contest a few years ago. The article reads:

> A Charlotte, North Carolina, lawyer purchased a box of very rare and expensive cigars, and then insured them against fire, among other things. Within a month, having smoked his entire stockpile of twenty-four cigars, the lawyer filed claim against the insurance company. In his claim, the lawyer stated the cigars were lost "in a series of small fires."
>
> The insurance company refused to pay, citing the obvious reason: the man had consumed the cigars himself—an insurance claim against fire damage cannot mean the same thing as the fire whereby he himself had consumed the cigars. The court sided with the lawyer and he actually won.
>
> In delivering the ruling the judge agreed with the insurance company that the claim was frivolous. The judge stated, nevertheless, the lawyer held a policy from the company in which it had warranted that the cigars were insurable and also guaranteed that it would insure them against fire, without defining what is considered to be unacceptable fire, and thus were obligated to pay the claim.

> [To the surprise of everyone,] the insurance company accepted the ruling and paid $15,000 to the lawyer for the twenty-four cigars lost in the "fires." The lawyer was rather proud of himself for his clever deed. After the lawyer cashed the check, the insurance company had him arrested on twenty-four counts of arson.
>
> With his own testimony used against him, the lawyer was convicted of intentionally setting fire to insured property twenty-four different times and was sentenced to two years in jail and a $24,000 fine.[9]

The lawyer was convicted by his own words.

Job is convicted by his own testimony. He had rather proudly demanded an audience with God:

> ***"Let the Almighty answer me! And the indictment which my adversary has written"*** (Job 31:35*b*).

These are brash words, "Let God give me an explanation."

God showed up.

Job soon realizes he has boxed himself in:

> ***"Once I have spoken, and I will not answer; even twice, and I will add nothing more"*** (Job 40:5).

"Lord, I've already said enough. I have nothing further to say or suggest to You."

Maybe the best time to put our hands over our mouths and stop talking is right now—no more arguments with God, no more claims of cleverness.

Our response should simply be silence, surrender, and submission.

15 *“Behold now, Behemoth, which I made as well as you; he eats grass like an ox.*
16 *Behold now, his strength in his loins and his power in the muscles of his belly.*
17 *He bends his tail like a cedar; the sinews of his thighs are knit together.* 18 *His*
bones are tubes of bronze; his limbs are like bars of iron. 19 *He is the first of the*
ways of God.”

–Job 40:15–19*a*

“Can you draw out Leviathan with a fishhook? Or press down his tongue with a
cord? 2 *Can you put a rope in his nose or pierce his jaw with a hook?”*

–Job 41:1–2

7 *“Can you fill his skin with harpoons, or his head with fishing spears?* 8 *Lay your*
hand on him; remember the battle; you will not do it again!”

–Job 41:7–8

18 *“His sneezes flash forth light, and his eyes are like the eyelids of the morning.*
19 *Out of his mouth go burning torches; sparks of fire leap forth.* 20 *Out of his*
nostrils smoke goes forth as from a boiling pot and burning rushes. 21 *His breath*
kindles coals, and a flame goes forth from his mouth.”

–Job 41:18–21

CHAPTER TWENTY-FOUR

DRAGONS & DINOSAURS

Job 40:15–42:6

THE GIANT CREATIONS OF GOD

God has finally spoken to Job. His speech still startles us. We have expected His long-awaited appearance and answer to Job's questions, but He, instead, begins asking them—seventy-seven in all.

God's litany of questions effectively took Job on a tour of the universe—from the massive constellations on high to the most infinitesimal dewdrop below. Then God took Job on a safari, showing him a dozen animals and more.

In doing this, God revealed to Job that He was in control of the animals' habitat, and He was in control of Job's. If a bird—from the raven to the eagle—had not escaped God's notice, Job certainly hadn't slipped off the divine radar, either.

God may be asking the questions, but His questions provided deep answers and rich assurances.

The lasting legacy of Job's tour is this: the Creator, who spoke the *first* words in human history, deserves the *last* word in every heart. Not surprisingly, Job is left with his hand over his mouth in muted awe, humility, submission, and reassurance at the end of God's first series of questions!

We can now understand a little better why Peter would connect God's creative power to assurance and hope in suffering:

> [T]*hose also who suffer according to the will of God shall entrust their souls to a faithful Creator in doing what is right* (1 Peter 4:19).

Our hope in suffering is literally bound up in the truth that God is the Creator of heaven and earth . . . and everything and everyone in them. When you are having trouble with the plan of God, take time to notice the power of God in creation.

Perhaps one of the best things we can do for spiritual refreshment is take a drive through the countryside, or sit outside at sunset. Take a bike ride or a hike in the woods; go camping overnight or walk around a nearby lake or pond. And don't just walk around it . . . observe, listen, and wonder. You just might be led to worship God with fresh perspective and gratitude.

David Atkinson challenged the believer when he wrote in his commentary on Job, "Sometimes it is by enjoying the Creator's handiwork that we often begin to feel again the touch of the Creator's hand."[1]

This is God's panoramic challenge to Job:

> ***"Have you really thought about snowflakes and raindrops and dew and wind? Have you considered the currents of oceans and the clouds passing overhead? Do you know who rules the planets and directs the lightning and the thunder? What about the lion crouching in his lair or the ostrich with her head in the sand? Can you figure out all the ways and wonders of My creation? I made all of it. And I made you—down to the last detail! If I would use so much creative energy in thinking up snowflake designs, what do you imagine I did in thinking you up?"*** (Paraphrased).

"If I care about the sparrows, imagine how I care about the saints—the sons and daughters of My own grace and glory *(John 1:12; Galatians 4:7)*—the new creations by My Spirit's power" *(2 Corinthians 5:17)*.

As we survey this section of Job's personal journal where God speaks comfort to him, God actually focuses Job's attention on two additional animals—big ones—who illustrate His power and providence. They are magnificent creatures simply known as ***Behemoth*** and ***Leviathan***.

BEHEMOTH

> ***"Behold now, Behemoth, which I made as well as you"*** (Job 40:15).

Now, if you are like me, you immediately think, *All right, from the last trip to the zoo I know a little bit about horses and ostriches and donkeys and ravens, but what in the world is a Behemoth?*

The word ***Behemoth*** is really just a transliteration of the Hebrew word. In fact, it is the plural form of the word we would normally translate *beasts.*

Because of this plural form in this text, some believe that God is only talking in general about large animals in this chapter and the next. The problem with that view is that God specifically describes these animals *individually.*

Scholars debate long and loud about ***Behemoth***. In fact, many evangelical authors have suggested this is the hippopotamus, the elephant, or the water buffalo.

The problem, again, is that the description provided for us doesn't quite fit any of these animals:

> ***"Behold now, his strength in his loins and his power in the muscles of his belly. He bends his tail like a cedar; the sinews of his thighs are knit together"*** (Job 40:16–17).

Hippos and elephants have tails that do not resemble a cedar tree.

> ***"His bones are tubes of bronze; his limbs are like bars of iron. He is the first of the ways of God"*** (Job 40:18–19*a*).

This land animal, which also evidently enjoyed the water, is first in rank—not according to chronology, but size and strength.[2]

Job also reveals that a raging Jordan flood would not budge him ***(Job 40:23)***, and traps can't catch him ***(Job 40:24)***.

I would agree with those who believe this animal fits our understanding of the dinosaur. Now there's an animal whose tail is like a tree and yet ***eats grass like an ox*** (Job 40:15*b*). This is the greatest land animal ever known to mankind.

You might say, "But I've never seen the word *dinosaur* in the Bible." You're right.

The King James Bible was first translated in 1611 and several revisions soon followed, along with a number of newer English translations that are also committed to translating from the original languages. None of them contain the word *dinosaur.*

It wasn't until 1842 that the name *dinosaur* was coined by Sir Richard Owen, a famous British anatomist who directed the British Museum of Natural History. He classified the huge creatures that were being excavated for the first time in a large group called Dinosauria. The word *dino* means *terrible* and *sauros* means *lizard.* Sir Owen combined the two to create a word that literally translated means *terrible lizard.*

After viewing the bones of Iguanodon and Magalosaurus, he realized that he was examining the remains of a unique group of reptiles that had never been classified before.

We could easily translate ***Behemoth*** as *great beast* or *dinosaur.*

We're not sure which dinosaur God was referring to when He spoke to Job; one author suggests it could be the Brachiosaurus, which weighed 90,000 pounds, was 75 feet long and over 40 feet tall . . . that's quite a lizard!

The problem for the average person today is that after a century of evolutionary conditioning, people have been led to believe that dinosaurs existed at least ten million years *before* mankind. Their excavated bones are dated using indirect methods that have been proven to be unstable and inconsistent in more recent years.

According to *Genesis 1*, the world and the universe were created with all the appearances of maturity and age. Trees were bearing fruit immediately upon creation. Light from the sun, moon, and stars was immediately cascading to earth. A man and a woman were formed walking and talking—not toddling and drooling. To answer the age old question: the chicken came first, then the egg.

Even bones that *seem* to be millions of years old were fossilized quickly by the right amounts of pressure, sediment, and water—explainable only in terms of a universal flood. This also explains how fossilized sea creatures have been discovered on mountain tops and in deserts.

We do not interpret the Scriptures through the lens of the universe—we interpret the universe through the lens of *Scripture.*

Job's tour of the universe will not be referenced in science textbooks any time soon; dinosaur bones are not as old as is being taught by the theory of evolutionists.

In fact, several years ago, scientists from the University of Montana found T-Rex bones that were not entirely fossilized; there were sections of the bones clearly considered fresh. If those bones were really millions of years old, the blood cells would have already totally disintegrated. A report by one of the scientists recorded:

> The lab was filled with murmurs of excitement, for I had focused on something inside the vessels that none of us had ever noticed before: tiny round objects, translucent red with a dark center—red blood cells! Blood cells are mostly water and could not possibly have been preserved in a 65-million-year-old tyrannosaur. They were indeed hemoglobin fragments.[3]

This discovery never made it to the local PTA meetings . . . it never showed up in scientific journals or middle school textbooks. And it never will.

Still, many have suggested that ***Behemoth*** in ***Job 40*** and ***Leviathan*** in ***Job 41*** are simply poetic creations to communicate the awesome power of God. They are not to be taken literally.

Why not? All the other animals presented to Job as proof of God's providence are considered historically accurate. In fact, the only animals we've never seen are the aurochs—the wild ox—which is now extinct.

Further, the detailed description of the anatomy of ***Behemoth*** and ***Leviathan*** suggest real, historical animals. And both animals are mentioned elsewhere in Scripture apart from any mythological context. *Psalm 104:26* speaks of ***Leviathan*** playing in the ocean and *Joel 1* tells of ***Behemoth*** (the beasts of the field) panting in need of God's provision. God even said to Job, ***"Behold now, Behemoth, which I made as well as you"*** (Job 40:15).

God obviously speaks as if Job *already knows* about ***Behemoth***. He commands, ***"Behold now . . ."*** or ***"Look now . . ."*** as if to say that Job could actually see the existence of this animal. This massive animal that is extinct in our generation certainly was not extinct in Job's generation.

And Job was probably grateful that God created this huge creature to be an herbivore rather than a carnivore!

Stone carvings and drawings of people who lived several thousand years ago—as well as drawings by Native Americans—show them hunting mammoths and antelope. And those drawings end up in our children's textbooks, while similar drawings on cave walls depicting huge animals that look distinctly similar to dinosaurs do *not* . . . an interesting and tragic deletion.

I need to warn you that if you are having trouble believing that God could create the dinosaur to roam the earth the same time as mankind, then you are really going to have trouble with the next animal God mentions to Job.

LEVIATHAN

God describes a water creature that is a fire-breathing dragon: ***Leviathan.***

> ***"Can you draw out Leviathan with a fishhook? Or press down his tongue with a cord?"*** (Job 41:1).

Before reading further, make note of the fact this passage is the longest, most detailed description of *any* animal in all of Scripture!

> ***"Can you put a rope in his nose or pierce his jaw with a hook?"*** (Job 41:2).
>
> ***"Can you fill his skin with harpoons, or his head with fishing spears? Lay your hand on him; remember the battle; you will not do it again!"*** (Job 41:7–8).
>
> ***"No one is so fierce that he dares to arouse him; who then is he that can stand before Me? Who has given to Me that I should repay him? Whatever is under the whole heaven is Mine"*** (Job 41:10–11).

In other words, "I, the creator of ***Leviathan***, am the controller of ***Leviathan***. You cannot control him, but I can."

> ***"Who can strip off his outer armor? Who can come within his double mail? Who can open the doors of his face? Around his teeth there is terror. His strong scales are his pride, shut up as with a tight seal. One is so near to another that no air can come between them"*** (Job 41:13–16).

> ***"His sneezes flash forth light, and his eyes are like the eyelids of the morning. Out of his mouth go burning torches; sparks of fire leap forth. Out of his nostrils smoke goes forth as from a boiling pot and burning rushes"*** (Job 41:18–20).

This is nothing less than a fire-breathing creature. And you might be thinking, *You can't be serious!*

Try explaining the tiny Bombardier Beetle, which fires at its enemies bombs made of powerful chemicals stored and mixed inside its body.[4]

Explain how a firefly can have a reaction that converts chemical energy to light energy without burning a hole in its abdomen. And it does this with 90 percent efficiency, whereas an ordinary light bulb burns with only about 10 percent efficiency.[5]

What we do know is that excavated dinosaur bones show a strange protrusion with an internal cavity on top of the head, which some speculate served as the mixing chamber for combustible gases that would ignite when exhaled.[6]

> ***"His breath kindles coals, and a flame goes forth from his mouth"*** (Job 41:21).

Isaiah called this animal *the dragon that lives in the sea* (Isaiah 27:1).

Leviathan was a real animal, now extinct. Undoubtedly in Job's world, it was the largest and fiercest of all the beasts that lived in or near the water.

Imagine: God concluded His tour of the animal world with a dragon—a fire-breathing, unstoppable, untamable, fierce, and fearful dragon.

Could it be (we do *not* know for certain) that God concludes with ***Leviathan*** simply because it is this animal, used throughout Scripture, that represents Satan?

In Revelation, Satan is referred to as the "red dragon" because of his lust for blood and murder. The Apostle John writes of the tribulation period:

> [T]*here was war in heaven, Michael and his angels waging war with the dragon. The dragon and his angels waged war, and they were not strong enough, and there was no longer a place found for them in heaven. And the great dragon was thrown down, the serpent of old who is called the devil and Satan, who deceives the whole world; he was thrown down to the earth, and his angels*

> *were thrown down with him. Then I heard a loud voice in heaven saying . . . "the accuser of our brethren has been thrown down, he who accuses them before our God day and night"* (Revelation 12:7–10).

One day, this dragon—Satan, the accuser of the brethren—will be defeated by the power of God. But for now, he still accuses the brethren.

This is the dragon who accused Job. In fact, this is how the Book of Job opens.

And now the book is coming to an end with a reference to God's victory and power over the dragon: ***"He is under My heaven"*** (Job 41:11).

I do not know if Job caught the analogy; he may have lacked the revelation we have been afforded to reveal the last days of the dragon. But we can be confident that the great dragon who accused Job would have been listening to this conversation between God and Job. He would not have missed a single word of it.[7]

The dragon knows his end, as do we, according to Scripture. Reformer Martin Luther rejoiced over the coming judgment of Satan in his hymn text:

And though this world, with devils filled,
Should threaten to undo us,
We will not fear, for God hath willed
His truth to triumph through us.
The prince of darkness grim—
We tremble not for him;
His rage we can endure,
For lo! His doom is sure—
One little word shall fell him.[8]

So, why would God choose to talk about these giant, fierce, fire-breathing animals? More than likely, because these animals—above all others—seemed uncontrollable . . . untamable . . . able to crush everything in their path. And yet, they were shown to be creations of God, the Tamer of Creation, whose power is greater than any creature—including Satan himself.

All the powers and forces and creatures of heaven and hell are under God's control.

This trip around the universe and the field trip to the zoo changed Job's attitude from worry to worship; from anxiety to adoration.

An hour or two in the presence of God, and God became everything Job needed for security.

Sarah Edwards was the faithful wife of Jonathan Edwards, one of the key architects of the spiritual Great Awakening of the 1700s in America. Just after assuming the role of president of Princeton College, he died unexpectedly from a reaction to a smallpox inoculation he had received one month earlier. Sarah wrote their daughter Esther, who was still grieving the loss of her own husband six months earlier:

> My dear child, what shall I say? A holy and good God has covered us with a dark cloud. O that we may kiss the rod and lay our hands upon our mouths [a reference to Job 40]. The Lord has done this. He has made me adore His goodness that we had your father so long. But my God lives; and He has my heart.[9]

This is the deepest faith that God beckons us to embrace: faith in God who created everything and controls everything He created . . . to bring about His sovereign purposes.

JOB'S RESPONSE

Affirmation

> ***"I know that You can do all things, and that no purpose of Yours can be thwarted"*** (Job 42:2).

Awe

> ***"Who is this that hides counsel without knowledge? Therefore I have declared that which I did not understand, things too wonderful for me, which I did not know"*** (Job 42:3).

Attention

> ***"'Hear now, and I will speak; I will ask You*** [the questions], ***and You instruct me'"*** (Job 42:4).

Adoration

"I have heard of You by the hearing of the ear; but now my eye sees You" (Job 42:5).

Apology

"Therefore I retract, and I repent in dust and ashes" (Job 42:6).

A tour of the universe has brought Job to his knees in repentance; he's come back into fellowship with God . . . He's come home.

A mom, dad, and three sons were personal friends with the commentator on the Book of Job. The oldest son was greatly gifted, both intellectually and musically, as a fine young scholar and a splendid violinist. Earlier in his high school years, the father—a medical doctor—had some trouble with the boy's spirit of submission. But we know what we do with our gifted children: we give them room and cut them a little too much slack. A proud streak soon accompanied this boy's independent spirit.

Upon graduation from high school, the son was accepted into a prestigious school on the West Coast—a very expensive and excellent university known for its academics. The physician father paid the full tuition, and the boy began his first year many miles from home. It was not long until he began running with a rough crowd. He continued his musicianship, playing violin in the school's orchestra, and did well academically. But while he was there, he cultivated an even deeper rebellious spirit.

Completing his freshman year, he returned home, bringing his proud and selfish spirit with him. It was not long before his mom, dad, and two younger brothers realized they had a real problem on their hands. The conflicts intensified. His arrogant, stubborn, and mean-spirited attitude disrupted the family harmony.

Late one afternoon, the father had had enough. He called the young man into his study, closed the door, pointed to a large leather chair, and said firmly, "Sit down."

He then delivered a speech the boy would never forget:

> Everything you own is mine. I bought every stitch of clothing you wear and everything that hangs in your closet. Your car

> in the driveway is mine—I paid for it. The money in your pocket came from my account.
>
> Now, I want you to empty your pockets and your wallet on my desk. Leave everything that is mine in this house, and I want you to leave. Leave all your clothing, give me the car keys, and leave your violin. I bought that, too. Leave everything behind that you have been using, which I am now claiming as rightfully mine. You can keep the clothes on your back and the shoes on your feet, but that is it. There is the door, you can leave now.
>
> By the way, if you decide to change your attitude and come back into this home with a cooperative, submissive spirit, we will accept you and we will welcome you back as part of this family . . . but not until then. I love you and always will, but you are not the son we raised, and I am not putting up with this any longer.[10]

The father told the commentator that the boy stood defiantly to his feet, put all his money and keys on the desk, walked to the door, and left the house without saying one word—not even goodbye. He proudly walked to the sidewalk out front, took a left, and went about three blocks down the street, then stood there motionless with his hands in his empty pockets. He began to think through all he would be facing as night was falling: the street life he knew nothing about; no money; no prospects; no car; no job; no food; no sophomore year ahead of him. After his dad had taken everything he owned, the young man realized he had nothing left.

When it was almost dark, he turned around, walked back home with his proud head hanging low and his heart truly repentant. He knocked on his own front door. His dad opened the door, his mom standing behind him next to his two younger brothers, who had already been thinking, *Who's going to get his room?*

Then came the words, "I'm sorry . . . I realize I need all of you . . . I love you . . . I've been wrong . . . I want you to forgive me for my attitude and my spirit."

They reached out and embraced him and welcomed him home.

Job speaks out of the same broken, submissive heart—with fresh awareness of God's unchangeable, unknowable, unspeakable, unsearchable, unbelievable power and purpose:

> Lord, I was wrong to demand my way, to command You to answer me. In spite of all my suffering, I had no right to challenge You or condemn You as unjust. Everything I have and everything I am, You gave me. You made me. You do not answer to me—I answer to You, my sovereign God and gracious Lord.

May our response be in like manner!

The hymn writer put it this way:

Have Thine own way, Lord!
Have Thine own way!
Thou art the Potter,
I am the clay:
Mould me and make me
After Thy will,
While I am waiting,
Yielded and still.[11]

7 It came about after the LORD had spoken these words to Job, that the LORD
said to Eliphaz the Temanite, "My wrath is kindled against you and against your
two friends, because you have not spoken of Me what is right as My servant Job
has. 8 Now therefore, take for yourselves seven bulls and seven rams, and go to
My servant Job, and offer up a burnt offering for yourselves, and My servant Job
will pray for you. For I will accept him so that I may not do with you according
to your folly, because you have not spoken of Me what is right, as My servant
Job has." 9 So Eliphaz the Temanite and Bildad the Shuhite and Zophar the
Naamathite went and did as the LORD told them; and the LORD accepted Job.
10 The LORD restored the fortunes of Job when he prayed for his friends, and the
LORD increased all that Job had twofold. 11 Then all his brothers and all his
sisters and all who had known him before came to him, and they ate bread with
him in his house; and they consoled him and comforted him for all the adversities
that the LORD had brought on him. And each one gave him one piece of money,
and each a ring of gold. 12 The LORD blessed the latter days of Job more than
his beginning; and he had 14,000 sheep and 6,000 camels and 1,000 yoke of
oxen and 1,000 female donkeys. 13 He had seven sons and three daughters. 14 He
named the first Jemimah, and the second Keziah, and the third Keren-happuch.
15 In all the land no women were found so fair as Job's daughters; and their father
gave them inheritance among their brothers. 16 After this, Job lived 140 years,
and saw his sons and his grandsons, four generations. 17 And Job died, an old
man and full of days.

–Job 42:7–17

CHAPTER TWENTY-FIVE

ALMOST HAPPILY EVER AFTER

Job 42:7–17

We have all grown up with fairytales in which the good guys win and the bad guys lose. Against all odds, the prince wins the princess and they ride off into the sunset to live happily ever after. The wicked witch gets it between the eyes, and the greedy king is left holding an empty bag.

The truth is we all know life is *not* a fairytale. "Happily ever after" needs to leave room for the realities, challenges, and hardships of life.

One author wrote,

> Do you remember your first home—perhaps you built it and called it your dream home. Shortly after moving in, some of the electric outlets didn't work, the roof sprung a leak, and one of the faucets wouldn't turn on.
>
> How about that new job? You believed it would make getting up in the morning easy. You expected it to fulfill you and confirm your love of your career. But many of the people there reminded you a lot of those you left behind, and the boss was not as perfect as you thought, and the health benefits were not all that great, either.

> And how about that new car? It smelled wonderful and ran beautifully—until that Monday morning it wouldn't start. Then there was the afternoon when a guy parked next to you at the mall and opened his door and gave you the mother of all dings on the side of your polished chariot.
>
> How about that new baby? Do you remember thinking how great it would be to start a family and have that adorable little chunk of love cooing at you from her crib in the newly decorated nursery? Everything was organized and clean and ready. Then the baby arrived—after thirty-six hours of labor. She refused to nurse and then had colic so badly she wouldn't stop crying for six months—and finally fell asleep and woke up thirteen years later as a teenager.
>
> Farewell to fantasy land. It is not an easy world.[1]

When we consider Job, we may be tempted to think, *Job had it tough, but wait—it ended happily ever after for him.*

At first glance, it did. But this conclusion is for shallow thinkers.

Ask someone who has lost a child if having another child erased the hollow place in their heart.

Ask someone who has suffered with a painful disease or been hurt in an accident if they ever completely forgot the effects.

Ask someone who has been abandoned by friends and family or been the victim of a crime or abuse if they look at life in exactly the same way they used to.

Now that we have come to the last chapter, let's not trivialize Job's troubles by saying, "Hey, he had more children, his diseases cleared up, and he got his money back."

Job will *never* look at life in the same way again—even regarding "good things." He will have a deeper appreciation for his health like he never had before. He will look at money, business, and wealth with an entirely different perspective. He will hold his children and grandchildren a little differently than he did in the past. He will do this because he knows what it is like to lose it all in 39 seconds—which is about the amount of time it took for the messengers to deliver the bad news.

It's not *quite* happily ever after, but many wonderful events *are* about to take place.

GOD SPEAKS ON JOB'S BEHALF

> ***It came about after the LORD had spoken these words to Job, that the LORD said to Eliphaz the Temanite, "My wrath is kindled against you and against your two friends, because you have not spoken of Me what is right as My servant Job has"*** (Job 42:7).

We can't help but catch the phrase that God used four times throughout verses seven and eight—***My servant Job***:

> ***"Now therefore, take for yourselves seven bulls and seven rams, and go to My servant Job, and offer up a burnt offering for yourselves, and My servant Job will pray for you"*** (Job 42:8*a*).

Can you imagine this scene? Nobody really knows where Elihu went—he seems to have disappeared as quickly as he had appeared—but here are these three friends . . . or former friends! These three have spent hours—one condescending, unfeeling, uncaring, super-spiritual speech after another—castigating Job as a rebellious man . . . one worthy of God's judgment.

Talk about kicking a man when he is down! They had added grief to Job's misery.

Eliphaz made up what he believed to be the horrible secret sins Job must have committed to have received God's terrible judgment. Eliphaz and the others implied that Job's sins were the reason his children had died and his fortunes were lost.

"Not so," God thunders, "not so. Job is ***My servant*** and you, Eliphaz, and your two friends need to come to Job, who is ***My servant***, and he will ***pray for you***!"

Is this the ultimate vindication, or what?

What do you think Job is doing? Is he hopping around saying, "I told you so!"?

No. Job has already repented of saying things he should not have said.

And for those who suffer, there are more important things than being right, like being satisfied completely with having the pleasure, smile, and commendation of God.

I imagine tears trickling down Job's cheeks as he hears God call him, ***My servant.*** Frankly, that's enough.

God has spoken on His servant Job's behalf.

JOB PRAYS ON HIS FRIENDS' BEHALF

Proof that Job is not gloating over them is the fact that he is now praying for them.

> ***The LORD restored the fortunes of Job when he prayed for his friends*** (Job 42:10*a*).

Job prayed, not for himself and not for his own restoration of fortune. He prayed for these men who had wronged him. He had forgiven them.[2]

Job was praying for God to show them forgiveness and mercy, too.

How does a person do this?

Job recognized that he had maligned God and had been forgiven, and he is now turning to forgive those who had maligned him.[3]

Our problem in forgiving others is that we have forgotten how much we have been forgiven. A truly repentant sinner is most willing to forgive other sinners.

GOD ACTS ON JOB'S BEHALF

> **[T]*he LORD increased all that Job had twofold*** (Job 42:10*b*).

What exactly does this twofold increase look like?

> ***Then all his brothers and all his sisters and all who had known him before came to him, and they ate bread with him in his house; and they consoled him and comforted him for all the adversities that the LORD had brought on him*** (Job 42:11*a*).

This is a surprise. I did not know that Job had brothers and sisters. Where were they when the chips were down? We really don't know. It may be that the family banded together and kept his wife from starving.

However, the Greek translation of the Old Testament (the Septuagint—a manuscript old enough for our Lord to actually quote from), includes a passage that indicates Job's wife had to go through the humiliation of cutting off her hair and selling it in order to buy food.[4]

We have every indication—although we cannot be certain—that Job's family had left them hung out to dry.

Frankly, I believe Job's family, like his three friends, was afraid of God's judgment, too. In other words, if Job is being judged by God, then any attempt to help him might incur similar judgment from God.

So, they all kept their distance. This means that in order for this family gathering, along with all their former friends, to take place with the level of fellowship that is indicated, there must have been apologies from and forgiveness demonstrated toward every family member and every estranged friend.

"Job, we're sorry; we didn't know what to do. Dinah (according to Jewish tradition, this was Job's wife's name), we're sorry for not helping you. We were wrong. We didn't believe you were innocent and we, like everyone else, thought you were under the judgment of God. We should have known better; we knew you walked with God. Please forgive us."

"Okay—c'mon over. I've finally gotten my appetite back . . . let's eat together and talk of all we've learned. And you are all *forgiven*."

Wow!

It isn't long after the reunion that Dinah announces to Job, "You won't believe it—we're expecting a child."

> ***He had seven sons and three daughters*** (Job 42:13).

This is the exact number of children they had raised before.

But wait—God had promised that He would double Job's fortune, and God did, indeed, double his ***sheep*** and ***camels*** and ***yoke of oxen*** and ***female donkeys*** (Job 42:12).

Job now has ten more children; which means that Job and his wife actually do double the number of children, because they did not entirely lose their first ten . . . they just lost *contact* with them.

Unlike camels and sheep and oxen and donkeys, his first ten children are counted because they are *still alive* . . . and he will see them in Paradise.

God also restores Job's financial security and adds to it:

> ***And each one gave him one piece of money, and each a ring of gold.*** (Job 42:11*b*).

The Hebrew text doesn't indicate a value for this that we can understand. All we know is that everyone gave Job a gift of money and a ring of gold. We *do* know that this was God's way of restoring Job's fortune; this freewill offering will allow Job to be able to purchase new livestock and get back on his feet financially.

One classic painting of this event shows Job all cleaned up and dressed in fine clothing, seated in a chair under a tree, with a long line of wellwishers ready to make amends.

However, don't overlook the fact that rebuilding will be a slow and tedious process. God didn't restore in one afternoon that which He had taken away in 39 seconds.

This displayed the wisdom of God. Job's healing and restoration included people; it was a restoration of relationships which Job now knew was far more important than wealth alone.[5]

Did you also notice that Job seems especially proud of his daughters?

> ***He named the first Jemimah*** ["dove"]***, and the second Keziah*** ["perfume"]***, and the third Keren-happuch*** ["horn of eye paint"] (Job 42:14).

"Horn of eye paint"? Was this third daughter being punished for something? Perhaps for eight months of colic? This phrase referred to a bottle of dye used to paint the eyelashes, eyelids, and eyebrows to make the eyes more attractive.[6]

For the dads who are looking for a verse against makeup and mascara, the godliest man in the East actually named one of his daughters "Eye Shadow." Sorry, dad!

> ***In all the land no women were found so fair as Job's daughters; and their father gave them inheritance*** [sweetened the pot] ***among their brothers. After this, Job lived 140 years, and saw his sons and his grandsons, four generations*** [his great-grandsons and his great-great-grandsons—four generations of sons]***. And Job died, an old man and full of years*** (Job 42:15–17).

This is the Hebrew way of saying, "He was satisfied with a full life."

If anyone qualified to live happily ever after, it would be Job. But even Job would eventually grow ill again. He probably stood by more fresh graves along the way to his own death.

Only then would he learn the whole story.

LESSONS LEARNED FROM JOB'S LIFE

Before we say farewell to Job, let's allow his life to echo once more across the span of some 4,000 years. There are still fresh principles and desperately needed truths.

I have twenty-five sermons preached by Charles Spurgeon on the life of Job. I wanted to see what this renowned preacher of the 1800s had to say in his last sermon on Job. The book is entitled *Suffering and the Sovereignty of God*. In this sermon, Spurgeon preached these words:

> This may seem to be a very trite observation, commonplace, and such as everybody knows, but, beloved, the very things that everybody knows are those which we need to hear . . . those old things which we did not care about in our prosperity are most valued when we are cast down by the terrible blows of tribulation.[7]

When I read this statement, it made me wonder where *you* were when we started this journey through the Book of Job.

Perhaps for you, these truths did not matter so much because suffering was far from your door—but not now. Perhaps now, Job has more to say to you than ever.

You may remember that this book began with Job making sacrifices for his children in case they had misspoken or acted improperly. His children were already out from under his roof, having their own homes and their own families, but Job was a shepherd. He cared about his children—not just physically but spiritually.

The book began by introducing us to the best representative of God's purpose for man on earth. This is what God intended a man to be—from his heart to his hands.

There was no question about it, Job was a godly man.

This led us to the rather unsettling observation that God's children are not immune to trials. Christians are not given some sort of flu shot against hardship. There is no such guarantee.

Maybe you have said under your breath, *Yeah, I believe that God's children can suffer great trials, but not His godly children. Godly people are given a hall pass against harassment.*

We had no idea that godly people actually *invite* harassment, even from fallen angels who hate God and His people.

The Accuser was after Job. If he could get Job to walk away from God, he would win the pleasure of seeing God robbed of worship—which is Satan's highest aim. Satan comes to God and accuses Job before God. Then Satan will come and accuse God before Job.

He does the same toward us as well. Satan is called, in the Book of Revelation, "the accuser of the brethren."

It is his mission to tell God we are not worth keeping and, then, to tell us that God is not worth following. Satan reminds God that we are sinful and repeats to us that God is absent. He whispers in the ear of God that we are unfaithful to Him, and then he whispers in our ear that God is uninterested in us.

However, Job will sing of God's faithfulness in those early days, and say,

"As for me, I know that my Redeemer lives" (Job 19:25*a*).

It is no wonder that Martin Luther, the great Reformer, would write hymn texts of Christ's victory over Satan and say to his congregation, "Let us spite the devil by singing praise to God."[8]

Imagine Luther composing these words in days of great difficulty and persecution, and even with the threat of losing his own life:

For still our ancient foe
Doth seek to work us woe—
His craft and pow'r are great,
And armed with cruel hate,
On earth is not his equal.

This great hymn is not just about the strength of Christ, but about the accuser and enemy of the believer who has not let up at all since the days of Job.

Luther concluded:

That word above all earthly pow'rs—
No thanks to them—abideth;
The Spirit and the gifts are ours
Through Him who with us sideth;
Let goods and kindred go,
This mortal life also;
The body they may kill:
God's truth abideth still—
His kingdom is forever.[9]

No matter what the accuser says; no matter what life delivers; no matter what trials may come; no matter that we may find ourselves with David, saying, "I am in the lowest pit and darkness is my closest friend" *(Psalm 88:6)*, these five truths may mean more to us now than ever before.

Whenever We Conclude that God Isn't Present, He Is!

> *For He Himself hath said, "I will never leave you nor forsake you"* (Hebrews 13:5*b* NKJV).

Whenever We Feel that Life Is Hopeless, It Isn't!

> *"I have plans for you . . . I have promised to give you a future and a hope"* (Jeremiah 29:11 paraphrase).

Whenever the Enemy of Our Souls Whispers that God Doesn't Care, He Does!

> [C]*asting all your care upon Him, for He cares for you* (1 Peter 5:7 NKJV).

Whenever We Believe that God Hasn't Heard Our Cries, He Has!

I cried to the LORD with my voice, and He heard me from His holy hill (Psalm 3:4 NKJV).

In my distress I cried to the LORD, and He heard me (Psalm 120:1 NKJV).

"I called out of my distress to the LORD and He answered me. I cried for help . . . [and] *You heard my voice"* (Jonah 2:2).

Whenever the Accuser Says that God Has Ceased Loving Us, It's a Lie!

For I am convinced that neither death, nor life, nor angels, nor principalities, nor things present, nor things to come, nor powers, nor height, nor depth, nor any other created thing, will be able to separate us from the love of God, which is in Christ Jesus our Lord (Romans 8:38–39).

Paul was convinced of this, not by the whippings and beatings he endured; not by the stoning he received; not by the storms and shipwrecks God could have kept from happening; not by the abandonment of the churches he planted and the believers he discipled. He was not convinced by any of those things, for what assurances can life provide for mankind? Paul was convinced because of the truth of God's revelation to him.

For our trials will one day seem light—and momentary—yielding eternally a weight of glory far beyond all comparison *(2 Corinthians 4:17).*

After you have suffered for a little while, the God of all grace, who called you to His eternal glory in Christ, will Himself perfect, confirm, strengthen, and establish you. To Him be dominion forever and ever (1 Peter 5:10–11).

Living happily ever after will *not* take place on earth. It will not take place until the earth is remade and we, along with all the redeemed, with our robes dazzling and clean, face eternity beside our sovereign Lord who has chosen to retain His wounds while healing all of ours.

Job 42 was not the end of Job's story, and ours will not be written any time soon. There is, for all of us who follow Christ, an ending like we cannot imagine. It will be far beyond a fairytale ending, and it will be for real:

- Our Prince of Peace will one day come.
- There will be a kingdom, a palace, and a throne.
- The streets will be made of gold.
- Our residence will be with our Lord.
- Our joy will be undiminished forever.

Our Prince *is* coming. He will set everything right, and we shall begin, one day, to live happily ever after . . . *forever*!

ENDNOTES

CHAPTER ONE

1 Jerry Bridges, *Trusting God: Even When Life Hurts* (Navpress, 1988), 9.

2 Elie Wiesel, *Night* (Hill and Wang, 1972).

3 Harold S. Kushner, *When Bad Things Happen to Good People* (New York, Avon Books, 1983), 43.

4 Steven J. Lawson, *Holman Old Testament Commentary: Job* (B&H Publishing Group, 2005), 1.

5 Charles R. Swindoll, *Job: A Man of Heroic Endurance*, (Thomas Nelson, Inc., 2004), 5.

6 J. Sidlow Baxter, *Explore the Book* (Zondervan, 1960), 26.

7 Henry Morris, *The Remarkable Record of Job* (Master Books, 1988), 13.

8 Lawson, 2.

9 Morris, 15.

10 John C. L. Gibson, *Daily Study Bible: Job* (Westminster John Knox Press, 1985), 6.

11 David J. A. Clines, *Word Biblical Commentary: Job 1–20* (Thomas Nelson Publishers, 1989), 12.

12 David L. McKenna, *Mastering the Old Testament: Job* (W Publishing Group, 1986), 30.

13 Lawson, 19.

14 Lawson, 21.

15 Lawson, 24.

CHAPTER TWO

1 Steven J. Lawson, *Holman Old Testament Commentary: Job* (B&H Publishing Group, 2005), 23.

2 *Sitting with Job*, Roy B. Zuck, ed. (Wipf & Stock Publishers, 1992), 145.

3 Charles Spurgeon, *The Suffering of Man & the Sovereignty of God* (Fox River Press, 2001), 7.

4 Charles R. Swindoll, *Job: A Man of Heroic Endurance* (Thomas Nelson, Inc., 2004), 8.

5 John C. L. Gibson, *Daily Study Bible: Job* (Westminster John Knox Press, 1985), 10.

6 Spurgeon, 10.

7 Charles R. Swindoll, 11.

8 Warren W. Wiersbe, *Job: Be Patient* (Victor Books, 1991), 16.

9 Spurgeon, 16.

CHAPTER THREE

1 Erwin Lutzer, *Where Was God?* (Tyndale House, 2006), 61.

2 Francis I. Andersen, *Tyndale Old Testament Commentaries: Job* (Inter-Varsity Press), 89.

3 Steve May, *The Story File* (Hendrickson, 2000), 236.

4 Andersen, 86.

5 Charles R. Swindoll, *Job: A Man of Heroic Endurance* (Thomas Nelson, Inc., 2004), 21.

6 Ibid., 21.

7 Charles Spurgeon, *The Suffering of Man & the Sovereignty of God* (Fox River Press, 2001), back cover.

8 Lutzer, 51.

9 Tom Vanderbilt, "Americans Are Storing More Stuff than Ever," July 18, 2005, http://www.slate.com.

10 John E. Hartley, *New International Commentary on the Old Testament: Job* (Eerdmans, 1988), 78.

11 A. M. Overton, 1932.

CHAPTER FOUR

1 Charles R. Swindoll,, *Growing Strong in the Seasons of Life* (Multnomah, 1983), 91.

2 Erwin Lutzer, *Where Was God?* (Tyndale House, 2006), xiii.

3 Paul E. Little, *Know Why You Believe* (Inter-Varsity Press, 1974), 83.

4 Lutzer, 5.

5 John Piper and Justin Taylor, *Suffering and the Sovereignty of God* (Crossway, 2006), 35.

6 Lutzer, 21.

7 Piper and Taylor, 18.

8 Lutzer, 18.

9 Ibid., 13.

10 Ibid., 12.

11 Jerry Bridges, *Is God Really in Control?* (NavPress, 2006), 57.

12 Mark Talbot, quoted by Piper and Taylor, 47.

13 Isaac Watts, "I Sing the Mighty Power of God," *Praise Songs and Hymns* (Zondervan, 1979), 9.

14 C. S. Lewis, *The Problem of Pain* (Harper/Collins, 1940), 91.

15 Lutzer, 71.

16 Ibid., 67.

17 David Miller, quoted by Lutzer, 57.

18 Charles R. Swindoll, *Hope Again* (Thomas Nelson, Inc., 1996), 83.

19 Lutzer, 74.

CHAPTER FIVE

1 "Boll Weevil Monument," http://www.encyclopediaofalabama.org/face/Article.jsp?id=h-2384.

2 Charles R. Swindoll, *Growing Strong in the Seasons of Life* (Multnomah, 1983), 265.

3 John MacArthur, *The Power of Suffering* (Victor Books, 1995), 26.

4 John E. Hartley, *New International Commentary on the Old Testament: The Book of Job* (Eerdmans, 1988), 79.

5 Warren Wiersbe, *Job*: *Be Patient* (Victor Books, 1991), 18.

6 Hartley, 81.

7 Ray Robinson, *Famous Last Words* (Workman Publishing, 2003), 101.

8 Mike Mason, *The Gospel According to Job* (Crossway, 1994), 44.

9 David L. McKenna, *Mastering the Old Testament: Job* (W Publishing Group, 1986), 47.

10 Wiersbe, 19.

11 Charles R. Swindoll, *Job: A Man of Heroic Endurance* (Thomas Nelson, Inc., 2004), 40.

CHAPTER SIX

1 Adapted from "Secondhand Smoke Fact Sheet," www.lungusa.org.

2 Ibid.

3 Adapted from Albert Barnes, *Notes on the Old Testament: Job, Volume 1* (Baker,1949), 118.

4 David J. A. Clines, *Word Biblical Commentary: Job 1–20* (Thomas Nelson Publishers, 1989), 53.

5 Scott Mitchell, "God's Job," October 16, 2013, http://pasturescott.org/2013/10/16/gods-job/.

6 John MacArthur, *The Power of Suffering* (Victor Books, 1995), 135.

7 Diane Johnson, "Blue Moods/Blue Skies."

8 Clines, 51.

9 Ibid., 54.

10 John E. Hartley, *Job* (Eerdmans, 1988), 84.

11 Adapted from Jill Briscoe, "In My Father's Arms," *preachingtoday.com.*

12 Charles Spurgeon, *The Suffering of Man & the Sovereignty of God* (Fox River Press, 2001), 18.

13 Charles R. Swindoll, *Hope Again* (Thomas Nelson, Inc., 1996), 210.

CHAPTER SEVEN

1 William Henry Green, *Conflict and Triumph* (Banner of Truth Trust, 1999, first published in 1874), 57.

2 John E. Hartley, *New International Commentary on the Old Testament: The Book of Job* (Eerdmans, 1988), 85.

3 Adapted from Roy B. Zuck, *Job* (Moody Press, 1978), 20.

4 Hartley, 86.

5 Adapted from Mike Mason, *The Gospel According to Job* (Crossway Books, 1994), 49.

6 Hartley, 85.

7 Adapted from Charles R. Swindoll, *Job: A Man of Heroic Endurance* (Thomas Nelson, Inc., 2004), 50.

8 Adapted from Warren Wiersbe, *Job: Be Patient* (Victor Books, 1991), 21.

9 Fritz Rienecker & Cleon Rogers, *Linguistic Key to the Greek New Testament* (Regency, 1976), 245.

10 Swindoll, 53.

CHAPTER EIGHT

1 John Piper, *The Roots of Endurance* (Crossway Books, 2002), 117.

2 John Piper and Justin Taylor, *Suffering and the Sovereignty of God* (Crossway Books, 2006), 179.

3 Steven Lawson, *Holman Old Testament Commentary: Job* (Holman Publishers, 2004), 33.

4 Ibid., 61.

5 Charles R. Swindoll, *Job: A Man of Heroic Endurance* (Thomas Nelson, Inc., 2004), 63.

6 Ibid., 61.

7 Roy B. Zuck, *Job* (Moody Press, 1978), 27.

8 Derek Thomas, *The Storm Breaks* (Evangelical Press, 1995), 64.

9 Ibid., 67.

10 Warren Wiersbe, *Be Patient* (Victor Books, 1991), 22

11 Derek Thomas, http://www.monergism.com.

12 Piper and Taylor, 192.

CHAPTER NINE

1 Roy B. Zuck, *Job* (Moody Press, 1978), 32.

2 David L. McKenna, *Mastering the Old Testament: Job* (W Publishing Group, 1986), 60.

3 Steven J. Lawson, *When All Hell Breaks Loose* (NavPress Publishing Group, 1993), 74.

4 Warren Wiersbe, *Be Patient: Job* (Victor Books, 1991), 27.

5 Adapted from Steven J. Lawson, *Holman Old Testament Commentary: Job* (B&H Publishing Group, 2005), 48.

6 Charles R. Swindoll, *Job: Man of Heroic Endurance* (Thomas Nelson, Inc., 2004), 88.

7 Adapted from Swindoll, 88.

8 J. Allen Blair, *Living Patiently* (Loizeaux Brothers, 1966), 39.

CHAPTER TEN

1 Joseph Caryl, *Practical Observations on Job: Vol. 2* (Reformation Heritage, 2001), 421.

2 J. Allen Blair, *Living Patiently* (Loizeaux Brothers, 1966), 53.

3 John E. Hartley, *New International Commentary on the Old Testament: The Book of Job* (Eerdmans, 1988), 140.

4 Warren Wiersbe, *Job: Be Patient* (Victor Books, 1991), 32.

5 Robert J. Morgan, *Then Sings My Soul* (Thomas Nelson, 2003), 207.

6 George Matheson, "O Love That Wilt Not Let Me Go" (1882), public domain.

CHAPTER ELEVEN

1 Adapted from Charles R. Swindoll, *Job: A Man of Heroic Endurance* (Thomas Nelson, Inc., 2004), 56.

2 Quoted by David L. McKenna in *Mastering the Old Testament: Job* (Word Publishing, 1986), 78.

3 Charles R. Swindoll, *The Tale of the Tardy Ox Cart* (Word Publishing, 1998), 191.

4 Adapted from J. Allen Blair, *Living Patiently* (Loizeaux Brothers, 1966), 54.

5 Adapted from Mike Mason, *The Gospel According to Job* (Crossway Books, 1994), 89.

6 Robert J. Morgan, *Nelson's Complete Book of Illustrations* (Thomas Nelson, 2000), 170.

CHAPTER TWELVE

1 "Romanian Prisoner Sues God," Oct. 18, 2005, http://en.ria.ru/world/20051018/41809986.html.

[2] http://www.angryandrew.com/lawsuit.html.

[3] Steven Lawson, *Holman Old Testament Commentary: Job* (Holman Reference, 2004), 83.

[4] Charles R. Swindoll, *Job: A Man of Heroic Endurance* (Thomas Nelson, Inc., 2004), 104.

[5] R. Kent Hughes, *Romans* (Crossway Books, 1991), 324.

[6] Fritz Rienecker and Cleon Rogers, *Linguistic Key to the Greek New Testament* (Regency, 1976), 738.

[7] Warren Wiersbe, *Job: Be Patient* (Victor Books, 1991), 44.

[8] Swindoll, 106.

CHAPTER THIRTEEN

[1] David L. McKenna, *Mastering the Old Testament: Job* (W Publishing Group, 1986), 99.

[2] Mike Mason, *The Gospel According to Job* (Crossway, 1994), 141.

[3] David J. A. Clines, *Word Biblical Commentary: Job 1–20* (Thomas Nelson Publishers, 1989), 266.

[4] Quoted by Charles R. Swindoll, *Job: A Man of Heroic Endurance* (Thomas Nelson, Inc., 2004), 111.

[5] "Only in America," Feb. 3, 2006, *PT.COM: The Week*, 6.

[6] Swindoll, 122.

[7] Erwin Lutzer, *One Minute After You Die* (Moody Press, 1997), 34.

[8] Ibid., 38.

[9] Sam Gordon, *Hope and Glory: Jesus Is Coming Again* (Ambassador International, 2005), 161.

CHAPTER FOURTEEN

[1] Charles R. Swindoll, *Job: A Man of Heroic Endurance* (Thomas Nelson, Inc., 2004), 138.

[2] Steven Lawson, *Holman Old Testament Commentary: Job* (Holman, 2004), 133.

[3] Warren Wiersbe, *Job: Be Patient* (Victor Books, 1991), 56.

[4] Wiersbe, 61.

[5] Quoted in Swindoll, 139.

[6] http://www.preachingtoday.com/illustrations/2000/january/5447.html.

[7] Lawson, 147.

[8] Adapted from Wiersbe, 65.

[9] Wiersbe, 65.

CHAPTER FIFTEEN

1 Knute Larson, *Holman New Testament Commentary: 1 Thessalonians* (Holman, 2000), 51.

2 Steven Lawson, *Holman New Testament Commentary: Job* (Holman, 2004), 122.

3 Warren Wiersbe, *Job: Be Patient* (Victor Books, 1991), 68.

4 "Messiah and George Frideric Handel," March 2007, http://www.christianity.com/church/church-history/timeline/1701-1800/messiah-and-george-frideric-handel-11630237.html.

5 Charles Haddon Spurgeon edited by Kerry James Allen in *The Suffering of Man & The Sovereignty of God* (Fox River Press, 2001), 161.

6 Ibid., 162.

7 Adapted from Steven J. Lawson, *When All Hell Breaks Loose* (NavPress Publishing Group, 1993), 149.

8 The Elisabeth Elliot Newsletter, Sept/October 1988, quoted in James Dobson, *When God Doesn't Make Sense* (Tyndale House, 1993), 106.

9 George Frideric Handel, "Hallelujah Chorus," (1741), public domain.

CHAPTER SIXTEEN

1 Steven Lawson, *Holman Old Testament Commentary: Job* (Holman, 2004), 67.

2 Warren Wiersbe, *Job: Be Patient* (Victor Books, 1991), 75.

3 Charles Spurgeon, *The Treasury of David, Volume 2* (Kregel, rep. 1968), 312.

4 Charles R. Swindoll, *Job: A Man of Heroic Endurance* (Thomas Nelson, Inc., 2004), 70.

CHAPTER SEVENTEEN

1 http://acronyms.thefreedictionary.com/Containment+Area+for+Relocated+Yankees.

2 Adapted from Charles R. Swindoll, *Job: Man of Heroic Endurance* (Thomas Nelson, Inc., 2004), 181.

3 Adapted from Steven J. Lawson, *Holman Old Testament Commentary: Job* (B&H Publishing Group,2005), 195.

4 Steven J. Lawson, *When All Hell Breaks Loose* (NavPress Publishing Group, 1993).

5 Marlin Vis, "The Blame Game" citation: preachingtoday.com.

6 Swindoll, 182.

7 John Rippon, "How Firm a Foundation," (1787), public domain.

8 Adapted from Charles R. Swindoll, *Getting Through the Tough Stuff: It's Always Something!* (Thomas Nelson, Inc., 2004), 224.

CHAPTER EIGHTEEN

1 "The Persians Invade Thermopylae," http://www.pbs.org/empires/thegreeks/background/20.html.

2 "Persian Wars Battle at Thermopylae 480 BC," http://ancienthistory.about.com/cs/weaponswar/p/blpwtherm.html.

3 Charles Swindoll, *Job: A Man of Heroic Endurance* (Thomas Nelson, Inc., 2004), 213.

4 A.W. Tozer, *The Knowledge of the Holy* (San Francisco, Harper, 1961), 6.

5 Swindoll, 213.

6 Steven J. Lawson, *When All Hell Breaks Loose* (NavPress Publishing Group, 1993), 190.

CHAPTER NINETEEN

1 Adapted from Warren Wiersbe, *Be Patient: Job* (Victor Books, 1991), 123.

2 Charles R. Swindoll, *Job: Man of Heroic Endurance* (Thomas Nelson, Inc., 2004), 248.

3 Steven J. Lawson, *When All Hell Breaks Loose* (NavPress Publishing Group, 1993), 206.

4 Adapted from Roy B. Zuck, *Job* (Moody Press, 1978), 150.

5 Adapted from John MacArthur, Joni Eareckson Tada, Robert & Bobbie Wolgemuth, *O Worship the King* (Crossway, 2000), 33.

6 Derek Thomas, *The Storm Breaks: Job Simply Explained* (Evangelical Press, 1995), 279.

7 Adapted from Wiersbe, 139.

8 Robert Grant, "O Worship the King," (1833), public domain.

CHAPTER TWENTY

1 "The World's (Un) Luckiest Man," http://www.neatorama.com/2007/10/17/the-worlds-unluckiest-man/#!oCrjj.

2 John MacArthur, *The Battle for the Beginning* (W Publishing, 2001), 20.

3 Henry Morris, *The Remarkable Record of Job* (Master Books, 1988), 94.

4 MacArthur, 56.

5 Derek Thomas, *The Storm Breaks: Job Simply Explained* (Evangelical Press, 1995), 286.

6 Steven J. Lawson, *Holman Old Testament Commentary: Job* (B&H Publishing Group, 2005), 333.

CHAPTER TWENTY-ONE

[1] John MacArthur, *The Battle for the Beginning: Creation, Evolution, and the Bible* (Thomas Nelson, Inc., 2001), 12.

[2] Ruth Kamps, National Public Radio, "Living Life with Grace and Elegant Treeness," Aug. 15, 2005.

[3] Joy Harjo, National Public Radio, "A Sacred Connection to the Sun," July 8, 2007.

[4] MacArthur, 14.

[5] MacArthur, 40.

[6] Henry Morris, *The Remarkable Record of Job* (Master Books, 1988), 40.

[7] MacArthur, 94.

[8] Morris, 102.

[9] John E. Hartley, *The Book of Job* (Eerdmans, 1988), 495.

[10] Ibid., 496.

[11] Morris, 166.

[12] MacArthur, 111.

[13] Hartley, 496.

[14] MacArthur, 114.

[15] Ibid., 114.

[16] "Huddled up with LISA," *The Wall Street Journal Online* (Jan. 20, 2005).

CHAPTER TWENTY-TWO

[1] James Montgomery Boice, *Genesis: Volume 1* (Zondervan, 1982), 14.

[2] Ibid., 15.

[3] Ibid., 15.

[4] National Public Radio, Morning Edition, May 6, 2004, http://www.npr.org.

[5] John MacArthur, *The Battle for the Beginning: Creation, Evolution, and the Bible* (Thomas Nelson, Inc., 2001), 83.

[6] Ibid., 82.

[7] Ibid., 81.

[8] Samuel Ridout, *The Book of Job* (Loizeaux Brothers, 1919), 222.

[9] http://aquasana.com.

[10] Henry Morris, *The Remarkable Record of Job* (Master Books, 2000), 38.

[11] Ibid., 39.

[12] David L. McKenna, *Mastering the Old Testament: Job* (W Publishing Group, 1986), 289.

13 John Phillips, *Exploring Genesis* (Loizeaux Brothers, 1980), 40.

CHAPTER TWENTY-THREE

1 John MacArthur, *The Battle for the Beginning: Creation, Evolution, and the Bible* (Thomas Nelson, Inc., 2001), 134.

2 Ibid., 134.

3 John C. L. Gibson, *Daily Study Bible: Job* (Westminster John Knox Press, 1985), 233.

4 Steven J. Lawson, *Holman Old Testament Commentary: Job* (B&H Publishing Group, 2005), 340.

5 Roy B. Zuck, *Job* (Moody Press, 1978), 171.

6 Derek Thomas, *The Storm Breaks: Job Simply Explained* (Evangelical Press, 1995), 293.

7 Zuck, 172.

8 Albert Barnes, *Notes on the Book of Job*, quoted by Zuck, 174.

9 Charles R. Swindoll, *Job: A Man of Heroic Endurance* (Thomas Nelson, Inc., 2004), 281.

CHAPTER TWENTY-FOUR

1 David J. Atkinson, *The Message of Job* (InterVarsity Press, 1991), 147.

2 Roy B. Zuck, *Job* (Moody, 1978), 179.

3 Ken Ham, *The Great Dinosaur Mystery Solved* (Master Books, 2000), 18.

4 "Bombardier Beetle," http://www.wikipedia.com.

5 Ibid., "Firefly."

6 Henry Morris, *The Remarkable Record of Job* (Master Books, 1988), 118.

7 Ibid., 123.

8 Martin Luther, "A Mighty Fortress Is Our God," (1529, Translation from the Pennsylvania Lutheran Church Book of 1868), public domain.

9 John Piper, http://www.desiringgod.org/Job_Wrestling.

10 Charles R. Swindoll, *Job: A Man of Heroic Endurance* (Thomas Nelson, Inc., 2004), 293.

11 Adelaide A. Pollard and George C. Stebbins, "Have Thine Own Way, Lord!" (1907, © Hope Publishing Company, 1935).

CHAPTER TWENTY-FIVE

1 Charles R. Swindoll, *Job: A Man of Heroic Endurance* (Thomas Nelson, Inc., 2004), 308.

[2] Ibid., 305.

[3] Roy B. Zuck, *Job* (Moody, 1978), 187.

[4] David J. A. Clines, *Word Biblical Commentary: Job 1–20* (Thomas Nelson Publishers, 1989), 53.

[5] Mike Mason, *The Gospel According to Job* (Crossway, 1994), 437.

[6] Zuck, 188.

[7] Charles Spurgeon, *Suffering and the Sovereignty of God* (Fox River Press, 2001), 370.

[8] Spurgeon, 7.

[9] Martin Luther, "A Mighty Fortress Is Our God," (1529, Translation from the Pennsylvania Lutheran Church Book of 1868), public domain.

SCRIPTURE INDEX

Reference	Page
Job 38:19–38	270
Job 38:22–23*a*	276
Job 38:24*a*	276
Job 38:25–26*a*	279
Job 38:26–27	278
Job 38:31–33	281
Job 38:37*a*	278
Job 38:37*b*–38	278
Job 38:39	287
Job 38:40	287
Job 38:41	287
Job 39:1–2	289
Job 39:5–7	289
Job 39:9–12	290
Job 39:13–17	291
Job 39:18	291
Job 39:19–25	292
Job 39:26–29	293
Job 40	301/305
Job 40:1–2	293
Job 40:1–5	284
Job 40:3–4	246/294
Job 40:5	295
Job 40:15	299/301
Job 40:15*b*	299
Job 40:15–19*a*	296
Job 40:16–17	299
Job 40:18–19*a*	299
Job 40:23	299
Job 40:24	299

Reference	Page
Job 41	301
Job 41:1	302
Job 41:1–2	296
Job 41:7–8	296/302
Job 41:10–11	302
Job 41:11	304
Job 41:13–16	302
Job 41:18–20	303
Job 41:18–21	296
Job 41:21	303
Job 42	74/321
Job 42:2	305
Job 42:3	305
Job 42:4	305
Job 42:5	306
Job 42:6	306
Job 42:7	313
Job 42:8*a*	313
Job 42:10*a*	314
Job 42:10*b*	314
Job 42:11*a*	314
Job 42:11*b*	316
Job 42:12	315
Job 42:13	315
Job 42:14	316
Job 42:15–17	316
Psalm 3:4 (NKJV)	320
Psalm 8:3–4	282
Psalm 13:1*a*	186
Psalm 18:6*a*	90

Reference	Page
Psalm 18:30	117
Psalm 19:1*a* (NIV)	44
Psalm 22:11–12	290
Psalm 33:6	282
Psalm 33:6–9, 11	267
Psalm 46:10*a* (KJV)	45
Psalm 49:14–15	150
Psalm 50:21	44
Psalm 65:8*b*	276
Psalm 69:32*b*–33	117
Psalm 73:3	186
Psalm 73:3–5, 13–14	99
Psalm 73:5	189
Psalm 73:13	189
Psalm 74:16*b*	276
Psalm 88	85
Psalm 88:6	319
Psalm 104:26	301
Psalm 119:71	51/229
Psalm 119:75	51
Psalm 120:1 (NKJV)	320
Psalm 147:8, 16–18 (NIV)	42
Proverbs 2:1, 6, 10	128
Proverbs 8:15–17	128
Proverbs 12:25	95
Proverbs 15:4	95/100
Proverbs 15:23	79/95
Proverbs 16:24	95
Proverbs 25:2*a*	44/80
Proverbs 25:11	79

Reference	Page
Ecclesiastes 3:11	148
Ecclesiastes 8:11	190
Isaiah 8:20	232
Isaiah 14:9	150
Isaiah 14:12 (KJV)	22
Isaiah 14:24 (NIV)	44
Isaiah 26:3 (KJV)	260
Isaiah 27:1	303
Isaiah 45:7 (NIV)	44
Isaiah 45:7*a*	276
Isaiah 45:15*a*	44
Isaiah 55:8	292
Isaiah 66:13	77
Jeremiah 29:11	86/116/319
Jeremiah 49:7	74
Ezekiel 14:14	13
Ezekiel 28	22
Joel 1	301
Amos 4:7 (NIV)	43
Obadiah 8	74
Nahum 1:3*b* (NIV)	44
Zechariah 3:1	21
Matthew 5:16	162
Matthew 5:45*b*	43
Matthew 6:26*a*	288
Matthew 6:26*b*	288
Matthew 9:12	129
Matthew 11:3	85
Matthew 12:24 (KJV)	22
Matthew 13:39	22

Reference	Page
Matthew 14	274
Matthew 21:14	252
Matthew 26:30	235
Matthew 27:46	281
Mark 4:39	274
Mark 6	252
Mark 10:6	249
Mark 14:33–34 (NIV)	90
Luke 5:12*c*–13	280
Luke 12:6	288
Luke 12:7*b*	288
Luke 13	46
Luke 16:22–26	151
Luke 16:24	151
Luke 16:27–30	152
Luke 19:10	139
Luke 22:31	21
Luke 23:46	69
John 1:1–3	249
John 1:12	298
John 2	252
John 8:44	23
John 9:3	55
John 11:25	154
John 11:35	80
John 11:36	81
John 11:43	280
John 12:31	22
John 14:6	136
John 19:30	281

Reference	Page
Acts 4:12	137
Acts 10:13	288
Acts 14:15	250
Acts 16	235
Acts 17:24–26	250
Romans 1:20	44
Romans 1:21–25	259
Romans 3:19	137
Romans 5:3–4	52
Romans 5:12, 15, 17	251
Romans 8:1	136
Romans 8:18	47/91
Romans 8:18–19, 22–23, 25	41
Romans 8:28	86
Romans 8:38–39	117/320
Romans 11:33	80
1 Corinthians 2:16	80
1 Corinthians 15:14	180
1 Corinthians 15:22	251
1 Corinthians 15:27*a*	180
2 Corinthians 4:4	22
2 Corinthians 4:17	320
2 Corinthians 5:8	153
2 Corinthians 5:17	298
2 Corinthians 10:5*a* (NIV)	89
2 Corinthians 12:7	230
Galatians 1:3–4*a*	137
Galatians 4:7	298
Ephesians 2:2	22
Ephesians 4:8 (NKJV)	154